A Way

in the

WORLD

A WAY
in the
WORLD

A NOVEL

V. S. NAIPAUL

ALFRED A. KNOPF
New York 1994

THIS IS A BORZOI BOOK
PUBLISHED BY ALFRED A. KNOPF, INC.

Copyright © 1994 by V. S. Naipaul

All rights reserved under International and Pan-American Copyright Conventions. Published in the United States by Alfred A. Knopf, Inc., New York. Distributed by Random House, Inc., New York.

Library of Congress Cataloging-in-Publication Data

Naipaul, V. S. (Vidiadhar Surajprasad).
A way in the world / V. S. Naipaul. — 1st American ed.
p.   cm.
ISBN 0-394-56478-2
I. Title.
PR9272.9.N32W39   1994
823'.914—dc20   93-44680
CIP

Manufactured in the United States of America

First Edition

And year by year our memory fades
From all the circle of the hills.

Till from the garden and the wild
A fresh association blow,
And year by year the landscape grow
Familiar to the stranger's child.

Contents

A WAY
in the
WORLD

CHAPTER I

Prelude: An Inheritance

I LEFT HOME more than forty years ago. I was eighteen. When I went back, after six years—and slowly: a two-week journey by steamer—everything was strange and not strange: the suddenness of night, the very big leaves of some trees, the shrunken streets, the corrugated-iron roofs. You could walk down a street and hear the American advertising jingles coming out of the Rediffusion sets in all the little open houses. Six years before I had known the jingles the Rediffusion sets played; but these jingles were all new to me and were like somebody else's folksong now.

All the people on the streets were darker than I remembered: Africans, Indians, whites, Portuguese, mixed Chinese. In their houses, though, people didn't look so dark. I suppose that was because on the streets I was more of a looker, half a tourist, and when I went to a house it was to be with people I had known years before. So I saw them more easily.

To go back home was to play with impressions in this way, the way I played with the first pair of glasses I had, looking at a world now sharp and small and not quite real, now standard size and real but blurred; the way I played with my first pair of dark glasses, moving between dazzle and coolness; or the way, on this first return, when I was intro-

duced to air-conditioning, I liked to move from the coolness
of an air-conditioned room to the warmth outside, and back
again. I was in time, over the years, and over many returns,
to get used to what was new; but that shifting about of reality
never really stopped. I could call it up whenever I wished.
Up to about twenty years ago whenever I went back I could
persuade myself from time to time that I was in a half-dream,
knowing and not knowing. It was a pleasant feeling; it was
a little like the sensations that came to me as a child when,
once in the rainy season, I had "fever."

It was at a time like that, a time of "fever," during a
return, that I heard about Leonard Side, a decorator of cakes
and arranger of flowers. I heard about him from a school
teacher.

The school she taught at was a new one, beyond the
suburbs of the town, and in what had been country and
plantations right up to the end of the war. The school grounds
still looked like a piece of a cleared sugar-cane or coconut
estate. There wasn't even a tree. The plain two-storey concrete building—green roof, cream-coloured walls—stood by
itself in the openness and the glare.

The teacher said, "The work we were doing in those early
days was a little bit like social work, with girls from labouring
families. Some of them had brothers or fathers or relations
who had gone to jail; they talked about this in the most
natural way. One day, at a staff meeting in that very hot
school with the glare all around, one of the senior teachers,
a Presbyterian Indian lady, suggested that we should have a
May Day fair, to introduce the girls to that idea. Everybody
agreed, and we decided that the thing to do would be to ask
the girls to make flower displays or arrangements, and to
give a prize to the girl who did the best display.

"If you had a prize you had to have a judge. If you didn't
have a good judge the idea wouldn't work. Who was this
judge to be? The people we taught were very cynical. They
got it from their families. Oh, they were very respectful and

so on, but they thought that everybody and everything was crooked, and in their heart of hearts they looked down on the people above them. So we couldn't have a judge from the government or the Education Department or anybody too famous. This didn't leave us with too many names.

"One of the junior teachers, very young, a country girl herself, fresh from the GTC, the Government Training College, then said that Leonard Side would make the perfect judge.

"Who was Leonard Side?

"The girl had to think. Then she said, 'He work all his life in flowers.'

"Well. But then somebody else remembered the name. She said Leonard Side gave little courses at the WAA, the Women's Auxiliary Association, and people there liked him. That was the place to find him.

"The Women's Auxiliary Association had been founded during the war and was modelled on the WVS in England. They had a building in Parry's Corner, which was in the heart of the city. There was everything in Parry's Corner, a garage for buses, a garage for taxis, a funeral parlour, two cafés, a haberdashery and dry-goods shop, and a number of little houses, some of them offices, some of them dwelling-places; and the well-known Parry family owned it all.

"It was easy for me to go to Parry's Corner, and I offered to go and talk to Leonard Side. The WAA was in a very small building from the Spanish time. The flat front wall—a thick rubble wall, plastered and painted, with rusticated stone slabs at either end—rose up directly from the pavement, so that you stepped from the narrow pavement straight into the front room. The front door was bang in the middle of the pavement wall, and there was a little curtained window on either side. Door and windows had yellow-brown jalousies, linked wooden cross slats you could lift all at once and use an iron pin to close.

"A brown woman was sitting at a desk, and on the dusty

wall—dust catching on the unevenness of the plastered rubble wall—were Information Office posters from England. The Tower of London, the English countryside.

"I said, 'They tell me I could find Mr. Side here.'

"'He over there, across the road,' the woman at the desk said.

"I crossed the road. As always at this time of day, the asphalt was soft and black, as black as the oil-stained concrete floor of the big shed of a garage where the Parry buses were. The building I entered was a modern one, with grey-washed decorated concrete blocks mimicking chipped stone. It was a very clean and plain kind of place, like a doctor's office.

"I said to the girl sitting at the table, 'Mr. Side?'

"She said, 'Go right in.'

"I went through to the inner room, and there I could hardly believe what I saw. A dark Indian man was doing things with his fingers to a dead body on a table or slab in front of him. I had gone to Parry's Funeral Parlour. It was a famous place; it advertised every day on the radio with organ music. I suppose Leonard Side was dressing the body. 'Dressing'—I just knew the word. I had had no idea what it meant. I was too frightened and shocked to say anything. I ran out of the room, and the front room, and got out into the open again. The man ran out after me, calling in a soft voice, 'Miss, Miss.'

"And really he was quite a good-looking man, in spite of the hairy fingers I had seen dressing the dead body on the table. He was very pleased to be asked to judge the girls' flower competition. He even said he wanted to give the first prize. He said that if we allowed him he would make a special posy. And he did, too. A little posy of pink rosebuds. Our May Day fair was a great success.

"A year passed. Fair time came again, and I had to go again and look for Leonard Side. This time I wasn't going to forget: I wasn't going to the funeral parlour. The only place

I was going to meet Leonard Side was the Women's Association. I went there late one afternoon after school, about five.
The little Spanish-style house was full of women, and in the
inside room Leonard Side was doing things with dough,
using those hairy fingers to knead dough. Using those fingers
to work in a little more milk, then a little more butter.

"He was teaching the women how to make bread and
cake. After he had finished doing the dough, he began to
teach them how to ice a cake, forcing with those hairy fingers
coloured icing out of the special cones or moulds he had. He
pressed on and then into the moulds with his hairy fingers,
and out came a pink or green rosebud or a flower, which he
then fixed with icing-flecked fingers on to the soft iced cake.
The women said ooh and aah, and he, very happy with his
audience and his work, worked on, like a magician.

"But I didn't like seeing those fingers doing this kind of
work, and I liked it less when, at the end, with those same
fingers he offered the women little things he had iced, to eat
on the spot, as a treat. He liked offering these little treats.
They were offered almost like a wafer in church, and the
women, concentrating, ate and tasted with a similar kind of
respect.

"The third year came. This time I thought I wouldn't go
to Parry's Corner to meet Leonard Side. I thought I would
go to his house instead. I had found out where he lived. He
lived in St. James, quite near where I lived. That was a surprise: that he should have been so close, living that life, and
I shouldn't have known.

"I went after school. I was wearing a slender black skirt
and a white shirty top and I was carrying a bag with school
books. I blew the horn when I stopped. A woman came out
to the front gallery, bright in the afternoon light, and she
said, 'Come right in.' Just like that, as though she knew me.

"When I went up the steps to the front gallery she said,
'Come in, Doctor. Poor Lenny. He so sick, Doctor.'

"Doctor—that was because of the car and blowing the horn, and the bag, and the clothes I was wearing. I thought I would explain later, and I followed her through this little old St. James wood house to the back room. There I found Leonard Side, very sick and trembling, but dressed for a meeting with the doctor. He was in a shiny brass fourposter bed with a flowered canopy, and he was in green silk pyjamas. His little hairy fingers were resting on the satin or silk spread he was using as a coverlet. He had laid himself out with great care, and the coverlet was folded back neatly.

"There were crepe-paper flowers in a brass vase on a thin-legged side table or vase-stand, and there were satiny cushions and big bows on two simple cane-bottomed bentwood chairs. I knew at once that a lot of that satin and silk had come from the funeral parlour, and was material for the coffins and the laying out of the bodies.

"He was a Mohammedan, everyone knew. But he was so much a man of his job—laying out Christian bodies, though nobody thought of it quite like that—that in that bedroom of his he even had a framed picture of Christ in Majesty, radiating light and gold, and lifting a finger of blessing.

"The picture was centrally placed above the door and leaned forward so much that the blessing of the finger would have seemed aimed at the man on the bed. I knew that the picture wasn't there for the religion alone: it was also for the beauty, the colours, the gold, the long wavy hair of Christ. And I believe I was more shocked than when I saw him dressing the body and later when I saw him using the same fingers to knead dough and then to squeeze out the terrible little blobs of icing.

"It was late afternoon, warm still, and through the open window came the smell of the cesspits of St. James, the cesspits of those dirt yards with the separate little wood houses, two or three to a lot, with runnels of filth from the latrines, runnels that ran green and shiny and then dried away in the dirt; with the discoloured stones where people put out their washing to bleach; with irregular little areas where the earth was mounded up with dust and sand and gravel, and where fruit trees and little shrubs grew, creating the effect not of gardens but of little patches of waste ground where things grew haphazardly.

"When I looked at those hairy fingers on the coverlet and thought about the house and the woman who had called me in—his mother—I wondered about his life and felt sorry and frightened for him. He was sick now; he wanted help. I didn't have the heart to talk to him about the girls and the May Day fair, and I left the house and never saw him again.

"It was his idea of beauty that upset me, I suppose. That idea of beauty had taken him to the job in the funeral parlour, and had got him to deck out his bedroom in the extravagant way he had. That idea of beauty—mixing roses and flowers and nice things to eat with the idea of making the dead human body beautiful too—was contrary to my own idea. The mixing of things upset me. It didn't upset him. I had thought something like that the very first time I had seen him, when he had left his dead body and run out after me to the street, saying, 'Miss, Miss,' as though he couldn't understand why I was leaving.

"He was like so many of the Indian men you see on the streets in St. James, slender fellows in narrow-waisted trousers and open-necked shirts. Ordinary, even with the good looks. But he had that special idea of beauty.

"That idea of beauty, surprising as it was, was not a secret. Many people would have known about it—like the junior teacher who had brought his name up at the staff meeting, and then didn't know how to describe him. He would have been used to people treating him in a special way: the women in the classes clapping him, other people mocking him or scorning him, and people like me running away from him because he frightened us. He frightened me because I felt his feeling for beauty was like an illness; as though some unfamiliar, deforming virus had passed through his simple mother to him, and was even then—he was in his mid-thirties—something neither of them had begun to understand."

THIS WAS what I heard, and the teacher couldn't tell me what had happened to Leonard Side; she had never thought to ask. Perhaps he had joined the great migration to England or the United States. I wondered whether in that other place Leonard Side had come to some understanding of his nature; or whether the thing that had frightened the teacher had, when the time of revelation came, also frightened Leonard Side.

He knew he was a Mohammedan, in spite of the picture of Christ in his bedroom. But he would have had almost no idea of where he or his ancestors had come from. He wouldn't have guessed that the name Side might have been a version of Sayed, and that his grandfather or great-grandfather might have come from a Shia Muslim group in India. From Lucknow, perhaps; there was even a street in St. James called Lucknow Street. All Leonard Side would have known of himself and his ancestors would have been what he had awakened to in his mother's house in St. James. In that he was like the rest of us.

With learning now I can tell you more or less how we all came to be where we were. I can tell you that the Amerindian name for that land of St. James would have been Cumucurapo, which the early travellers from Europe turned to Conquerabo or Conquerabia. I can look at the vegetation and tell you what was there when Columbus came and what was imported later. I can reconstruct the plantations that were laid out on that area of St. James. The recorded history of the place is short, three centuries of depopulation followed by two centuries of resettlement. The documents of the resettle-

ment are available in the city, in the Registrar-General's Office. While the documents last we can hunt up the story of
every strip of occupied land.

I can give you that historical bird's eye view. But I cannot
really explain the mystery of Leonard Side's inheritance. Most
of us know the parents or grandparents we come from. But
we go back and back, forever; we go back all of us to the
very beginning; in our blood and bone and brain we carry
the memories of thousands of beings. I might say that an
ancestor of Leonard Side's came from the dancing groups of
Lucknow, the lewd men who painted their faces and tried to
live like women. But that would only be a fragment of his
inheritance, a fragment of the truth. We cannot understand all
the traits we have inherited. Sometimes we can be strangers to
ourselves.

CHAPTER 2

History:
A Smell of
Fish Glue

ON MY seventeenth birthday I became an acting second-class clerk in the Registrar-General's Department. It was a filling-in job, between leaving school and going away to England, to the university; and it was one of the most hopeful times in my life. The Registrar-General's Department was in the Red House, in St. Vincent Street. This was one of the first streets I had got to know in Port of Spain.

I was a country boy, and still am in my heart of hearts. Only a country boy could have loved the town as I did when I came to it. This was in 1938 or 1939. I loved everything about the town that was not like the country. I liked the paved cambered streets and even the open kerbside gutters: every morning, after they had done their sweeping and gathering, the street-cleaners opened the water hydrants and flooded the gutters with fresh, clear water. I liked the pavements. Many of the houses had decorative fences of a particular style, with a big carriage or cart-gate at the side, usually of corrugated iron, and an elegant small gate in the middle, leading to the front door. These front gates were of stiff patterned wire within a tubular frame and with a metal arabesque at the top. Sometimes they had a bell. I liked the way the pavements dipped outside the big side gates (to let in the

carts or cars to the yards, though very few people had cars).
I liked the street lamps; the squares with their trees and paved
paths and benches; the routine of the town day, from the
street-cleaners' brooms in the early morning, to the newspaper being thrown onto the front steps, to the horse-drawn
ice-cart in the middle of the morning. Port of Spain was
small, really, with less than a hundred thousand people. But
to me it was a big town, and quite complete.

My father was my guide to the city in the very early days.
One Sunday afternoon he took me to the city centre and
walked me down two or three of the principal streets. Sunday
was such a quiet day that you could—for the sake of doing
something unusual—get off the pavement and walk in the
street itself. Frederick Street was the street of the big stores.
More interesting to me was St. Vincent Street. At the lower
end, near the harbour, it was the street of the newspapers,
the *Trinidad Guardian* and the *Port of Spain Gazette,* facing one
another. My father worked for the *Guardian.* It was the more
important and more modern paper. From the pavement you
could see the new machines, the big rollers, the big unwind-
ing ribbons of newsprint, and you could get the warm smell
of machines and paper and printing ink. So, almost as soon
as I had come to the city, this new excitement, of paper and
ink and urgent printing, was given to me.

Later I got to know the higher or upper parts of the street.
The tailor who made trousers for me had his shop in St.
Vincent Street. My father took me there one day. The tailor's
name was Nazaralli Baksh. His shop faced west and was
shaded from the afternoon sun by a white canvas blind hanging vertically over the pavement. His name was painted on
this blind. He was a small, slender Indian man, standing some
way inside his shop, perhaps because of the sun. He had a
fined-down face, with dark shining eyes set in darker sockets,
and with his thin hair brushed back flat: a severe man, friendly
to my father, but more matter of fact with me than I expected

adults to be. I expected adults who had been properly introduced to me to be a little awed by me, and my "brightness."
The thin tape measure hanging round Nazaralli Baksh's neck
was like part of the severity of his appearance.

I don't know how good his tailoring was; but this introduction made him the man I thought of as "the tailor." I
thought of no one else as a tailor in quite this way; every
other tailor in Port of Spain seemed to me counterfeit. I
understood at some stage that he was a Mohammedan. This
didn't at first make him less close; but then, with Indian
independence, and the religious partition of the sub-
continent, the idea of difference began to attach to him,
though I never stopped going to him for my clothes. It was
Nazaralli Baksh who made the clothes I took with me when
I went away to England.

I heard later that a lot of his work was for the local police
force; he made uniforms for them. For us who were his fellow
Indians this would have been part of Nazaralli Baksh's legend
and success. Police Headquarters was just across the road
from his shop. It was an important Port of Spain building. It
was distinctive, with a high grey wall of stone and rubble.
Later knowledge told me that it was a British colonial building in the Victorian Gothic style. At the time that rough
grey front wall and those pointed reddish arches in the open
galleries at the back seemed to be just what you would expect
to find in Police Headquarters.

A small town, a small street; but it took time to know. I
had no interest in the law or lawyers, for instance, and for
many years I paid no attention to that part of the street,
opposite the courts, where the lawyers were. Then one day
I went to the "chambers"—quaint word—of a famous black
lawyer.

This happened quite late, shortly after I had left school. I
had been successful at school; it was known—people took an
interest in these things—that I had won a scholarship and was

going to go abroad soon. The lawyer's son had been right through school with me, and one day he said he wanted to take me to meet his father. We went to his father's chambers. These chambers were in St. Vincent Street and occupied the whole of a very small house, a real Port of Spain miniature from the Spanish time. It would have been one of the earliest residential houses, built perhaps in the 1780s, not long after the city had been laid out. I suppose a number of these early houses were as small and squashed as they were because only short stretches of the streets had been made up; bush and plantations would have been quite close.

The little front room of the chambers was full of black people, ordinary people, sitting very close together on two benches, bench facing bench across bare floorboards. The slats of the jalousies of the little front window were coated with dust from the street; you could see on the distempered walls where over the years the people on the benches had rested shoulders and heads. The people I saw were as silent and patient as people waiting for free medicine in a Health Office. Bright eyes, shining faces, reverential expressions: black people coming to one of their own, not minding the discomfort and the stillness and the wait, and not resenting the young boy who, just arrived, simply went into the inner room where the great man was. The atmosphere of the narrow little waiting room was new to me.

In the more open, cooler room at the back the lawyer was in shirtsleeves, with his lawyer's jacket on a hanger. The lawbooks and old folders with old papers, the general scruffiness of the chambers, the worm-eaten boards of the partition, made the lawyer's profession seem a very dull one: it was hard to imagine that anything done in this room could generate real money.

I didn't know what to say to the lawyer, after the courtesies, which went on for a while. And he seemed equally at a loss; he seemed content just to look at me. I myself had a wish to look below the desk at the lawyer's shoes. His son had told me, years and years before, when we were both in the fourth or fifth standard at the elementary school, that you could always tell a gentleman by the way he kept his shoes.

My friend didn't help with the conversation. His manner had altered in the inner office. He had become very much the son, the family treasure, the person who didn't have to try. He seemed now to be more interested in finding a cold drink. He was very casual with the great lawyer.

The lawyer was famous for his first name, which was Evander. And all I could think of, at this artificial moment, was to ask how he had been given it.

He said, "My father worshipped education. It was his way of giving me ambition. He was not an educated man. But he was born in 1867 or 1870. That's a long time ago for us. If you look it up, you'll find the name in Homer. Book four or book five."

It was surprising, that this famous man hadn't gone into his unusual name, didn't know that the name came from Latin and Virgil, and had simply tried to bluff me. He was a self-made man. He hadn't had anything like a formal education; all his energies had gone into his profession and making his way. But this flaw in his character, so casually revealed, was worrying. While I was getting used to that new idea of him, he was taking the conversation, by ways I cannot reconstruct, to something else.

The moment came when he leaned back in his Windsor chair, thrust his big white-sleeved forearm across the table, in a gesture of strength, and said, with a smile, and as a kind of pledge, "The race! The race, man!"

The black race, the African race, the coloured races: I suppose that was what the lawyer meant, and that was why I had been brought to his chambers.

I looked at his son. His face registered nothing, as though he hadn't heard what his father had said and hadn't noticed the gesture he had made.

I didn't believe that, didn't believe that blank face. At the lower end of St. Vincent Street I had years before smelt paper and ink and warm printing presses, and certain fantasies had come to me. In this back room of the chambers, with the jalousie-strained light, were other fantasies, subterranean emotions that had to be hidden from the light of St. Vincent Street, from the colonial reality of that street.

This was in the late 1940s. Few black people at that time could see a way ahead. How strange, then, to find an old man, a man born in the last century, to whom the way ahead was clear, something he could even toast, with an instinctive gesture across the desk that twenty years later might have been seen as a black-power salute. What was stranger was that the public idea of Evander, my friend's father, was not like this at all. In the gossip Evander was the self-made black man who wanted only to be white, wanted to have nothing to do with black people, and in everything he did was fighting only for himself.

This other dream was like a family secret, which father and son were now admitting me to. I was moved, but at the same time embarrassed. I understood their feelings, shared them to some extent, but I wished, even with that under-standing, to belong to myself. I couldn't support the idea of being part of a group. I would have felt tied down by it, and I thought Evander's idea of a great racial movement forward too sentimental.

THE CIVIL service didn't employ anyone under seventeen, and in the next year, on my seventeenth birthday, I went to work in the Registrar-General's Department, and got to know St. Vincent Street in quite another way.

The department was on the ground floor of the Red House. The Red House was the principal building of the administration. It was one of the biggest buildings in the island and we all thought it was beautiful. I am not sure whether its dull red colour came from paint or from something that had been mixed into the plaster. It was one of the buildings that made Port of Spain Port of Spain. You saw it from the harbour, from the hills, and from across the Savannah.

It was in the Italian style, we were told. It was on two floors, with open galleries on both floors, and with a dome. It was as wide as a block, and there was a walkway, below that red dome, between St. Vincent Street and Woodford Square, on the other side. That walkway gave a special big-town feel. You went up stone steps, and then you walked in an echoing openness past a fountain and then down other steps to the other side. The fountain didn't work—one of the interruptions we associated with the war—but the marble, though iron-stained and tide-marked, was still beautiful, and the idea of the fountain was somehow still there.

On either side of the empty fountain big, free-standing, wooden notice-boards, head-high, were set in front of the open doors of government departments. These notice-boards also served as screens, shielding clerks and typists and other civil servants from the gaze of the people passing to and fro. At the back of the notice-boards were bicycle-racks, where the civil servants chained up their bicycles. Notice-boards and bicycle-racks took away something of the openness of the walkway below the high pierced dome. So already there was a feeling of a fine building not being seen in all its beauty, and beginning to be misused.

The notice-boards didn't carry government instructions. The pinned-up posters were about health care and the importance of vaccinations, things like that. Many of them came from London, and didn't always completely apply to local conditions; but we were used to that. These notice-boards and posters were the work of the Information Office, a department that had been established during the war—in a timber building set down on the lawn of the Red House—to give out pictures and booklets about the war and about life in England. These posters and notices about health and blood-tests and X-rays and clean water were a peacetime continuation of that work. You saw these posters only in the Red House; you didn't see them anywhere else. I never thought they meant anything; but they introduced me to the idea of government as a benevolent agency, concerned about people.

This idea of government shouldn't have been new to me, after all that I had learned at school. But in every practical and concrete way it was new. It must have been that I carried in my blood and brain very old Indian ideas about the indifference or the arbitrariness of rulers and governments. They were simply there; you looked to them for nothing. Or it might have been that—without any words being spoken—I had grown up thinking of cruelty as something always in the background. There was an ancient, or not-so-ancient, cruelty in the language of the streets: casual threats, man to man and parents to children, of punishments and degradation that took you back to plantation times. There was the cruelty of extended-family life; the cruelty of the elementary school, the bad beatings by teachers, the bloody end-of-term fights between boys; the cruelty of the Indian countryside and the African town. The simplest things around us held memories of cruelty.

The Registrar-General's Department was to the right of the fountain, if you entered the Red House from St. Vincent Street. If you walked right through you ended in Woodford Square. This was the most beautiful square in Port of Spain, and it was named after the very young English governor who in the second decade of the nineteenth century brought order and law to the colony after the anarchy that followed the British conquest. The Spaniards lost Port of Spain almost as soon as they had laid it out. Woodford Square, at that time, would have been nothing, empty ground. It had been embellished by the British, and we thought it of a piece with the splendour of the Red House. It had a bandstand, a fountain like the one in the Red House, benches, decorative iron rails, paved paths; and it was full now of old, shady trees.

Always beautiful, always a glorious thing of the town, yet even when I had first seen it, that Sunday before the war when my father took me on a walk through the town centre, this square was one of the places in Port of Spain where homeless people lived. Most of these people were Indians. Many of them would have been indentured immigrants from India who had served out their indentures on the sugar estates and then for one reason or another—perhaps they had become drinkers; perhaps they hadn't been given their promised passage back to India; perhaps they had quarrelled with their families—had found themselves with nowhere to live. These people were without money, job, without anything like a family, without the English language; without any kind of representation. They were utterly destitute. They were people who had been, as in a fairy story, lifted up from the peasantry of India and set down thousands of miles away—weeks and weeks of sailing—in Trinidad. In the colonial setting of Trinidad, where rights were limited, you could have done anything with these people; and they were tormented by the people of the town.

We all lived easily with this kind of cruelty. We saw it, but we seldom thought about it. Eventually these people from India died out; by the late 1940s they would nearly all have died. In the early 1940s my father talked to some of them and wrote an article about them for a local Indian magazine. When I went to work in the Red House they were no longer there in Woodford Square. What I remember were the black madmen, two or three of them, one of them with tangled long plaits or tails of stiff hair, grey-brown with dirt and dust and oil, and wearing a Robinson Crusoe–like set of clothes, an accumulation or improvisation not of skins but of rags that had all lost their original colour and turned black and greasy. Perhaps he was harmless; but he had the madman's assurance, and people walking through the square kept away from where he was, and tried to avoid his bright, inward-seeing eyes.

This was where I went to work every day, in the Registrar-General's Department, between St. Vincent Street and Woodford Square.

MY JOB as an acting second-class clerk was to make copies of birth, marriage and death certificates. People who needed these certificates came to the Red House and made an arrangement with one of the freelance searchers who hung about the entrance to the department, near the notice-boards, waiting for customers. These searchers, after they had been given possible dates by their customers, then used stamped forms to requisition various volumes of certificates; the department's messengers brought out the thick, heavy bound volumes, more wide than high, from the vaults; the searchers sat in the outer office on a polished long brown desk and searched through the volumes. In this room—with a view through the tall windows of the lawns of the Red House and the trees and iron rails of Woodford Square—there was an unexpected atmosphere of the classroom, with grown and sometimes elderly black men sitting side by side at the long desk, some-times for a whole morning, as if under an enchantment laid on them at school, and turning the very wide pages of very big books, one page at a time. In a separate area of the outer office lawyers' clerks looked for deeds. These men sat at single desks and some of them wore ties. They were al-together a higher class than the birth-and-death certificate-searchers, who really were in business—making a small, insecure living—because they could read and write, and many of the people who wanted certificates couldn't.

When a searcher found what he was looking for, he made

a request for a copy; and a messenger brought the request and the appropriate volume to my table. A table, rather than a desk: I was only an acting second-class clerk, a stop-gap, and I sat at a narrow table near the vault, and did my work facing the green-distempered wall. The messengers passed behind me all the time on their way to and from the vault. The volumes I had to copy from were placed in a pile on my right; when I was finished with them I put them in a pile on my left. The piles were high: each volume was three or four inches thick, and about fifteen inches wide.

The volumes smelled of fish glue. This was what they were bound with; and I suppose the glue was made from a boiling down of fish bones and skin and offal. It was the colour of honey; it dried very hard, and every careless golden drip had the clarity of glass; but it never lost the smell of fish and rottenness.

I had been told that everything printed in the island was lodged in the vault. All the records of the colony were there, all the births, deaths, deeds, transfers of property and slaves, all the life of the island for the century and a half of the colonial time. I would have liked to look at old things, old newspapers, old books. But the smell of fish glue was very strong in the vault. That, together with the smell of old dust and old paper, the airlessness, which became worse the deeper you went in, the dim light, and the sheer quantity of old paper, was too much for me.

Morning and afternoon the copies I had written out were checked and initialled by a senior clerk, who came and sat at my table, like a teacher in the kindergarten. Then they were taken for signature to the desk of the big man of our office: the deputy registrar-general or sometimes the acting deputy registrar-general, in whose full name I had had to write out the copies. Then stamps were stuck on, cancelled with the raised letters of the iron seal of the department; and the copies were at last ready to be handed out.

All of this searching, writing, checking, signing, the attentions of so many people—for a job that might nowadays be done by one person and a computer. All of that fetching and carrying by the messengers: they were on their feet for much of the day, tramping between the vault and the outer office, cradling those bulky, awkwardly shaped volumes in their arms. Theirs was technically an office job, but it required strength and stamina, and they were powerfully built men.

I would try sometimes to imagine myself spending all my life in that department. A working life of checking and being checked, of writing out certificates in the names of one's seniors: I thought I could see how, after longing for the security of the civil service job, the job could get at you and you would become full of hate, and not only for the people whose full name you wrote out, as though your own didn't matter.

There were two people in the office, a brown man and a Chinese woman, who had served many years and whose thoughts were now of retirement. They had probably entered the government service during the First World War. It was hard for me to think back so far, to imagine that stacking up of the weeks and months and years; it was hard enough for me to go back just ten years, to my discovery of the city, and the first time I had walked down St. Vincent Street with my father. But now for these two people the years had passed. They had seen the job through, and the job had seen them through. Age and endurance were now like a kind of luck that lifted them above other people, above office strife and ambition. They made small, unhurried movements, as though the job and the years had taught them patience.

The woman—her desk was directly below the front counter: she gave out the completed certificates—was motherly, tender with everyone, as though the job had brought out all her feminine instincts. But the gentleness of the man had been given him by drinking. He was known for it; he would come in on a Monday like a man both revivified and rested, worn a little finer by the drinking of the weekend.

Sometimes, near pay-day, there was drinking in the office after office hours. It seemed to be a recognized office facility. The drinkers—some with a towel over their shoulders: that towel an emblem of the end of the working day—the drinkers would sit on desks or with their legs over the arms of chairs, and drink seriously for half an hour or so. I was not a drinker; it was the seriousness of these occasions that I remember. There was no humour, no friendship. It was as though the rum went straight to the soul and privacy of every man.

In the department there was a black boy from St. James. We had been street acquaintances, no more, for some years. I knew he lived near me, but I didn't know exactly where, and I felt he wanted to keep it like that. He talked sometimes about his mother, and I imagined him living alone with her in a crowded backyard, in one of those tottering old St. James shacks. The difference between us, though, lay not so much in money as in our prospects. I was a college boy, aiming high; he was an elementary-school boy, accepting his limitations. That was the basis of our street relationship, and I had thought of this boy, tall and thin and seemingly uncoordinated, riding a lady's bicycle, as a jester, a loud-mouth from the backyards. It was only now, seeing the seriousness with which he drank, and seeing how the rum altered him, seeing how he became red-eyed and unfunny, that I felt that he was serious about himself, about his job, his duties as a clerk, about his own ambitions, in a way I had never supposed. He was not at all content. His jester's personality, the personality of a man not expecting much, not aiming high, was a cover; he didn't really mean many of his jokes.

Belbenoit—one of the senior clerks who sometimes checked my certificates—didn't have this cover. He was a middle-aged "coloured" man. On both sides he would have been of mixed race for some generations; he was fair-skinned.

He had no particular qualifications, but he didn't think he had done well enough. Though every kind of racial assumption showed in his own querulous face, he felt he had been discouraged for racial reasons from aiming higher: at the time when he had entered the service, the best jobs were reserved for people from England. That was no longer so; but the changes had come too late for Belbenoit. He was famous in the office for being a disappointed man; and people treated his unhappiness like an illness, though it was no secret that Belbenoit (with all his old assumptions) felt he hadn't had the treatment due to his fair colour, and felt his position in the office was in the nature of a racial disgrace.

His unlikely ally in the office—in office politics, and in representations of various kinds to the civil servants' council—was Blair. Blair was a black giant, smooth-skinned, erect, with powerful shoulders. His manners were perfect; he could be very serious; he could also laugh easily, but always with control. He had an immense confidence. He came from a purely black village somewhere in the north-east of the island. This made him unusual: he didn't have the combativeness and nerves of black people who had grown up in mixed communities. At the same time, because of that isolation, Blair had started school late. But he had made up for that. He was already a senior clerk, and everybody in the office knew he was studying now for an external degree of some sort, looking for the qualifications that Belbenoit never had. Blair sometimes checked my certificates. That very big man had the tiniest and neatest initials: they spoke to me of his ambition and strength.

Blair was courtesy itself to me; but I felt about him that, though we met with ease in the government office, there was much in his background I could never get to know. That all-African village in the north-east, isolated for some generations, without Indians or white people, would have had its own subterranean emotions, its own faith and fantasies. Blair no doubt felt the same about me; my Indian and orthodox Hindu background might have seemed to him even more closed. But in the neutral ground of the department we didn't have to worry about these home matters; we got on, as far as we had to get on. In a civil service way Blair was perfection—and not without the disquietingness of such perfection. Just months out of school, and having only that experience to judge outsiders by, I thought of him (in spite of Belbenoit's apparent alliance with him) as a kind of head boy: someone who could be one of the boys and at the same time represent authority.

He lived out what I felt about him then. Seven years later he abandoned the civil service, gave up that fine career, abandoned that restrained departmental demeanour, and went into local politics. He judged the moment well. He shot up, and then, in a decolonizing world, he rose and rose. He was to have an international career. Nearly twenty years later we were to meet in an independent East African country. He had gone there to work for the local government on a short-term contract. He would have been especially pleased by this assignment in independent Africa; but it was there, not long after we had met again, that he was to die, murdered by the agents of some wild men in the government who felt threatened by him. For two days Blair's big, mangled body lay undiscovered in a banana plantation, partly covered by dead banana leaves. A career is a career; and death is inescapable. I do not know whether the ironies of his death made a mockery of that career or undid the virtue of it. But that matter will be raised in this book in its place.

Remember him now, in the office at the Red House: at that mid-point in his career, when with his extraordinary gifts he could have gone one way or the other. Remember him (like me) trailing all the strands of his own complicated past, animated by that past, feeling the current running with him (as the lawyer Evander did), and feeling (again like me) as he studied after work that he was at the most hopeful time of his life.

WHEN I HAD free time—usually an hour or two a day—I did my writing, the way Blair did his studying. But I had nothing to write about: I was just preparing to be a writer. I kept a kind of notebook and in turquoise ink wrote comments about books I had read and thoughts about life. What I wrote was pretentious and false; I thought of it like that even when I was doing it, and wouldn't have wanted anyone to see it, though with a small part of my mind I was hoping it was profound. Sometimes I wrote descriptions of landscapes: the Petit Valley woods, remnants of old cocoa estates in the hills to the north-west of the city, after afternoon rain. Sometimes I did Port of Spain scenes: the Western Main Road in St. James at night, after rain (more rain), the red neon Coca-Cola sign on the Rialto cinema flicking on and off, the shiny uneven asphalt reflecting the lights of cars and open shops, the naked light bulbs in the parlours, the flies sleeping on the hanging electric cord, rough with their droppings, the bald head of the Chinese parlour-keeper, the smeared glasscase with stale, floury cakes and soft coconut turnovers. I liked doing those tableaux. I liked even more correcting them, for the sake of the appearance of the corrected page. Artificial, but everything I worked on in this way stayed with me, and years later those descriptions were to be a key to events and moods I had thought beyond recall.

I went one Saturday or Sunday to a black beauty contest at the Rialto. I went for the material; I hadn't gone to any beauty contest before that. It was a shabby occasion, shabby to everyone except perhaps one or two of the girls. It wasn't really funny; I hadn't found it so; but I tried to write a funny piece about it. There had been no twist, but I tried to give it one: I made the queen cry because of the hoots of the crowd.

The writing took two or three weeks, too much time for the simple or flat things I had to say. I wrote with pen and then on an office typewriter, correcting and correcting, deliberately lengthening out the writing time. The correcting didn't help; it made the essay more and more of a school-magazine piece, with the humour depending more on words than on observation or true feeling.

I concentrated in what I wrote on the master of ceremonies: his formal clothes, his ungrammatical speech, his vanity. I showed the finished article to a black woman typist in the office whom I had got to know. She held the sheets against her high standard typewriter and read them through. I thought she smiled once or twice, but at the end she said, "If it was an Indian man, you wouldn't have written like that."

It was the last comment I was expecting. I had offered her a piece of writing, and was expecting her to judge it in a higher way. And though what she had said wasn't true, I grew to feel after some weeks there was something wrong with the writing. What was the basis of the writer's attitude? What other world did he know, what other experience did he bring to his way of looking? How could a writer write about this world, if it was the only world he knew? I never formulated the questions like that; the doubts were just with me.

IT WAS some time, six years, before I worked through those doubts. I was in England then, and the first true book that came to me was the one prompted by my discovery of Port of Spain before the war, my delight in the city. To me then it was like going back to the very beginning of things, the Sunday walk down St. Vincent Street with my father, the visit to Nazaralli Baksh's tailor shop: things barely remembered, things released only by the act of writing.

After that writing I went back to Trinidad for a few

weeks. I went by steamer. The clock was put back every
other day; the weather slowly turned. One evening on deck
a breeze started up. I braced myself for the chill, but the wind
that played about my head and face was warm. I felt when I
arrived, and went visiting, and found people becoming less
dark than they seemed on the streets, that an age—a vanished
adolescence, a forced maturity, England, a book—separated
me from the people in the Registrar-General's Department.
But for them only six years had passed. Dingier walls; a more
crowded office; more tables. Blair had gone, but so many of
the others were still there: Belbenoit, the long-limbed boy
(or man) from St. James with the lady's bicycle, the typist
who hadn't liked what I had written. They were friendly.
But there was something new.

I had heard on the steamer that a new kind of politics had
come to Trinidad. There were regular meetings in Woodford
Square, across the road from the Red House, which the Spaniards had laid out in the 1780s as the main city square, and
which the British had later embellished; where the destitute
Indians, refugees from the plantations, had slept until they
had died out; and where later the black madmen had come
to camp. In that square now there were lectures about local
history and slavery. People were being told about themselves,
and black feeling was high. This was the politics that had
claimed Blair.

I went to a meeting one night. The square, its scale already
altered for me, looked different again now, with the electric
lights, the speakers and the microphones on the old bandstand
(which I had found so beautiful the first time I had seen it,
and now saw as the Victorian or Edwardian bandstand of an
English city park); and the dark, scattered, unreadable crowd.
The big trees threw distorting shadows and looked bigger
than in daylight. Some people stood at the very edge of the
square, against the railings; there were some white people
and Indians among them.

The men on the bandstand spoke of old suffering and current local politics. They spoke like people uncovering a conspiracy. They were at one with their audience. They made jokes easily; and laughter, or a kind of contented humming, came easily to the crowd. The people who spoke were not all black or African, but the occasion was an African one; there could be no doubt of that. (I didn't see Blair on the bandstand. He was never an orator or front-of-house man; he didn't have the manner.)

I knew few of the speakers; I couldn't pick up the references and the jokes. It was like entering a cinema long after the picture had started, but I felt that what was said didn't matter. The occasion itself was what mattered: the gathering, the drama, the mood: the discovery (and celebration) by many of the black people in the square, educated and uneducated, of a shared emotion. Of aspects of that emotion I had had many intimations long ago, before I had gone away.

Intimations: people had lived with this emotion as with something private, not to be carelessly exposed. Everyone— the typist in the office, the black boy or man from St. James, Blair, even the master of ceremonies at the Miss Fine Brown Frame contest, the mocking crowd there, and some of the self-mocking contestants—everyone had lived with it according to his character and intellectual means. Everyone you saw on the street had a bit of this emotion locked up in himself. It was no secret. It was part of the unacknowledged cruelty of our setting, the thing we didn't want to go searching into. Now all those private emotions ran together into a common pool, where everyone found a blessing. Everyone, high and low, could now exchange his private emotion, which he sometimes distrusted, for the sacrament of the larger truth.

In the square, romantic with its lights and shadows, they talked of history and the new constitution and rights; but what had been generated was more like religion. It wasn't something that could be left behind in the square; it couldn't be separated from the other sides of life. And I understood the exaltation, and distance, I had sensed in people when I had visited my old office in the Red House.

In the outer office of the Registrar-General's Department I had remembered the lawyer's clerks sitting like students at their sloping desks and searching for deeds in large bound volumes. They were modest but self-respecting people; some wore ties and white shirts. They had a kind of ambition, like everybody else. Sometimes they pretended to be more ambitious than they were, but many of them knew they weren't going far, and they were reconciled to it, as you could see when sometimes an older man—of a generation without possibilities, a generation now more or less finished—came to do some searching, and led them all into a kind of pointless barber-shop chatter, like servant-room gossip, full of knowingness and conspiratorial hints, but really quite empty, mere words.

(I had got to know about this barber-shop gossip even before I went to work at the Red House. After I had applied for my little temporary clerkship, word was sent back to me, through a cousin, from someone said to be in the know, someone deep in the machinery of the Red House: "Pereira is the man he have to see. All those papers pass through Pereira hand." Pereira was a clerk in some department. One midday a man cycling down the Western Main Road was pointed out to me: "Look. Pereira." The great man, just like that, in the Western Main Road, with everybody else! He was a mixed man, more Indian-looking than Portuguese, not old, and I suppose he was cycling home from the Red House for lunch. He had no hat and, in all the hot sun, he was taking his time, sitting upright on the saddle of his heavy, pre-war English bicycle, pen and pencil clipped to the pocket of his shirt, and with his socks pulled up over his trouser bottoms, which were neatly folded back over his shins. In another memory of this sighting, Pereira was on a slender-framed racing cycle, crouched over the dropped handlebars, sitting high on the narrow, ridged saddle, and pedalling away. The second memory is probably satirical and mischievous. I don't know. I never saw Pereira again; I don't even know whether the man pointed out to me was Pereira. I got the job because my former school principal recommended me for it, and no one talked to me about Pereira again.)

Some of those search clerks in the Registrar-General's Department were still there. They were easy with me; they were ready to chat. But there wasn't the barber-shop slackness about them. I thought I detected a new intensity, a new stiffening; and I felt that that intensity—hidden, unacknowledged—had always been there, and even in the older man.

I felt this even when I met simpler people. Like the paunchy department messenger, pleased to make the same joke he had made six years before ("You always query me. Why you query me so for?"). Or the elderly, sour-faced freelance searcher, waiting every day outside the office door for illiterates to come and give him work, living on the edge when I knew him, occasionally needing the gift of a drink, and now a little more broken down, his services less and less needed. Or the old Barbadian mason who had done work for our family. I used to like to see him at work; I liked his songs; and I liked the way the hairs sprouting out of his nostrils were dusted with cement, like a bee's legs with pollen. He came to see me now. He stood on the pavement and leaned on the gate. He didn't want to come into the yard because he had come to ask for money. Times were hard, he said. The lighter colour on his nostril hairs was not cement now, but the grey of grey hair. Even in these people I felt the new sacrament of the square, a little new glory.

Much of this feeling might have been in me—I was full of nerves on this return, for all kinds of reasons—but I believe I was only amplifying something that was true. The history of the place was known; its reminders were all around us; scratch us and we all bled. The wonder was that it had taken so long for black people to arrive at this way of feeling. In our colonial set-up the champions of black people had been white men or coloured men like Belbenoit. Black men, with their self-distrust, had looked to such people to be their leaders. Political life had come late to black people; confidence had come late; too many generations had had to bury or mock their emotions in barber-shop gossip. There had been a big strike in the oilfields in 1937, but the leader there, a man from one of the smaller islands, had been more of a country preacher, uneducated and a little mad, quickly going idle after his initial political inspiration, and offering his followers only a kind of religious ecstasy. The new sacrament of the square went far beyond that.

On this return everything I had known, every street, every building, shrank as soon as I saw it. I liked, as I travelled about, to play with this shift of scale, to compare what existed in my memory, from childhood and adolescence, with what existed now, as if suddenly, before me. In some such way every black or African person from my past altered. And I felt a double distance from what I had known.

At the meeting I had gone to in the square I had seen a white family walk out in an interval between the speeches. They were an old trading family. I had had some slight dealings with them. For a few weeks, just before I went to work in the Red House, I had been a tutor to one of their children. I felt I had been tricked by them into accepting very low payment for what I did. They had left it to me to fix the fee, and I, not yet seventeen, hadn't known what to ask. I had given a very low figure, moved by some absurd idea of honour. They hadn't sought to match that idea of honour; they had paid me the very low fee I had asked, and no more. Old shame and rage (an aspect of the very mood of the meeting in the square) came back to me when I saw them.

They had been standing at the edge of the square, noticeable, confident, respectful of the occasion. Perhaps they had gone for the show. But then, like me, they might have felt excluded; they might have felt the ground move below them. White people in the colony were very few, though; and they were not really threatened. Much of the hostile feeling released by the sacrament of the square would have focussed on the Indians, who made up the other half of the population.

The town had been important to me. Its discovery had been one of the pleasures of my childhood: the discovery of fine buildings, squares, fountains, gardens, beautiful things meant only to please people. Yet I had known the colonial town for only ten years. To me it had always been a strange place, a place I had come to from somewhere else, and was still getting to know. Now on this return I felt it had passed to other hands.

In a few weeks I left. It was four years before I returned. And then I came and went irregularly, coming back sometimes for a few days, staying away once for more than five years. It was from this distance, and with these interruptions, that I saw this place I knew and didn't know, which continued in its state of insurrection. People fell away, retired, died, went abroad. The time came when there were no offices for me to visit or people to call on.

As with those pre-war pads of photographs showing a cricketer in action—pads of twenty or thirty photographs in sequence which you flicked to see, jerkily, Constantine bowling or Bradman holding the bat high up the handle and doing a cover drive—my vision of the place began to run fast.

IT WENT into independence in its state of black exaltation— almost a state of insurrection—and with its now well-defined racial division: the Indian countryside, the African town. And soon the town I had known began to change.

Black people from the smaller islands to the north came

to settle. There had always been this movement of people from the islands; during the war they had come in some number to work on the American bases, and they had then built a sensational-looking, grey-black shanty town, of old wood and packing cases and rusty corrugated iron, on the bad-smelling swamp to the east. This immigration had never been legal, but now it increased. The immigrants were drawn into the local mood; they added something of the passions of their small islands, their small shut-in African communities.

The immigrant shanty town spread, on the filled-in swamp and on the hills above it. To the west, at the same time, the town spread, with new middle-class developments along the coast (where there had been bathing places) and in the valleys of the Northern Range, where there had been plantations of cocoa and citrus until the Depression.

The small town the Spaniards had laid out in the eighteenth century had had many squares or open spaces between its residential blocks; and there had been countryside and plantations all around. Now there wasn't that kind of countryside, and the town itself began to feel choked. Already, during the war, the Americans had put up big two-storey buildings on some of the central squares, near the harbour. At about the same time the local government had built the Information Office on one of the Red House lawns; and some of the Office's wooden notice-boards had been set up around the unplaying fountain in the open walkway of the Red House, under the pierced dome. Now, where there had been the notice-boards, there were rough and awkward wooden extensions to government departments, and they looked like big crates. The elementary school I had gone to was extended and extended; the grounds where we had played disappeared.

Eventually there was no longer a division between town and country. That was a loss: as a child I had loved the separate ideas of town and country. In my memory I had made a journey from the country to the town; and then from the town I had made occasional holiday journeys to the

country. If you were going to the east, you stood in the queue
at the George Street bus station. Not long after you left the
slums around the wide concrete canal known as East Dry
River, you began to see big trees, patches of bush, and then
you had glimpses of the sugar-cane plains to the south. To
the west, the ending of the town was even more dramatic:
there was, suddenly, a coconut plantation, and no house was
to be seen.

Now to east and west it was all built up, with no open
spaces, no green breaks. There were just houses and houses;
sometimes the plots were very small. There was always noise,
no rest from noise. The impression was of people cooped up
and constantly agitated in their small spaces. But new roads
continued to be cut, especially in the narrow valleys to the
west of the city; more hillsides were graded away; and the
hill landscapes I had known (and written about in my spare
time at the Red House) were so altered, so much a place now
where I was without my bearings, so much the landscape
now of other people, that I preferred for many years to stay
far away.

A new rubbish dump was established in the black-water
mangrove swamp at the east end of the city, on the other side
of the highway that ran through the shanty town—officially
recognized, officially added to sometimes, but always a
shanty town, and always growing, spreading over the hills.
The fires of the rubbish dump burned night and day. The
smoke was black turning to dark brown; it often billowed
over the highway; the smell was high; you had to turn up
your car windows. The people of the shanty town, men and
women and children, worked in this smoke—emblematic
silhouettes—raking over the rubbish for things that could be
salvaged and sold. The local corbeaux, black, heavy,
hunched, hopped about the slopes of rubbish; the children of
the shanty town ran between the traffic on the rubbish-strewn
highway to get to the dump.

It was as though, with the colonial past, all the colonial

landscape was being trampled over and undone; as though, with that past, the very idea of regulation had been rejected; as though, after the sacrament of the square, the energy of revolt had become a thing on its own, eating away at the land.

IN THE square, at the beginning, all those years before, in the glamour of the lights—and where the beauty of the paved walks and the fountain would have been an aspect of the richness of the world that was about to be inherited—the speakers on the Victorian bandstand had talked of history and suffering and the great conspiracy of the rulers, and had suggested that redemption had at last come.

It came for many. But that promise of redemption was so large that some people would have felt defrauded by what had followed. These people would have continued to find virtue in the original mood of rejection; and over the years they would have grafted on to that mood the passions of more extreme and more marginal and more publicized black causes from other places. So disaffection grew, feeding on an idea of an impossible racial righteousness; and there was always the threat of an insurrection within the insurrection.

One year there was a serious revolt. The government survived, and afterwards the last big open space of the eighteenth-century Spanish city was blocked up. What had been the Calle Marina, the Marine Street, the wide square that ran the length of what had been the sea front, was offered as a market-place to the mutinous, dreadlocked people of the hills and the shanty town to the east. To enable them to compete with the established merchants of the city, the big square was built up with little wooden shacks, and there the shanty folk sold or offered for sale the simple leather and metal goods they made.

This led to the further isolation of the city centre, the

place we used to call "town" (and where, newly arrived in the city, I had gone walking one quiet Sunday afternoon with my father, so quiet that we had walked in the street, and I had seen our undisturbed reflection in the store windows). Shopping plazas and malls were established in the new settlements west and east of Port of Spain. There was no need to go to the centre; and sometimes now, when I went back to Trinidad for a few days, I never went to the city at all.

People continued to live on their nerves. They did so even during the oil boom, when it seemed that money, given away every day in doles to everyone who claimed it, had come like a reward for their passions, their loyalty to their sacrament. When the Depression came, and times became harder than people remembered, the mood of rejection and righteousness was there again as a balm. But now there was a twist that the first speakers in the square would not have dreamed of.

There began to appear, in Port of Spain and country towns, black men and women dressed like Arabs, the men in long white gowns and with white skullcaps, the women with black veils, men and women noticeable in the street, self-consciously righteous and apart.

These people were Mohammedans of a new kind. They were not Mohammedans by inheritance, like some of the Indians of the island: people like Leonard Side of Parry's Funeral Parlour and Nazaralli Baksh, the tailor of St. Vincent Street from fifty years before. Nor were they like the Black Muslims of the United States. These people gave the impression of being in direct contact with the Arab world. Here and there in the city centre, in what in colonial days had been a fashionable area, important property had been bought by these Arab-style Muslims. These buildings had their windows and verandahs blanked out, and they displayed green and white boards with Arabic lettering.

They had occupied open public land in Mucurapo, near St. James, and built a little settlement and a mosque. This was not far from the cemetery of Mucurapo, with the very old and tall royal palms, and not far from the little house on the half-lot where, up to twenty years or so before, Leonard Side had lived with his mother. During the war the land had been occupied by the Americans. They had built enormous brick warehouses on it, like hangars. One such building had become the USO building, the entertainment centre for the Americans, very bright and glamorous to us, on the other side of the guarded fence. The land had been reclaimed from the shallows of the Gulf of Paria before the war: land built up on pebble-less and very soft black mud exposed at low tide. I remembered the reclamation taking place, the dredged-up black mud of the Gulf drying out in cracked grey cakes. (And long before that, and for hundreds of years, all this area, St. James, Mucurapo, Conquerabia, Conquerabo, had been Cumucurapo, an aboriginal Indian place.)

People were nervous of this settlement, which appeared to be ever growing, to have money, and to obey its own laws. There was a school in the settlement. The group were keen on schooling; when you saw them at the end of the morning doing their shopping in the markets of certain country areas, they—adults, men and women—were like children after school, with textbooks and exercise books in their hands. But the books were in Arabic, and their schools were said to be Koranic schools. This idea of learning was distasteful to many local people; and, added to the Arab clothes they wore, further set the group apart. The mosque they had built was not like the usual local Indian mosque, a rectangular concrete structure with domes on top, and painted green and white. This was taller, more angular, and more flashily coloured. Local people didn't know where the style had come from. I thought it might have been from North Africa; but I wasn't sure.

Late one afternoon, after they had said their prayers at this mosque—all this is as it was later reported—about a hundred of the men of the sect went with guns and explosives to St. Vincent Street. They assaulted Police Headquarters and set off a big explosion near the armoury. A number of policemen died in this first assault. Later or at the same time an assault was made on the Red House, obliquely opposite. The parliament was sitting. Shots were fired; people were hit. And then, as so often happened during slave revolts in these islands, the rebels appeared not to know what to do: all energy and exaltation had been gathered up and consumed in the drama of the attack, the surprise, the drawing of the first blood, the humiliation of the people in authority. For six days or so the rebels besieged the Red House and held the ministers of the government and everyone in the building hostage.

The Red House and St. Vincent Street smelled of death. Some fifteen people had died in the late-afternoon assault, it was said; and a number of the bodies had begun to rot. There were stories that some of the bodies had been put in the Red House vault, near the entrance to which I had for some weeks had my table while I wrote out copies of birth and death certificates. How true the stories were I don't know. But when the rebels had surrendered, and the siege was over, and the local papers carried photographs (taken from far away) of people leaving the Red House with handkerchiefs to their noses, I remembered the smell of the fish glue in which I had worked; and thought of the dimly lit, airless, oddly quiet vault, full of paper, where I had been told all the records of the British colony were stored, all the records, that is, since 1797, records of surveys and property transactions and then the records, starting later, of births and deaths, together with a copy of everything that had been printed in the colony.

I was told that the smell of death lingered for days in that area where, thirty-five years or so before, the fathers and grandfathers of some of the rebels (many were very young, boys in their teens) might have once partaken of the sacrament of Woodford Square.

I had never thought of St. Vincent Street—so calm and
quiet in my first memory of it—as a place where men might
fight so desperately. But all scenes of human habitation are
touched by violence of this kind. Nearly every town has been
besieged and fought over and has known this kind of blood.
And as soon as I thought back, even to my own nerves at the
time of my first return from England, I saw that there was
an immense chain of events. You could start with the sacrament of the square and work back: to the black madmen
on the benches, the Indian destitutes, the plantations, the
wilderness, the aboriginal settlements, the discovery. And
you could move forward from that exaltation and that mood
of rejection to the nihilism of the moment.

As soon as the siege began there was no effective government. It took a little while for this to be understood; and then
the effect on black communities—local and immigrant, in the
capital and all those contiguous settlements at the foot of the
Northern Range, north of the mainly Indian countryside,
which remained quiet, untouched by the frenzy to the
north—the effect on these communities was extraordinary.
They were like people who had been granted a moment of
pure freedom. They formed looting gangs. It was of this—
of the inflamed, unrecognizable faces of the looters, the glittering eyes—as much as of the siege at the Red House that
people spoke when I went back. For six days or so whole
communities had lived with the idea of the end of things, a
world without logic, and they had been lifted out of themselves. At least twenty-nine people died during this looting.

For many years I had accepted that the city I had known
as a child no longer existed and what was there now belonged
to others. Nazaralli Baksh, who had made the clothes I had
gone away in, had ceased for some time to be a name in St.
Vincent Street. But to see the destruction around where his
shop had been was to be reminded of him more than ever.
Across the road, the Victorian Gothic Police Headquarters—

he used to make uniforms for them—had been blasted in at one side. The grey outer wall, where it still stood, was blackened; smoke had poured out of the pointed arches. It was unsettling to see what had been city—regulated, serviced, protected, full of wonder and the possibility of adventure— turn to vacancy, simple ground. The commercial streets of the centre had been levelled. You could see down to what might have been thought buried forever: the thick-walled eighteenth-century Spanish foundations of some buildings. You could see the low gable marks of early, small buildings against higher walls. You could look down, in fact, at more than Spanish foundations: you could look down at red Amerindian soil.

There had been blood here before. Where the shacks of immigrants now scaffolded the hillsides there had once been aboriginal people. The eighteenth-century Spanish city had been laid out on a wilderness the Spaniards had themselves created two centuries before, when they had taken over the aboriginal settlement of Cumucurapo. The Spaniards, always legalistic, nearly always had a notary on hand to "give faith" to what he witnessed. "*Doy fe*," the notary would write: "I give faith," "I give witness." And there was a notary who recorded the names of the Amerindian chiefs of Cumucurapo who had surrendered their land to the Spaniards; the notary said that they had done so willingly, and that the people had "rejoiced." The names of these chiefs were confirmed by an extraordinary accident. A short while later an English marauder came raiding. The Spaniards, who had so recently taken "true possession," were themselves now put to flight; and, in the jail of the new Spanish settlement beyond the hills, five of the dispossessed chiefs were found, with the very names the notary had recorded, the last aboriginal rulers of the land, held together on one chain, scalded with hot bacon fat, and broken by other punishments.

CHAPTER 3

New Clothes: An Unwritten Story

SOME WRITING ideas go cold on you when you try to work them out on the page. Other ideas you simply play with in your mind, and don't do more about, perhaps because you know you won't get far. Most of these unattempted ideas fade; but one or two can stay with you. This is an account of an idea that has stayed.

The first impulse came to me in the first or second week of 1961, when I was in the Guiana Highlands, an Amerindian no man's land on the frontiers of Venezuela, Brazil and what is now called Guyana.

I hadn't been to South America before, had never travelled in wilderness. I had never, in fact, done any kind of serious travelling; and the writing wish that came to me was less an idea for a story than an excitement about where I was.

Once for nearly a whole day I was in a small boat on a highland river, moving upstream through tall, cool woodland. The river here was the merest tributary of a tributary. It was shallow, widening out sometimes over a cluttered rocky bed, with occasional deep pools where fallen trees or branches made perfect reflections, together with big fissured boulders. These boulders, grey, scoured clean, were sometimes so neatly cracked apart—like some kind of enormous petrified fruit—that they became things of beauty in themselves. The river water was reddish (from rotting leaves and tree-bark), transparent in sunlight, and clean enough to drink.

Brightly coloured birds followed our boat. We had a man with a gun with us, an Amerindian. He fired at the birds, for sport. After every shot he looked down at the boat, at no one in particular, and gave a nervous laugh. The birds didn't take fright; they stayed with us; you could hear their wings flapping steadily on.

Once or twice during the day we stopped at an Amerindian village. At these village sites the river bank was higher, with a ramp or path zigzagging down to where the village dugouts were tied up. The people were pale, with black hair. Animated among themselves, exchanging food and goods and news, they managed at the next moment to be distant with the rest of us: holding themselves with an extraordinary stillness on their tree-shaded bank, and looking down without expression at the boat.

That was the setting. I would have liked to do something with it, but every piece of invention that came to me seemed to falsify what I had felt as a traveller.

Six or seven years later, when I was writing another kind of book, I did some detailed reading about the area. I went back to the earliest records, concentrating on the period between 1590 and 1620. Among the Spanish documents were accounts of the formal foundation of Spanish towns in Amerindian wilderness, reports of expeditions (most of them ending in death or despair), petitions of colonists to the king (read by the king or an official perhaps a full year later): curiously informal and fresh, these old Spanish cries from the other end of the world, the complaints and deceptions of hungry, quarrelsome, self-righteous, stoical people.

I looked also at the accounts of foreign adventurers. Foreigners—other Europeans—were barred by Spanish law from the Spanish empire. They risked death or the Inquisition if they were picked up. But this was a neglected corner of the Spanish empire, and the interlopers, as they were called, kept on coming, from France and Holland and England. Most came to trade (bringing in African slaves, taking out salt or tobacco); but a few had the idea of setting up colonies or kingdoms of their own, and came to find allies and subjects among the Indians.

I wondered at the fortitude of all these people. I remembered what I had first seen of the continent, a very small corner of it, from the low-flying aeroplane in the last week of 1960: miles of muddy wild beach with collapsed big trees where perhaps no traveller had set foot and no tourist ever would; tight forest; the vast half-drowned confusion of meandering rivers. It would have been achievement enough to get there and survive. The people whose words I was reading went there to intrigue, to look for gold, to fight.

A story shaped in my mind, over some years. But it never clothed itself in detail, in the "business" necessary to a narrative, even though this business fades as the narrative moves on—much as the oil or alcohol that carries a longer-lasting perfume fades.

My idea remained an idea, and (partly working it out for the first time) I write it down here.

THE NARRATOR is going up a highland river in an unnamed South American country. Who is this narrator? What can he be made to be? This is often where fiction can simply become false.

To make the narrator a writer or traveller would be true to the actual experience; but then the fictional additions would be quite transparent. Can the narrator be a man in disguise, a man on the run? That would be true about the region. In 1971 Michael X, the Trinidad Black Power man, after he had killed two people in Trinidad, went to Guyana (physically like the country of the narrative) and made for the interior, to hide. And many years before, one of the last men of the Frank James gang, looking for a sanctuary outside the United States, fetched up in the Guiana savannah country, lower down from the forest. (So I had heard when I went there on my own journey. Local people were proud of the connection; and I, too, thought it glamorous, having seen as a child the Tyrone Power and Henry Fonda films about Frank and Jesse James.)

A man on the run would have been true to the place. But narrative has its own strictness. It requires pertinence at all times, and to have given that character to the narrator would have introduced something not needed, a distraction, something that wouldn't have tied up with what was to come at the end of his journey.

Better, instead of a man on the run, have a narrator who is a carrier of mischief. A revolutionary of the 1970s, say. A man seeking the help of up-country Amerindians to over-throw the African government on the coast. Such a situation wouldn't only echo the truth of more than one country in the region. It would also hold certain historical ironies.

In the late eighteenth and early nineteenth centuries, at the time of the Dutch and British slave plantations on the coast—the Dutch and British no longer interlopers on the Spanish Main, but sovereign powers—when slaves ran away to the interior, Amerindians hunted them down for a bounty. Now, at the time of the story, the Africans on the coast, descendants of the slaves, have inherited the authority of the old colonial government. They have a substantial educated and professional class. They are the rulers now; and the Amerindians are culturally what they were two hundred years before.

So for this narrator—who is more than a traveller look-ing for new sights—everything seen on the river has many meanings.

At the stern of the boat there is a man with a shotgun. From time to time he fires at the birds following the boat; and after every shot he laughs. It was perhaps with this sense of sport that his ancestors hunted down African runaways. Not with guns then, but with arrows—delicate little wands with the merest metal tip, not at all dangerous-looking, looking more like toys. They are still made: the arrows and quivers in the craft shops on the coast are exactly like the real things, fifty or sixty years old, that can be seen, coated with dust, in the ramshackle little museum—hardly touched since colonial days—in the capital.

And—perhaps, perhaps, the narrator thinks—this old instinct, this old attitude to the African, can be revived now, to serve a higher cause. Though when the boat stops at the villages, and the narrator considers the blank faces, the stillness of the staring people (after the first agitation), he has his doubts, comparing these withdrawn, passive river people with the Africans on the coast, and with the liveliness of revolutionary tribal people in other continents.

The once-a-week boat on this river is a cause for excitement at all the villages. At one shady village a woman comes down the zigzagging yellow ramp with a basket of food for the man with the shotgun: various things in tins and wooden bowls, separately tied up in cloth. The man doesn't look at the woman when he speaks a few words to her; and later she comes down again with some cassava bread, two halves of a big stiff whitish disc about half an inch thick, with something of the appearance of granulated polystyrene.

The man breaks these halves into smaller pieces and wedges them between the bowls and tins and the side of the basket—roughly, as though the wrapping up of food in cloth is something that only women do. Later, when they are on the smooth river again, and the time has come to eat, the man unties all the dishes and—with sudden seriousness—breaks off small pieces of bread to dip into them. Cassava bread is part of every mouthful that he chews. It is the staple; it bulks out the meal.

The narrator asks for a piece, to try. The man laughs, pleased to be of interest. Below the unexpected sourness of the bread there is almost no taste.

The light alters; the mood of the day alters. The sun, more directly overhead, strikes down between the forest walls, and the river becomes full of glare. The river changes. The man with the gun, his meal finished, the dishes rinsed in the river and put back in the basket, is now sitting in the bow looking out for snags. He sits and watches and never stirs.

The narrator, with the sourness of the cassava bread lingering in his mouth, and a memory of its grittiness, thinks of the world's staples. Rice and wheat and other kinds of grain are grasses. Cassava—a cousin of the red-leaved poinsettia— is more miraculous. It is a root, and it has a poison. It would have taken centuries for the remote ancestors of these forest people, after the crossing over of their ancestors from Asia, to have made their way down the continent to these forests and rivers. How many centuries more before the discovery of cassava? And how many centuries after that for the folk invention of the simple tools for getting rid of the poison?

Thinking like this, thinking of all the inventions of these isolated people, the narrator begins to think of the antiquity of the forest. Not new, not virgin. Those villages on the river would have been like the towns of the classical world, rising for millennia on the middens of their predecessors.

All at once, then, the light altering again, acquiring colour after glare, the river journey is over. It is about four o'clock, two hours to sunset. There is a new clearing in the forest, with a damaged stretch of low dirt-yellow bank—not the high bank of the Indian villages. There is no well-made ramp, just a number of crumbling chutes. After a day of river and sun and forest and Indian faces, the narrator is startled to see two almost naked white boys with bows and the small Indian arrows hiding behind the grass and boulder at the water's edge. Not the arrows of the craft shops on the coast: the real arrows, from the forest. For a moment or two it is like being taken back to the beginning of things. Before white skins turned another colour, and yellow hair turned black. There is no mystery: the children are from the new settlement in the clearing. They are playing at being Indians. The narrator is expected.

The narrator will stay for a few days here. The settlement is not his final destination. He will rest, take guides and go on. He will have to go on foot. The river cannot be navigated beyond this point. Beyond this are the boulders and the shallow rapids.

The settlement is the site of a religious mission. It is a newish religion, with a Christian basis. It has established itself in the country, both on the coast, where its followers are African, and in the interior, where it is getting Amerindian converts.

On the coast, among the Africans, it is even popular, because it promotes the idea of voluntary service as a two-way traffic, a form of international exchange. This means that the local country doesn't simply receive foreign volunteers. Favoured local people who accept the religion can be sent abroad as service volunteers, to Europe, the United States, Canada, and even West Africa. Since few people on the coast have the means to travel (and most of the black population want to migrate to northern countries), there are any number of Africans, among them the relatives and friends of local politicians, who want to be volunteers and go abroad.

So the church has some authority and, in this country which is officially hostile to white people, the service volunteers who come from abroad have a good deal of freedom. These are the people who have been infiltrated by the revolutionaries. The disguise is almost perfect. Both groups have the same kind of dedication; both talk about racial brotherhood; both talk about the wastefulness of the rich and the exploitation of the poor; and both deal in the same stern idea of imminent punishment and justice.

The narrator is one of these infiltrators. Who the others are at this mission station he doesn't know. They will declare themselves to him in time. Now, at this moment of arrival, shouldering his rucksack, allowing himself to be marched off as a prisoner by the boys with the bows and deadly little Indian arrows, he is concerned to act only as a religious volunteer.

He is led to a cabin in the centre of the clearing. It is a rough timber cabin, but it is on tree-branch pillars about four feet high, and it easily dominates the other, smaller cabins which are flat on the rough ground. The clearing is still littered with the finer debris of felled trees, still with the marks of bush-clearing fires, and the salty smell of those fires. On three sides the forest wall, with many tall, thin, white-trunked trees close together, looks freshly exposed.

The narrator is expecting some kind of welcome, after his long journey. But the heavy white man, in jeans and washed-out tee-shirt, who comes out of the kitchen shed at the back of the central cabin, simply says to the boys, "Take the man to his house." It is a foreign voice, central or eastern European, overlaid by American or Canadian intonation; and the narrator doesn't know whether the abruptness has to do with the lack of language or whether it comes out of aggression. As the narrator walks away the man calls out: "Dinner here at five-thirty. That's the rule here."

That gives the narrator just over an hour. The cabin to which he is taken is small and roughly floored. Four Indians are sitting or squatting on the floor, among their bundles. One is darning, one is making a toy (a tribal back-pack), and the other two are just waiting—their food is being got ready somewhere on the station—and they are as passive and unnoticing as the Indians on the river. The cabin smells of tree-bark and sawn wood and dirt and oil and rotting leaves; and just as all the colours in a paint box if run together make a dead brown, so all these smells combine with the salty smell of the dead bush-fires outside to make a very deep smell of stale tobacco.

After a wash in the river—the water is cool: the sun is going down fast—it is time for the narrator to go to the big cabin. There are eight people there, all of them passing as service volunteers, all of them foreigners from different countries, no Amerindians. So in spite of the jeans and the beards and the casual clothes, the big cabin has a colonial feel.

They have a language problem. The heavy man with the rough manner, who is the head of the station, comes from Czechoslovakia. He doesn't say so directly; it comes out from what other people say; there is some talk of the town of Pilsen. His wife or friend, the one woman at the table, and no doubt the mother of the boys, doesn't speak English at all.

She is a big woman, with very blond hair. She is not good-looking, and she says nothing; but she is the only woman at the table, and there is something about her that draws attention: this big woman with the shiny high cheekbones, the heavy twisted mouth, oily now with food, the big smooth hands, the big, ugly red feet.

In this strange colonial setting where, as the narrator thinks, she has no competition, this woman radiates sexuality in a way she wouldn't at home. There is something else. In this setting, where she is without language, the woman has become her sexuality: to look at her and her thin cotton dress is to be aware of nothing else.

The narrator recognizes that the revulsion he feels is a way of fighting his fascination. With what? With appetite: this woman, newly out of her country, with all its disciplines and narrowness, has become all appetite. The same, he thinks, is true of her husband; and when he looks up at the big man he catches his assessing gaze.

There is much talk at the table while the daylight lasts. Afterwards, in the yellow light of the hurricane lantern, which throws enormous shadows on the rough-sawn timber walls, everyone is more subdued; and the narrator feels isolated from everyone else.

The dinner ends. To step out from the house and the light of the hurricane lamp is to step out into blackness that feels for a second or so like a blow. Little yellow lights in the cabins all around. The forest is singing: the noise is like something imagined, something in the head. It is only half past six. Ten or eleven hours of darkness before it gets light again. Using his flashlight to pick his way back to his cabin, the narrator gets the smell of stale tobacco as he enters. That was the smell of the food he ate; it was the smell of the river water; it is the smell of the forest; it is his own smell now. He wonders whether he will ever get used to forest life. But then, thinking of the big silent woman, and excited by that idea of appetite, he falls asleep.

In the course of the next few days two of the infiltrators reveal themselves to him. There should be a third, the regional commander. He will not reveal himself to the narrator, but the narrator has a good idea who he is.

The narrator finally gets his orders. He is told where he has to go. It is just a name to him. Indian guides will come to take him there.

There will at the end be about a dozen agents like the narrator, and a dozen bases in the forest. On a given day there will be a dozen incidents; the rivers will be watched at strategic points; the few airstrips will be overrun; the forest area, the greater part of the country, will be effectively cut off from the African-ruled coast. The country doesn't have the military resources to re-occupy the forest; elements of the foreign press will ensure that there is sympathy for the Indian cause, and lessen the possibility of outside intervention.

The narrator is relieved to be moving on. The mission

station is oppressive to him, because of the Czech couple, and because of the glumness of the Indians. For this the narrator blames the Czechs. There is nothing like joy in the Czechs. Authority, and being out of their setting, have only released appetite in them. It is this quality of appetite that has given them away to the narrator.

There are daily religious services for the Indians; there are regulated hours of work. On some evenings in the open space in front of the big cabin—with a smoky brushwood bonfire (to keep away the insects) adding to the stale tobacco smell— television videos are shown. American thrillers, with a black slant. Not as harmless as they appear: they are part of the anti-African indoctrination of the Indians. The Indians are shocked by the guns and the fighting and the speeding cars; they sigh and call out. Sometimes, to break the tension, some- one plays a flashlight on a black face; there is laughter; then many flashlights play on black faces on the screen; and the film is made harmless, becomes a film again, and animation makes the Indians like people with possibilities again.

The guides eventually come. They are two young Indian boys, Lucas and Mateo. The narrator leaves with them one morning. One boy walks ahead of the narrator, one behind him.

Soon they come to a wide forest trail, and there they are never absolutely alone. In the forest gloom it seems that there is always someone in the distance: someone always breaking out of the camouflage of leaves and shadow. Some of them are carrying big loads in their back-packs or back-panniers, models for the toys which the Indian in the narrator's cabin had been making: a flat timber frame with flexible woven walls at the sides and the bottom, the walls laced up over the load with forest-made twine. A further cord or rope attaches both sides of the pannier to a band over the carrier's forehead. So head and back bear the strain of the load. The carriers' backs are bent, and at the same time they lean forward against the pull of the band on the forehead. It seems painful; the carriers are dwarfed by their loads; but it is a posture with a balance of forces—a posture that fits the device, which must have evolved over the centuries—and it enables the carriers to walk for hours.

This forest trail is very old, the narrator reflects. How far back would it go? Would it go back to the colonization of the forest by the remote ancestors of these men? Or would some climatic change have intervened?

When the porters or load-carriers (perhaps carrying their own things) pass, they grunt out greetings to Lucas and Mateo, and sometimes from below their taut forehead bands they look up at the narrator. Their faces are the faces of old men. The narrator thinks of the peasants and carriers in Japanese woodcuts; the resemblance is quite remarkable. And just as in woodcuts by Hokusai of rural scenes everything belongs—straw and roofs, trees and the timber of bridges—and nothing is imported, so here in this scene in which he is walking, almost everything belongs—except for the narrator himself, the clothes and canvas shoes of Lucas and Mateo, and the tins and sometimes the printed cardboard boxes in the carriers' loads. A hundred years before, the narrator thinks, everything in this scene would have belonged; and a hundred years before that.

They stop for a while to rest and eat and drink a little. Lucas and Mateo use their machetes to trim a place for the narrator to sit. As they walk on again, the narrator surrenders to the idea of the antiquity of the forest and this trail. He begins to wonder about the idea of time that men must have in this setting.

When men know their world well; when they know every tree and flower; all the foods and poisons; all the animals; when they have perfected all their tools; when everything exists in balance, and there is nothing from outside to compare, what idea can men have of the passing of time? It is the things we pass that give us an idea of speed. When there is nothing to compare, men must exist only in their own light and the light of the people they know—the narrator thinks of the dim lights in the blackness of the mission clearing, thinks of the play of his flashlight and the others' as they pick their way back to their cabins. Beyond that, backwards and forwards, there must be nothing.

The narrator wrestles with this difficult idea, very strange in the bright light. While the sun is still high the march ends. It is the rule. Two hours before sunset. They camp beside a stream. The sun strikes through the shallow reddish water; inches below the surface webs of light dance over the crushed grey and red rock at the bottom. Beauty; but it is only Lucas and Mateo who have made it safe. Lucas and Mateo are like people to whom the forest is home. Very quickly now, using their machetes, they trim slender tree branches, sharpen one end, bury it in the earth, and put up a low shelter, roofed with the fronds of the wild banana.

They light a little fire. Lucas and Mateo prepare their own food; the narrator prepares his own, using the river water. The sun begins to go; very quickly it falls out of the sky. The evening melancholy, the long hours before daylight, cast a gloom on the narrator.

Mateo is whittling away at a toy dugout-paddle.

The narrator asks Mateo, "What does your father do?"

A foolish question to ask in the forest: the narrator feels it as soon as he talks.

"My father dead."

"How did he die?"

Mateo puts down his paddle and throws a twig on the small fire and says, "Kanaima kill him." Mateo speaks like a philosopher, like a man resigned to grief.

The kanaima is the spirit of death of the forests. It inhabits the body of a living man. Somewhere in the forest is the killer who looks like a man, looks like Mateo and Lucas and all the others, and kills all men. In a world without time, where men live only in the present, by their own light, as it were, all a man's life is spent in this fear. Without the kanaima, a man could truly be happy; might live forever.

Impossible to enter this way of perceiving. The narrator asks, the little twig fire dying down, the night stretching out ahead, "Are you married, Mateo?"

The other boy answers, "How can he be married?"

And Mateo says, "Indian girls foolish. They know nothing."

The narrator is filled with shame and grief for the people of the forest. They are very far away, these people who can see everything in the forest, who have so many talents, and have perfected so much in their isolation. They are beyond reach. They are further away than any group the narrator has known; perhaps even the revolution will not reach them. Everywhere else, in Asia, Europe north and south, Africa, tribes and peoples have been in collision since the beginning of time. These people, after the migration of their ancestors from Asia, have become people entirely of themselves, without resilience or the talent to adapt. Once their world was broken into, they lost their wholeness.

The little fire dies down. Lucas and Mateo stretch out away from the hut. The forest sings; from time to time, for some reason, the singing subsides for a split second and the river sound is heard. The narrator tries to imagine himself living in that setting for some years; for the rest of his life; for five hundred years. He feels an artificial touch of stress. He takes a sip of whisky from his bottle.

One of the boys sits up straightaway and says, "You drink rum, sir?"

"Not rum."

"You give us rum, sir."

"No rum."

The boy lies down again, sighing like a man.

The narrator is awakened by the sound of rain, falling loudly on the wild-banana fronds of his hut roof. He awakens to his earlier stress, his own feeling of dislocation.

One of the boys is standing in the darkness outside. He says, "Can Lucas and I come here, sir?"

They come in, and the narrator is enveloped in the smell of stale tobacco, enveloped in the idea of appetite: appetite the antidote to stress.

He lets his hand fall on the body next to him, not knowing to whom it belongs. The boy is passive. Appetite grows on the narrator; and even while his fallen hand opens, against the hardness of the body, a finer version of a body like his own, a body therefore more than half known, the narrator's thought is of the grossness of the big blond woman at the station now a day's march away. Appetite, appetite: the passivity of the boy feeds it.

When he gets up in the morning the narrator finds himself alone in the little leaf-and-branch shelter. He has a moment of alarm. But the boys are higher up the river, preparing for the day. The narrator still doesn't know which of the two had been beside him.

The time comes to leave. With their machetes Lucas and Mateo—following some forest rule, perhaps—cut down the little shelter. So protecting during the night, but so flimsy, really.

The march begins. The narrator is no longer at ease, no longer the man he had been. The path moves away from the upland river to the forest. Such beauty there; but something of the safety and wholeness of the previous day has left the narrator. Something nags; he never has to search far for the reason. As often as he rejects it, as often as he applies his mind to it, unease returns, to come between him and the moment; and below all of this now, and adding to his agitation, there is the idea of his cause, the starting point of the journey.

Tossed about, sickening inwardly in a familiar way as

the day wears on, he ceases to look about him. He walks mechanically between the two boys, fixing his eyes on the heels (in dirty canvas shoes) of the boy in front of him.

The boys, on the other hand, are today more animated, cutting switches with their machetes, flicking leaves and small insects from the path, sometimes using their machetes to cut, very swiftly and neatly, light trail-marks on trees, talking loudly in their own language over him, as it were, as though it is important to make a human noise in the forest. There is a different swing to their gait; it is as if they were alone. They call out from afar to the people they see on the path; and sometimes, seeming to follow abrupt hunches of their own, they leave the path and—holding themselves still at a particular spot, as though they wish not even to disturb the air just then—they stand looking at something or for something.

In mid-afternoon they halt for the day. Today, though, the boys make no sign of building a shelter. Instead, they leave the narrator in the camp-site and they wander off—always the two together—and come back and wander off again. The day before, the narrator hadn't expected a shelter; today he does. He feels disregarded; it spoils the moment, the view, the yellowing light.

For the first time that day he asserts himself. When the boys come back he says, "Lucas, build the hut."

And it is really very easy. The boys obey, with no change of mood: they might have been waiting for his order. Talking in their language, in their new loud way, as though it is important to make noise, they cut and trim branches. The sharp blades ring as they slice through sappy wood, and in no time the timbers are ready, the uprights forked at the top, and sharpened at the end where they are to be buried in the soft forest earth. Quickly then, almost without searching—as though in their wanderings they have taken stock of every-thing and now know exactly where they have to go—the boys fetch the wild-banana fronds and the big, hollow-ribbed, heart-shaped leaves to hang on the roof frame.

When they are finished they lay the narrator's pack in the shelter. It is like a delicate attention; but then the narrator sees them get their own packs and set them down next to his: the three packs lying, quite formally, side by side, in a repetition of the previous night's arrangement: as though that was also contained in the narrator's orders.

They light a fire. The flame hardly shows in the afternoon light. They separately prepare their food, the boys theirs together, the narrator his. The light fades fast, the fire shows, and then, abruptly, night comes. The forest begins to sing. Soon it is like a noise in the head.

Lucas whittles at his toy paddle. He asks the narrator, "Where you come from?"

"England."

Mateo asks, "Why you come here?"

The narrator gives the reply he has been trained to give: "I will tell Alfred. He will tell you." Alfred is the headman of the village where they are going.

Lucas says, "You want to build houses here?"

"Alfred will tell you." And to cut the questioning short the narrator asks, "How did kanaima kill your father, Mateo?"

The faces of both boys, tanned, shiny, reflecting the fire, become very serious, resigned.

Lucas speaks first. "Kanaima was looking for him. He had a sign."

"But then he forget," Mateo says. "One day a cloth-seller come. My father *want* to look at the cloth. He don't know that kanaima come with the cloth-seller. When my father was looking at the cloth kanaima hide in his room. When my father come back with the new cloth kanaima kill him. That is all. Afterwards we burn the cloth."

They all look at the fire.

Lucas says, "You live in a *house* in England?"

There is such an emphasis on the word the narrator wants to say no, he lives in a flat; but that would be confusing. So he says yes.

Lucas says slowly, as though he is repeating a lesson, "I want to live in a house."

Such a simple ambition, but so far away, and at the moment so unlikely: the narrator finds himself moved by these boys in a way that goes beyond his political cause.

Mateo says, "You know that kanaima come for Lucas, sir?"

The narrator says, "Lucas?"

Lucas shaves with his sharp knife at his paddle, and throws the shaving into the fire. "I was walking. From very far I see something on the track that didn't have to be there. But I don't think. I go on, and see the thing that wrong. Was a little white flower. By itself. I turn and run. But was too late."

It is on Lucas's body—lying beside him—that the narrator's hand falls later that evening in the hut. He is moved now by more than appetite, the excitement of the earlier evening: the passivity of the boy adds to the narrator's mood, builds up to tenderness, made deeper by a feeling of being unable to help, tenderness that turns to a melancholy like the melancholy he had seen earlier in Lucas's face in the firelight.

Some time later Mateo sits up abruptly. He says, "Sir, you must take Lucas with you to England."

It is something that would have just struck Mateo, the narrator thinks: it is a way Lucas might be saved. The narrator doesn't answer.

A long time later Mateo says, "Sir?"

The narrator says, "Yes."

The word has no meaning. It is just a sound, an acknowledgement. But Mateo gives a contented sigh and settles down to sleep.

The boys are all friendliness the next day. They do not talk loudly over the narrator as on the day before; they do not abruptly leave the narrator and the line of march; they try to bring the narrator into all that they do. Their faces are brighter, less resigned-looking. One of the things the narrator has come out to do is to win the trust of people like Lucas and Mateo. But this trust is of another sort. He feels undermined by it; at the same time he doesn't see how he can reject it. And it is as if some exchange has been made, as if something of the oppression that has left the boys now sits on the narrator's shoulder.

He begins to feel, too, that the journey is lasting too long. They are meeting fewer people on the forest path now, and there are fewer tins and printed cardboard boxes strapped up in their back-packs. But the boys reassure the narrator. It's all right; he is not to worry; they are looking after him.

So for two or more days they walk and camp: make-believe in the evening (the leaf shelter in the forest, the little fire, safety in the night), turbulence and doubt in the day, day and night now like two sides of the narrator's spirit, one growing out of the other: the narrator at night wishing that make-believe could be all, the complete reality, and then in daylight wondering how he could disengage from the trust the boys have placed in him. More: almost without his being aware of it, the daylight doubt is widening. He begins to wonder—at first in a lightheaded way, and as though the idea is quite absurd—what would happen if he were to withdraw from what he has undertaken to do.

At last, at about noon one day, after four or five hours of marching, they arrive. They turn off the path and go through the forest and up to a little plateau where there is a village of old grey-brown grass huts, some of them open with tree-branch poles, some conical and closed.

Lucas and Mateo are home. People call out to them: they call back: animation such as, many days before, at the start

of his travel in the deep interior, the narrator had seen at the
village landing-stages on the river.

The narrator is taken to the hut where he is to live. There
is an overpowering smell of earth and stale tobacco. People
who have lived in the hut before have left pieces of cloth and
whittled wood wedged between the trimmed rods of the
frame and the old grass of the roof. The narrator becomes
very tired. He sleeps almost as soon as he lies down, relieved
to be at last alone.

When he gets up he finds that the light is the light of
mid-afternoon, the sun about to decline: the time when on
previous days they would have stopped marching, and Lucas
and Mateo would have been building their shelter: a toy
version, as the narrator now sees, of the huts here.

After days of forest and gloom, the smoke from the cooking fires in front of the open kitchen hut seems to the narrator
to be remarkably blue, a colour on its own, not a tone of
grey or brown. The narrator is also aware that the ground
below his feet feels hollow: footfalls even some distance away
make a dull drumming sound. The ground has been disturbed
or built up in some way. The narrator, considering the plateau
or platform of the village open space, feels that the site is old,
that for some way down the earth would contain debris or
relics of scenes, repeated through the centuries, like the one
around him now.

Some of the women are making cassava bread. Finished
rounds are on the grass roof. At the side of the kitchen hut
hangs the long plaited tube which can be twisted or wrung
by means of a horizontally fitted stick, to squeeze the poison
out of grated cassava: a poison caught in a wooden dish on
the ground. Because this poison is valuable: it can preserve
meat for up to a year.

On the ground is a cassava-grater. It is a beautiful object:
sharp chippings of granite fixed in hardened pitch, the pitch
set in a shallow rectangular trough in a flat piece of wood.

The pitch would have come from far away; a precious lump would have been imported; so, too, the granite chippings. The pitch would have been boiled into a liquid, then poured into the hollow in the wood; as it cooled, the granite chippings would have been set in it one by one.

The narrator looks up. The women and girls are delighted by his contemplation of this kitchen object. The narrator thinks, "I love these people." Then he questions himself, "What do I mean by that?" Looking at the women in the blue smoke, he thinks, "I want no harm to come to them."

Lucas and Mateo appear. Without their loads and travelling hats, and in fresh clothes, they look like young men of some standing in the village. They take the narrator down to the river. There is a deep part where he can dive, they say. They go down with him, when he is ready. They will not leave him alone; they will not do that with the kanaima prowling about; they will offer him their protection.

The sun is going down. The water, reddish from leaves, gets darker as the light goes. The water is cool, too cool for the man-eating small fish, the boys or young men say.

The narrator sinks into the red water. The pool is as deep as the young men say. Soon the light fades from the water. Soon it is utterly black. Soon it is of a black so deep that it is without colour: it is nothing, however much you concentrate on it. In this nothing the narrator feels he has lost touch with his body; water blocks sensation. He is just his eyes concentrating on nothing; he is just mind alone, a perceiving of nothing. He is quite frightened. He somehow gets in touch with his will again and pulls himself up, to the yellowing light.

He is glad to see the boys. They wait while he dresses, and then they walk him back up to the village. The best protection against the kanaima is company: once the kanaima is seen by a third party, the kanaima's power is lost. Yet the need for company also reinforces the kanaima's power. And the narrator feels that, like Lucas with the flower on the path, he has had a brush with his kanaima: an emotion, a moment, that will come back to him in dreams and states of blurred consciousness, something he will now not lose touch with, and which when it returns will carry with it the setting and all the extreme emotions of the last few days, including the emotion of this moment: the love for these people, which contains the wish that no harm should come to them, and is already as a result more pain than love.

It is pain rather than love which now suffuses the narrator's vision, and corrupts everything that he sees. It is all like something he has already lost: the late afternoon light, the friendly women and children, the very blue smoke. And now all the half-formulated doubts, mere impulses, of the last few days harden into a determination to turn his back on these people, to put them out of his mind.

Hard to formulate, harder to carry out. The narrator cannot simply go away. He doesn't know where he is. He will need guides to go back, people who will make the forest safe for him. Alfred, the village captain or headman, wouldn't let him go just like that. Alfred would worry about the consequences, worry about what reports would get back to the coast. There would also be the Czech at the mission settlement. He wouldn't let the narrator get away so easily.

So the narrator will have to stay. He will have to stay and get started with the organization and the other things he has been detailed to do. Perhaps later, when activity begins, it might be easier for the narrator to leave. To leave the forest, the country, the movement.

But now he will have to stay, for some weeks, some months. The people of this village and others will get to know him very well. He is already a stranger, an extraordinary being. And they, people without writing and books, depend completely on sight and memory; they have greater gifts that way. They will commit an infinity of details about him to memory: his voice, gait, gestures. He will exist in the minds of these people as he will exist nowhere else. And after he has gone away they will remember him as the man who stayed long and wasn't straight with them, who promised many things and then went away.

There is an hour or so to go before sunset. Lucas and Mateo come to take the narrator to the village captain. They say they will interpret.

The narrator says, "But they told me Alfred spoke English."

Mateo says, "This isn't Alfred."

"He is my uncle," Lucas says. "My father brother."

The uncle is not very old. He is in an open hut, a place of reception rather than sleeping, with a hammock for himself in one corner, and with low hardwood stools, each carved out of a solid piece of wood, for visitors. He is of a beautiful colour, the pores clean and separate on his fine skin. He is wearing new jeans and a flowered shirt: clearly the cloth-seller from the other side makes regular visits.

What he says in his language, which Lucas and Mateo turn into their own kind of English, is like this: "I heard from Alfred that Lucas and Mateo had gone to get you. But I never believed you would come. This sort of thing has been going on for so long. So much talk, so little done. But now you're here. I hope you will act carefully. You came the hard way. There is another way, an easier way. It is through the savannah. My wife's father told me he heard from his father that once some people were coming through there to look for gold."

"Djukas?" the narrator asks, using the local word for the descendants of the African runaways who had settled in some parts of the forest.

"Djukas, people from the south—I can't remember what my wife's grandfather said. These people were coming to look for gold. And I don't have to tell you what that would

have meant for us. Do you know what the villagers did? It
was the dry season. They set the savannah alight. It blazed up
for miles. My wife's grandfather said birds were always a little
ahead of the fire, picking up the snakes and other little animals
running away from the fire. The same fire burned every one
of the men coming to look for gold. After that everybody had
to leave the villages and hide in the forest for two years. Do
you think it will be like that this time? Are you sure you know
what you are doing? We are brave people. But—" He breaks
off. Then he says, "Where do you come from?"

"England."

"Lucas told me. My grandfather went to England. Did
Lucas tell you?"

Lucas licks his top lip, and looks down.

"He went with an Englishman who liked him, and
wanted him to learn English. He spent three years in England.
They wanted him to marry an Englishwoman. That was part
of the original idea. They even found a woman, but then at
the last minute, before they came back, she became frightened. The plan was that they would come back and build
houses here." He used the English word, but in his pronuncia-
tion it sounded like part of his own language. "One of the
things my grandfather said about England when he came
back was that the captain of the country was a woman. Was
that true?"

"It was true."

"I am glad to hear it. Some people said he was making it
up. Some people didn't even believe he had gone to England,
though he came back with printed books to show. He came
back and waited for the English people to come out here and
build *houses*. Every year or so somebody came out. Not by
the way you came, but by the other way, the savannah way
I told you about. They always brought the same message to
my grandfather: next year, next year. Is that the kind of
message you will be bringing us?"

"No," the narrator says. "It's going to be different this time. We are different people."

"People began to mock my grandfather. They said he was going to get us in trouble with the government for nothing at all. One time when an Englishman came out there was an eclipse of the moon. You know what people do when that happens? They shoot flaming arrows at the moon, to light it up again. My grandfather was ashamed. He told me so. He begged the Englishman to forgive them for behaving in that childish way. But the Englishman only laughed and said that there would be no trouble with the government. What you have just said. He said that the place was good for *houses*. It is what I hear people are telling Alfred now. And then something happened. There was a war or something, I suppose, and English people stopped coming. Nobody came even to say 'next year.' But my grandfather never stopped believing that they would come back. He went foolish with that belief, but there are people who still believe that. Lucas believes. And I'll tell you something. Kanaima has come for Lucas. You know that. He must have told you. He told me he told you. And when kanaima came for Lucas, he said, 'I will get away. I know that. I will go to England. My grandfather's friend will send for me.' And now you have come. Did Lucas tell you? They used to send clothes for my grandfather. Not our kind of clothes, but modern clothes, for the *houses* they were going to build. I still have some of them. Let me show you."

He undid the bundle beside him. A wild-banana leaf, cured in some way, with its browned ribs giving the effect of papyrus, was folded over the garment. He lifted out the material, fawn-coloured, perished, but recognizably a doublet of Tudor times, new clothes of three hundred and fifty years before, relic of an old betrayal.

CHAPTER 4

Passenger: A Figure from the Thirties

I THOUGHT THAT before I settled into the writing of this book I should go and look at old scenes. And, when I was in Trinidad, I did the longish drive one day to the north-easternmost point of the island, Point Galera, Galley Point. Columbus gave the name.

An asphalt lane led off the main road to the Point itself. After the forest of the last few miles, the lane felt high and exposed. The light was harder; the asphalt looked very black; you could hear the wind and the sea. Half-stripped old coconut trees were on one side of the lane, untrimmed bush on the other side, with many young guava trees (no doubt seeded by birds, always overhead), and with a wind-blown drift of browned newspaper and bleached, flattened cardboard packets.

At the end of the lane was a disused lighthouse. A little way up its cracked white bulk it was marked—in raised plaster or concrete—with a date, 1897, a simple diamond shape, and the letters VDJ. The letters stood for "Victoria Diamond Jubilee." It was a double celebration: 1897 was not only the year of the Diamond Jubilee of Queen Victoria; it was also the centenary of the British conquest of Trinidad from the Spaniards.

A path led down the broken cliff to the rocks the light-house used to warn against. Some young black men and boys (immigrants, legal and illegal, from the small islands to the north) were standing or sitting on the upper rocks and look-ing down at a man who, with a footing just above the spray, was fishing for baby shark, with the help of an assistant.

The assistant stood a safer distance away, higher up and a little to one side of his principal, and took the strain of the line when a shark bit. The hooked shark looked small and playful in the white water between the rocks, really a baby, not strong or smart, not worth catching. But after it had been landed and killed it looked big and heavy, especially when the assistant—as serious as his master and the silent watchers (scattered about the rocks, as if for privacy, each watcher with his tight midday shadow)—lifted the shark on to his shoulder to take it up to where the rest of the catch was.

Wind and beating sea, over the centuries, had caused the cliff to crumble at this Point. But plant life hung on wherever it could. A kind of grass had knitted itself together into de-pressions in the upper rocks. On rock formations a few hun-dred feet out in the sea, long ago cut off from the Point, strange-looking trees, wet with the spray, stunted and twisted by the wind, stood firm, and even now would have been screening the young trees that would in time replace them.

I couldn't have put a name to the trees. They were not part of the imported vegetation we knew very well, like the coconut, mango, breadfruit, bamboo. The trees on the rocks flourished where they did because they were native to those rocks, the Point, the island, the continent. And it occurred to me that, in spite of everything that had happened here, in spite of everything at our backs, what I was looking at was, miraculously, a version of the very first thing Columbus had seen after his crossing of the Atlantic on his third voyage: not the same rocks, but rocks created out of those he had seen, and wind-beaten trees like the ones before me, ten or twelve or fifteen cycles before.

The story was that he had called the point the Galley, Galera, because what he had seen looked like "a galley under sail." There is no such shape on the island itself, in this north-eastern part; and in the nineteenth century, after the island had become a British colony, people began to feel that the old maps had got it wrong, that in the two hundred and fifty years of depopulation and wilderness that had followed the discovery—the island ravaged at the edges, never properly settled or administered or explored by the Spaniards—knowledge of Columbus's landfall had been lost. The "galley" Columbus had seen was thought to refer to a formation on a long sandspit at the south-eastern tip of the island.

But I thought now, looking down with the others at the shark-fishing in the bloodied white water between the rocks, and looking beyond that to the rocks and the twisted trees out in the sea, that I was seeing what Columbus had seen. He would have seen the cliff and the rocks and the beating sea from far out. He would have kept well clear of the Point. A few hours' sailing would have taken him to the easier south-eastern tip of the island; just around that, and now close enough to the shore to see the vegetable gardens of the people, he would have seen the three low hills that would have suggested the name of the Trinity for the island. A few hours on from that, he would have had his first glimpse of the South American continent. He would have taken it for another island, and given it the name of Gracia, Grace.

Things had gone badly for him. He hadn't on his two previous journeys found much gold, and the colony he had founded on Haiti had gone wrong. Now, third time lucky with the sighting of new territory, his thoughts were of religion and redemption, of things at last being put right for him. But until just a few hours before, he had been more of a sailor; and to his fifteenth-century Mediterranean eyes the black rocks and twisted trees off the point of the island would have reminded him of a galley under sail: the rocks standing for the galley, the twisted trees standing for the sails.

I suppose that people had been looking for a galley shape on the island itself; they would have been looking for something big and noticeable. They wouldn't have considered the worn rocks out at sea, which the admiral would have seen from the other side. The caravels were small; the galleys would have been even lower.

It occurred to me that from that side, the ocean side, that first, fifteenth-century Mediterranean view might still exist; whereas from my position on the rocks I was looking at a remnant of the aboriginal island.

It was hard to hold on to that romantic way of looking. I had never tried to do that as a child: pretend I was looking at the aboriginal island. No teacher or anyone else had suggested it as an imaginative exercise. It was something I had found myself trying to do, on visits, many years after I had gone away. And now, to leave the Point, to travel back along the county roads, the overgrown cocoa estates with their weathered grey-black cocoa drying-houses, the villages with the little wooden or concrete houses in dirt yards, to the crowded towns beside the highway, was to be taken back into a version of the colony I had known as a child. It was to be taken back to old ways of feeling, where no moment of beginning, no past, seemed possible, and the aborigines might never have existed.

I USED TO feel—in the way of childhood, not putting words to feelings—that the light and the heat had burnt away the history of the place. I distrusted the ideas of glamour that were given us by postcards and postage stamps (ideas repeated by our local artists): certain bays and beaches, the Pitch Lake, certain flowering trees, certain buildings, our mixed population.

Many years later I thought that that feeling of the void had to do with my temperament, the temperament of a child of a recent Asian-Indian immigrant community in a mixed population: the child looked back and found no family past, found a blank. But I feel again now that I was responding to something that was missing, something that had been rooted out.

Like people of small or far-off communities, we liked the idea of being visited. And though I distrusted tourist-board ideas of glamour, I feel that without these ideas (if only as things to reject or react against), without the witness of our visitors, we would have been floating people, like the aborigines first come upon below Point Galera, living instinctive, unobserved lives.

I suppose visitors, tourists, began to come in number when steam replaced sail. The tourists at the turn of the century didn't come for the sun. They came for the sights; they protected themselves against the sun. With Edwardian layers of clothes, and with hats and umbrellas and parasols, they came to look at the diggings for the Panama Canal; they walked on the hard surface of the Pitch Lake; they looked at cocoa pods and coconuts growing on trees (crops requiring abundant plantation labour).

They also came for the history. They wanted to be in the waters of the great naval battles of the eighteenth century, when the powers of Europe fought over these small, rich sugar islands of the Caribbean. After the First World War, that idea of glory vanished. The naval battles and the once great names of the eighteenth-century admirals were forgotten. The tourists came for the sun, to get away from winter and the Depression; they came to be in places that were unspoilt, places that time had passed by, places, it might be said, that had never been discovered. So history was set on its head; the islands were refashioned.

EVERY YEAR the cruise ships brought one or two writers who were keeping journals and taking photographs for their "travel books." These books, though descended in form from

Victorian travel journals, were not like the books of Trollope or Charles Kingsley or Froude of fifty or sixty years before. There were no imperial "problems" now about the islands and the Spanish Main: no Victorian gloom about labour shortages after the abolition of slavery, about neglected or disaffected colonies, the rivalry of other powers, no nerves about an empire shrinking.

These cruise books, though very much about travel in the colonies, were about a part of the world that had, as it were, been cleansed of its past. The grainy photographs of, say, the fortifications of Cartagena in Colombia were photographs of an antiquity, something dimly connected with gold and galleons and the Spanish. The ruins of the black Emperor Christophe's Citadelle in Haiti were like an Egyptian mystery. This world was dead and safe.

These cruise books resembled one another. They couldn't have made much money for anybody, and I suppose they were a product of the Depression, written by hard-pressed men for public-library readers who dreamed of doing a cruise themselves one day in warm waters somewhere. Though this particular travel form required the writer to be always present, and knowledgeable, and busy, the books they wrote were curiously impersonal. That might have been because the writers had to get in everything earlier writers had got in; and also, I feel, because the writers of these travel books were really acting, acting being writers, acting being travellers, and, especially, acting being travellers in the colonies.

The Trinidad chapter of such a book would begin with an account of docking in the morning. It would speak of the mixed population in the streets. One writer might observe African people walking about and eating bananas; another would notice East Indian women with their jewellery and Indian costumes. There might be a visit to the Angostura Bitters factory; the Pitch Lake and the oilfields; a bay; a visit to a calypso tent or, if it wasn't the calypso season, a visit to a yard connected with one of the ecstatic local African sects, Shango or the Shouters.

There would be a well-connected local guide in the background. He had acted as guide for other writers and knew the Trinidad drill. Apart from him—and he would be white or mulatto and slightly aloof—the local people were far away, figures in the background. Of these people anything could be said. The Africans who had been seen eating bananas by one writer might, by another writer, be put into two-toned shoes. They might be put into new and squeaky two-toned shoes; and the writer might go on to say that Africans were so fond of squeaky shoes that they took brand-new shoes to shoemakers and asked them to "put in a squeak." As for the Indians of the countryside, they were a people apart; very little was known about their language or religion; and it was felt by the writer and his guide that this kind of knowledge didn't matter.

These books didn't cause offence. Very few local people read them. Some of the more extravagant things—like the squeaks in the two-toned shoes—chimed in with the local African sense of humour, the calypso fantasy. And then— hard to imagine now—local people lived with the idea of disregard. You could train yourself to read through this disregard in books and find things that were useful to you.

A book about Trinidad in the early 1930s had the pidgin or creole title of *If Crab No Walk*. It was by Owen Rutter, a name which has no other association for me. In his book Owen Rutter wrote this sentence: "The trains are all right, but the buses are a joke." My father hung a whole article for a local magazine on these words of Owen Rutter's. This would have been not long after I was born. Some years later—still a child—I came upon the magazine in my father's desk. I was entranced by the article, with its comic drawings and its examples of the wit and nonsense destination-rhymes of local bus conductors. I looked at this article many times; I suppose it was one of the things that helped to give me an idea of where I was. Without the Rutter book my father might not have seen that the local buses were something he could write about. So there is a kind of chain.

I am not sure, but I believe it was words of Owen Rutter's again that a local literary magazine put below a photograph of a Trinidad beach: "The desolate splendour of a palm-fringed beach at sunset." That was set next to a photograph of a sunset sky with some words from Keats below it: "While barrèd clouds bloom the soft-dying day." Beaches and sunsets were beautiful, of course; but those words of Keats (though they didn't match the photograph, and were mysterious) and Rutter's foreign witness were like an extra blessing.

We were not alone in this need for foreign witness. Even someone like Francis Parkman, with all his Boston security, when he was on the Oregon Trail in the 1840s, felt on occasion, in the splendour of the American wilderness, that in order to show himself equal to a particular scene he had to make some comparison to Italian painting, which at that time he would have known only in imperfect reproductions.

Perhaps there is no pure or primal gift of vision. Perhaps vision can only be tutored, and depends on an ability to compare one thing with another. Columbus saw a fifteenth-century galley where I, standing on the other side, saw a tumble of black rocks with trees that I would not have been able to recognize in another setting. Not many hours after seeing that galley, he was sailing close to the southern coast of the island, and he saw aboriginal village gardens as fair as those of Valencia in the spring. It was a comparison he had made more than once before, about islands far to the north, which are physically quite different. But it was the only way he had of describing vegetation he hadn't seen before, and it is all that we have of the first sighting of the untouched aboriginal island.

Centuries on, we needed our visitors to give us some

idea of where and what we were. We couldn't have done it ourselves. We needed foreign witness. But disregard came with this witness. And that was like a second setting of history on its head. Because in this traveller's view—this distant view of people eating bananas and wearing squeaky shoes, this view of a smallness that a cruise passenger could take in in a morning or a day—we, who had come in a variety of ways from many continents, were made to stand in for the aborigines and were held responsible for the nullity which had been created long before we had been transported to it.

AND THEN in 1937 a young English writer called Foster Morris came and wrote *The Shadowed Livery*, which was another kind of book. There was a big oilfield workers' strike in Trinidad that year. I don't know whether Foster Morris knew about local conditions before he came. But the strike and its personalities were at the heart of his book.

Oil had been discovered early in the century; and much of the south of the island (where Columbus had seen the beautiful Valencia-like aboriginal gardens) had been turned into an oil reserve. Most of the oilfield workers in Trinidad were Africans from the small island of Grenada to the north. Local people, East Indians or Africans, could have been used; but the radicals said (and I suppose they were right) that the authorities didn't want to disturb the local labour market and preferred to have an isolated labour force in the oilfields.

Local people told stories about the poverty and ignorance of the Grenadians. A story I heard as a child (without fully understanding it, not knowing at that time who or what Grenadians were) was that they lived off ground provisions, which they cooked in a "pitch-oil" tin. Ground provisions were tubers—yams, eddoes, cassava, sweet potatoes. The "pitch-oil tins" were originally the tins in which vegetable oil was imported. Normally in Trinidad those tins were used afterwards for storing "pitch-oil," which was the word we used for kerosene. So the story about the Grenadians boiling whole pitch-oil tins of ground provisions was not only a story about the grossness of their taste, the sheer bulk of the rubbishy food they could put away, but also a story about their poverty. They were too poor to buy proper enamel or black-iron Birmingham-made pots, like the rest of us; they cooked in tins that the rest of us used for pitch-oil.

(I heard this story about the Grenadians from a quarrel-some aunt—and in my memory the aunt, as she told this story, in her usual shrieking voice, was using a woven coconut-leaf fan to get a Birmingham black-iron coalpot go-ing on the concrete back steps of a small house in Woodbrook in Port of Spain. For two or three years many segments of our extended family, refugees from the countryside, were living squashed together in that Woodbrook lot, where there was as yet no proper sewerage. Some years later this aunt migrated to Canada. There, liberated from crowd and pov-erty and general wretchedness, she became an alert, generous, elegant woman—but nothing of that human possibility is contained in my memory of the shrieking woman fanning her coalpot on the back steps.)

This story about the Grenadians and the pitch-oil tins I heard during the war, some years after they had made a name for themselves in the strike of 1937. So in the years before 1937, when they would have been even less regarded, things would have been very hard for them. And then, from among them, in all their isolation and backwardness, a leader appeared.

The leader was a small bearded man with a long name, Tubal Uriah Buzz Butler. He was a preacher, and there was something in his passion or derangement that took the oilfield workers to a pitch of frenzy. He attracted other people as well. Many radicals, people who described themselves as so-cialists or communists, attached themselves to him. The strike he and the trade unions called came close to being an insurrection. A policeman was burned alive in the oilfield area. The government began to recruit and arm volunteers. The atmosphere would have been like that of 1805 or 1831, when there was talk of a slave revolt. And then, as happened in the slave days, passion died down, and people returned to being themselves.

This was the subject of Foster Morris's book. He wrote about Tubal Uriah Butler and the people around him. He wrote of them with the utmost seriousness. He gave them families, backgrounds; he treated what they said without irony. Nothing like this had been written about local people before. He wrote of them as though they were English people—as though they had that kind of social depth and solidity and rootedness.

It was well-intentioned, but it was wrong. Some of the people he wrote admiringly about, like certain lawyers and teachers, were even embarrassed by Foster Morris's misplaced social tributes. What was missing from Foster Morris's view was what we all lived with: the sense of the absurd, the idea of comedy, which hid from us our true position. The social depth he gave to ordinary people didn't make sense. That idea of a background—and what it contained: order and values and the possibility of striving: perfectibility—made sense only when people were more truly responsible for themselves. We weren't responsible in that way. Much had been taken out of our hands. We didn't have backgrounds. We didn't have a past. For most of us the past stopped with out grandparents; beyond that was a blank. If you could look down at us from the sky you would see us living in our little houses between the sea and the bush; and that was a kind of truth about us, who had been transported to that place. We were just there, floating.

Foster Morris, with all his wish to applaud us, didn't understand the nature of our deprivation. He saw us as versions of English people and simplified us. He couldn't understand, for instance, that though Tubal Uriah Buzz Butler was a kind of messiah, though in the high moments of the strike educated people like lawyers attributed to him almost miraculous powers, and felt that where he led no harm could come, these very people felt at the same time, in their bones, that he was a crazed and uneducated African preacher, a Grenadian, a small-islander, an eater of ground provisions boiled in a pitch-oil tin.

It was that idea of the absurd, never far away, that preserved us. It was the other side of the anger and the passion that had made the crowd burn the black policeman Charlie King alive. Foster Morris didn't appear to understand that Charlie King wasn't hated in Trinidad; that he was to become, in fact, in calypso and folk memory, a special sacrificial figure, as famous as Uriah Butler himself, and almost as honoured, and that the place on the road where he was burned was to be known as Charlie King Corner: a little joke about a sanctified place.

In 1937 I was five years old. So all this knowledge of the oilfield strike came to me later, when there was the war to worry about, when the Americans were in Trinidad, and the place was full of money; and the Butler affair (at least in the mind of a child) was receding fast.

All through the war Butler was interned. There was a little excitement when he was released; but only a little. The man who had gone in as a revolutionary came out as a clown, a preacher with a grey beard, a fly whisk, a fondness for suits. He was an embarrassment to the lawyers and others who had drawn strength from him in the great days of 1937. He had brought on a new kind of politics; but he had himself become an anachronism. There was a new constitution; there were elections. Butler re-started his party—it had the absurd name of the British Empire Workers and Citizens Home Rule Party—and he won a seat in the new legislature; but there

were more important parties now. As a member of the legislature he did nothing. He went away for long stretches to
England, "to take the cold," as it was said; and he was supported by contributions from his old Grenadian supporters.
Once, when he came back, he insisted on thanking the crew
of the aeroplane.

The Foster Morris book which had seen in this man a
revolutionary, a figure like Gandhi, a man who had thought
out his position, someone contributing to the general unravel-
ling of the old order, now seemed even more wrong. By the
time I had left Trinidad in 1950 the book had faded, like *If
Crab No Walk* by Owen Rutter, and all the pre-war cruise
books with titles like *Those Wild West Indies*.

LATER IN England, and especially after 1954, when I left
the university and went to live in London and was trying to
write, I began to know a little more about Foster Morris. In
Trinidad we had seen him as a kind of English renegade,
someone who went against all the racial ways of our colony.
In England things looked differently. He had written a book
about growing up, in the vein of Alec Waugh's *Loom of
Youth*, and some novels in the style of early Graham Greene.
He had a reputation of sorts. He was a man of the thirties,
very much part of the intellectual current of the time, one of
the radicals waiting for the war, each man in his own way,
and in the meantime going abroad on travels, not the cruise
travels, not the travels of Victorian times, but travels that
were helping to undermine the nineteenth-century European
empires. Auden and Isherwood went to China; Orwell and
others went to Spain. Graham Greene went to West Africa
and then to Mexico. Geoffrey Gorer went to West Africa and
wrote a new kind of book about Africa, *Africa Dances*. And
Foster Morris went to Trinidad and wrote *The Shadowed
Livery*.

He had receded a little since, not having built on that good pre-war start. In the mid-1950s his name was still around, but it was attached to reviews, to talks on the radio; it was no longer the name of a book-writer. Still, it was a name in the papers and on the radio. And over and above that—however muffled his name in England, however little found in articles or books about the thirties—he existed for me in a special way, an important figure from the past, someone from my childhood, someone who had come to us in Trinidad from the void around us.

I had a small part-time job in the BBC in 1955, working on a half-hour weekly literary programme for the Caribbean. Some book about post-war English fiction had to be reviewed, and the producer said, "I think this would be something for Foster Morris."

I could hardly believe it, hardly believe that my producer could speak the name so casually, and that the man was so accessible.

The producer said, "It's the kind of thing Foster could do standing on his head."

I was living in an old house in Kilburn, just behind the Gaumont State cinema. There was a public library not far away, in a couple of houses on a side street on the other side of the main road. It was a good place to use. The better books were hardly touched, and the art books were as good as new. And when I went to the library I found that in spite of the war, in spite of everything else, and after seventeen or eighteen years, *The Shadowed Livery* was still on the shelves. It had been taken out quite a few times before the war and during the war, but then it had been left alone.

It was strange to touch the faded cloth-bound book which I had read, in another climate, with other thoughts and ambitions in my head. Strange to see the name stamped on the spine, to see the good-quality pre-war paper, the pre-war date, the list of the author's books. And embarrassing and moving at the same time, flicking through the pages, to see the references to the names and incidents of the great Butler strike. The title of the book came—I had forgotten this— from *The Merchant of Venice*, from the speech of the Prince of Morocco, one of Portia's suitors:

> *Mislike me not for my complexion,*
> *The shadowed livery of the burnished sun,*
> *To whom I am a neighbour, and near bred.*

I began to get an idea. Foster Morris knew what I had come from. I would turn to him for help. I needed help very badly at that time.

I was holding on by my fingertips in London. In the Kilburn house I had a two-roomed second-floor flat, sharing bathroom and lavatory with everybody else. Not that this was bad; in fact, I thought I was lucky; few people let rooms to non-Europeans in those days; and what I had in Kilburn was better than what I had had in my last two years at Oxford. But I couldn't see a future. My BBC job was very small and uncertain. Everything depended on my writing—that was the whole point of my being in London, living that life— and, for many months now, so far as my writing went, I had lost my way. I was as far away as ever from getting properly started.

In Trinidad, at that time of optimism between leaving school and waiting to go to England and Oxford, I had started, light-heartedly, like a man with all the time in the world, on a novel, a farce with a local setting. I had thought— sitting in the Red House, in the midst of the African clerks gossiping portentously about this and that—of a local African who for political reasons had given himself the name of an African king. It was a good thing to think about in 1949; but at that age, seventeen, I really didn't know what to do with the material. But I wrote on, and I took what I had written to Oxford. Two years later, in the dreadful solitude of the long summer vacation, I pushed the work to its end. It wasn't of any value (though there would have been things hidden in it); but the fact that I finished the book—two hundred or so pages of typescript—was important to me.

When I left Oxford and went to London I started on something else. Not farce this time, but something very serious. The character I fixed on was someone like myself, working as a clerk in the Registrar-General's Office in Port of Spain. I didn't know what attitude to take to the character or the setting. I couldn't see it clearly; I must have lied and boasted a lot, must have tried very hard in the colonial way to separate my character from his setting, to set him up a little higher. And all I could think of in the way of narrative was a day in the life of this character. The pages piled up.

The fact was that at the age of twenty-two, unprotected, and feeling unprotected, with no vision of the future, only with ambition, I had no idea what kind of person I was. Writing should have helped me to see, to clarify myself; but every day as I wrote my novel (when I wasn't doing little things for money at the BBC), the fabrication, the turning away from the truths I couldn't fully acknowledge, pressed me down further into the little hole I had created for myself.

Just six years before, at the door of the vault of the Registrar-General's Department in Port of Spain I had—with what pleasure, what a vision of the future—pretended in my spare time in the office to be a writer, filling paper, correcting, making a page look like a page of manuscript. Now it was a desperate matter.

This was my mood when in the Kilburn library I looked at *The Shadowed Livery*, the work of a published writer, and decided to turn to Foster Morris for help.

On the day of the recording I went to the studio and sat behind the glass with the studio manager and the producer.

Foster Morris was a stockyish, grey man with a broad

face, dim-eyed, withdrawn. I suppose he would have been fifty. The dimness of the eye, the withdrawal, the man removed—that made an impression on me, as did the story he told when he was asked to speak some words to the microphone for the voice-level test.

He said, "I was lunching with Victor Gollancz the other day. He told me this joke. A farmer was had up for having sex with an under-age girl. The farmer told the judge he wasn't to blame, because the village girls had been stealing his apples and he had warned them that he was going to screw any of them he caught stealing apples. The farmer got off. But then the judge said to him, 'Mr. Roberts, you should be careful. Otherwise, you won't get to see many of your apples.'"

It wasn't much of a joke, but the name of the publisher was impressive. So Foster Morris was more than a man from the past; he was a man still in casual touch with great names.

In the shabby canteen, still with its rough-and-ready wartime feel, I said to him, "I've read *The Shadowed Livery*. And I looked at it the other day again."

His dim eyes lightened. He seemed even abashed. A kind of old-fashioned courtesy came to him. He said, "Oh, is that still around?"

That was also impressive: dismissing a whole published book, a book that had required two two-week journeys by steamer and taken weeks of writing. And I remember thinking, "When my turn comes, this is how I must behave."

I walked out with him to the Oxford Street lobby.

I said, "I've been writing a book for nearly a year. I don't know how to go on. Will you have a look at it for me?"

He agreed. He wanted me to send it to him at a publisher's where he said he looked in once or twice a week, but then he said I should send it to his house. As he was writing out his address, he said, "Whatever happened to that white-nigger fellow?"

I was stumped. I didn't know who he was talking about,

and I had never heard that combination of words in Trinidad. Probably the words came from another island; or probably Foster Morris had simply forgotten. But I understood—though he had been scrupulous in his book in the other direction, not appearing to notice a person's race, and hardly mentioning it—he was making a heavy kind of local joke with me. I knew he would have been referring to some light-skinned mulatto—in Trinidad people like that were described as "red," without insult—and then I understood he was talking about a well known radical who had taken part in the great Butler strike. Foster Morris had written in his admiring way about this man; and I felt I was caught a little off balance, not knowing about one of the important figures in *The Shadowed Livery*.

This was a bad moment, but I let it pass. I sent him my manuscript. He didn't keep me waiting. Within days he had sent it back, with a long typed letter, a page and a half in single spacing. The first sentence of his letter was: *I have read your book and my advice to you is to abandon it immediately.*

He was right. I knew that. But I had been hoping—just a little—for some kind of magic. And I was full of anger and hurt. I remembered that bad moment with him in the lobby; I remembered the one-sidedness and subtle wrongness of *The Shadowed Livery*. I thought of his unimportance. But it didn't help. I knew he was right.

All my life I had felt myself marked, destined for achievement. I had known doubts, long depressions; but I had been a student then, not a man in my own right. Now at last I was in the world, a doer: my moment should have come.

I spent a bad two or three weeks. I felt dreadfully abased. For some reason the moments on buses, going between Kilburn and the BBC on Oxford Street, were the worst. And yet at the same time I couldn't help feeling relieved. I didn't have to write that book. I didn't have to face that manuscript.

I read Foster Morris's letter many times. It was really

quite packed, and even at the first reading I had seen that, after the brutality of his first line, he wanted to help. His letter was full of instruction, of a sort no one before had given me. He wanted me to read certain writers—Chekhov, Hemingway, and his beloved Graham Greene—and he wanted me to pay attention to the way they wrote. He wanted me to think more about writing. And he was right. I had read only in a gobbling, inconsequential way. As for writing, I had thought of it as something that would come naturally to me. I hadn't thought of it as something I would have to learn about and try to understand. I hadn't foreseen the problem I was having with my material and the uncertainty of my writing personality.

But I was at the age when every day is long. It is hard when days are so long to hold on to gloom. And it must have been just three or four weeks after receiving Foster Morris's letter that, out of the misery of those bus rides up and down the Edgware Road, I decided to make a fresh start as a writer. I thought I would turn away from what I had done, and go back to the beginning: try to see whether I couldn't make writing out of plain concrete statements, adding meaning to meaning in simple stages.

At about this time something else happened. At tea in the BBC canteen one day we were talking about George Lamming's autobiography, *In the Castle of My Skin*. The producer who had introduced Foster Morris to the programme wanted to talk only about a small, comic episode in the book—about a boy climbing up a tree. I noticed the producer's laughter, his admiration, and I learned as a new truth what I really had always known, and what so far in my writing (veering between farce and introversion) I had suppressed: that comedy, the preserver we in Trinidad had always known, was close to me, a double inheritance, from my story-telling Hindu family, and from the creole street life of Port of Spain.

Within days I had begun to write about Port of Spain street life, setting my narrator in a street such as the one where once (in my memory or fantasy) my aunt had fanned her coalpot and talked about Grenadians. And I set my narrator at the level of the street. I found an immense freedom in this touch of fiction. The material bubbled up; the stories bubbled up; the jokes made themselves, two or three to a page. Day by day my book grew; I felt myself becoming a writer, someone in control, someone more at ease. In six weeks, no more, my book was done. My life in London at last had purpose. And I blessed the name of Foster Morris, this unlikely figure from the past who had set me free.

IT WAS four years before that book was published. The publisher required something less unconventional in form first, something more recognizable by the trade as a novel. When the street book was published I sent a copy to Foster Morris, with a letter. I reintroduced myself; told him about his letter, the pain it had caused, the release it had given. The book, I said, was an offering to him. And there was this extra interest: the book embroidered on memories, my own, that began almost at the time of his visit to Trinidad for *The Shadowed Livery*. So, although he was nearly thirty years older, it could be said that as writers our paths had long ago crossed. He would have seen as an adult certain things—Port of Spain streets, houses, backyards—which I had seen with the freshness and wonder of a child, an Indian child moving from the country to the city.

He replied beautifully. He was pleased that he had been of help. He had kept his eye on me. He had read reviews of the books I had published; he had read some of my own reviews in the *New Statesman* (sometimes, he said, he thought I out-*Staggered* the *Staggers*); and he loved the book I had sent him. He invited me to lunch. He belonged, he said, to something which no gentleman could call a club, but which he had become a member of because he had a "pash" on the waitress, who "must have been quite a hit at the Alhambra before the Great War." I recognized his heavy joking style; I felt it might have been something he had picked up from an older person in his family.

There was no sign of the waitress, but the place (it was in South Kensington, and when I next saw it, some years later, it had been turned into a second-rank hotel) was as decrepit as he had said; there had been no fresh paint or wallpaper since long before the war.

There I noticed what I had noticed four years before: the thin long strands of hair that fell over his forehead and seemed slightly to cobweb his dim eyes. All the time I was with him I wanted to lean across and brush that hair away.

We talked about writing and writers. We had the profession in common now. We could talk—or, at any rate, I could attend—in a more man-to-man way than when we had met four years before. He was contemptuous of C. P. Snow. Of Angus Wilson he said, "If you're going to leave the British Museum and set up as a writer in the country, at least you should first learn to write a decent sentence."

Both those writers were very famous at the time. I had read four books by Angus Wilson and one by Snow. I had lost my way in the plottings of the Snow. The Wilson I had read with something like awe. The awe was really for his success. I felt as separate from his English world as—travelling between the BBC and my lodgings, working at the material from the quite different world I carried in my head—I was separate from London and English life.

Literature wasn't a neutral subject, after all. Background entered into it. So our talk at lunch was unbalanced. He had read an immense amount in the English writing of the century, and he still kept up. I didn't feel this need. I was too concerned with my own writing, with finding ways of deal-

ing with the—unwritten-about—material I had begun to
glimpse four years before.

The other side of this was that I wasn't worried, as Foster
Morris was, by the fame of C. P. Snow and Angus Wilson.
And I remember how clearly the thought came to me—the
first moment of uncertainty at our lunch, but perhaps really
the second or third or fourth uncertainty about Foster Morris—that the careers of Angus Wilson and C. P. Snow were
not going to be affected in any way by what was said of them
in that dreary dining room.

He gave off a gloom. It began to call up some of my own
anxieties, never far away; it dulled the good mood I had
brought to our meeting. I took him as I saw him: I didn't
then have the knowledge of England to make a pattern of
what he had revealed of his life: the suburban address, the
heavy old-fashioned jokes, the visits two or three times a
week to publishers' offices, the occasional review or BBC
talk about the thirties. And at that time I didn't have the gift
of enquiry. Perhaps before you start enquiring it is necessary
to have a certain amount of knowledge.

I asked him about *The Shadowed Livery.*

He said, "It was Graham's idea." Graham Greene. "He
had gone to Liberia the previous year. He thought I should
go to the other side of the Atlantic to see where the ex-slaves
had come from. He thought I might find a book. I had run
into a bad patch." He paused. "They were a bunch of racial
fanatics."

"Who?"

"Butler and a lot of the crowd around him."

But he hadn't written that.

"How could one write that? You have no idea what it
was like out there in 1937. The oilfields were like a colony
within a colony. Few people outside understood that. A lot
of people in Port of Spain didn't know. Almost all the south
of the island was one big oil reserve. There were a lot of

South Africans there. I don't know why. Some of them didn't mind the strike at all. They loved it when the government asked for volunteers. They could hardly wait to start shooting niggers."

This touched a memory. One day in 1945—easy for me to date things at school—our English-history teacher, a white-mulatto man, began to talk about the 1937 strike, for no clear reason. I don't remember all he said. I remember only the rage of his last words: "And I wasn't going south to shoot niggers." I had never before heard language like this in the classroom. The teacher was in his late forties. He loved the school, and was a great promoter of good manners and good form. His family was well known; a number of his relations were in good positions in the civil service and city council—in such positions as were open to local people. Something must have taken that sedate man out of himself just before he came into the classroom that day.

Remembering him now, and what he said, I felt Foster Morris's words about "shooting niggers" hadn't just come to him, but must have been current among white people in Trinidad in 1937. And I understood again how much of my setting had been hidden from me as a child.

I told Foster Morris about the teacher.

He said, "They didn't treat people well." Then he went back to his own thoughts. "You couldn't go away and write that Butler was a crazy black preacher. That was what the oilfields people were saying. Perhaps it's the kind of thing you might write nowadays. I don't know.

"Let me tell you about something that happened not long after the burning of Charlie King. Butler had been arrested, and people were confused. Though I should tell you this: some of them were a little bit on a high after the Charlie King business, wanting things to go forward, even if they didn't see where they were going. At the same time everyone was frightened. In fact, things were beginning to wind down pretty fast. You could feel that people were getting quieter in themselves.

"There was a little gathering of Butler people one evening. Nothing to do with the strike this time. The opposite, in fact: this was to give people a chance to be together and drink a little rum and forget the trouble they were in.

"We were in a small Trinidad wood house in the country somewhere. Black old wood, corrugated iron, gaps in the plank floors. Oil lamps. In spite of everything, the atmosphere was good. I made notes. Then I simply enjoyed myself. I had got to like the local rum. It was light and nice. And then—it was as if time had jumped—I became aware that the half-white people and the brown people and the one or two Indians had gone away, and that everybody in the little room was black, except for me.

"Why did I feel that? Simple: they made me feel it. I knew a lot of those people very well. They knew where I stood, and once or twice in difficult situations with English officials I had been able to help them. But now the people around me were making racial jokes about me and they weren't letting go of those jokes. This went on and on. They were like schoolboys. They were ganging up on me. I began to find it hard to keep on smiling. The room was full of big criss-crossing shadows from the oil lamps. The thought came to me that one of those black men might reach out and touch me in this new aggressive way, and then anything might happen. I might be the white Charlie King.

"One of the men was called Lebrun. He was a Trinidadian, but he had grown up in Panama. His family had gone there to work on the Canal, just as the Grenadians had come to Trinidad to work on the oilfields. Lebrun was a communist of a kind you got in the thirties. I actually thought he was the most dangerous man around Butler. He was a fluent Spanish speaker and his business was to travel round Central America and the West Indies and West Africa and talk revolution. He knew how to talk to local people, and at the same time he was able to pitch everything he did and said at some very special people in Moscow or wherever who were his patrons. He was actually a very handsome man, very educated and polished.

"In this dark little house now Lebrun began to taunt me sexually. I wasn't ready for that at all. I was white: women came easily to me: that was what he was banging away at. Can you imagine?"

After more than twenty years, the comment of Lebrun's—the taunting, as Foster Morris saw it—still rankled, and when I looked at Foster Morris's dim eyes, cobwebbed by the thin strands of dry hair falling over his forehead, the rather flat, wrinkled, pasty face, his air of withdrawal, I thought I could still see the emotional incompleteness that Lebrun had tried to play on.

"The taunting got worse and worse. I thought I would have to leave. Lebrun began to say that black men lived with sexual deprivation. That was a pretty original thing for a black man to say in 1937, though it was strange to hear it from Lebrun. He was very good-looking and I'm sure he did very well that way. A strange idea came to me, with the rum and the surprise and with all those men so close to me: it was that Lebrun was really a white man, imprisoned in this other body. As soon as I thought that, I found words for it. Almost as soon as I began to speak the words, I thought I was making a big mistake. The words would have been good in the Oxford Union ten years before, but they were going to be terrible here. I said, 'I'm sorry, Lebrun. I can't kiss you and make you a prince.'

"To my surprise, everybody laughed. It was a joke with a delayed charge, you might say, because the key word was missing. Some people caught on later than the others, and the laughter went on. The taunting stopped, people pulled away. I could breathe again, and it was all right. It was as though nothing had happened, and we were as we had always been. But I knew that something had happened. I knew I had been close to something nasty. And I knew that Lebrun would never forgive me.

"That was something else you couldn't write about. It may be that there are some things you can't write about. I tried later to make a story of that episode. Once I set it in pre-war Berlin. It became too Isherwood. Then I set it in France, and Lehmann published it during the war. But the transposition was difficult. I was never happy with it. The thirties were a difficult time for a writer, and one of the big problems about going to a place like Trinidad was that black people were simply not a subject. No one was interested in the subtleties. I don't think Graham managed it in his Liberian book—he didn't know whether he was Somerset Maugham or Sanders of the River. Perhaps it's easier now. Perhaps it will be easier in twenty years. I don't know.

"In Port of Spain, when they were talking down south about shooting niggers, there was a Potogee trade-union feller who had a moustache and smoked a pipe and tried to look like Stalin. You could do that in farce. But then you can't recover and do something serious. You just become sentimental. Like Evelyn. In *The Shadowed Livery* I had to tone it down. I had to make the Stalin man more serious."

I HAD GONE to the lunch out of a sense of duty, out of a sentimental regard for the man who had appeared at such a bad moment in my life and set me right. I had expected a stiffish occasion with a much older man. But he had made it reasonably enjoyable. I was overwhelmed by his fluency and knowledge, the subtlety of some of the things he had said; and, unexpectedly, by the beauty and measure of his old-fashioned voice.

But when I "played the newsreel back"—a metaphor I

used in those days for the memory drill I instinctively practised (and had done since childhood) after every meeting:
trying to remember words, gestures and expressions in
correct sequence, to arrive at an understanding of the people I had been with and the true meaning of what had been
said—when I played the newsreel back a few times, I began
to feel that he had not spoken as spontaneously as I had
thought.

He had come prepared to defend the incompleteness (or
the simplicity) of his Trinidad book, which at our first meeting he had appeared—so grandly, in my eyes—to dismiss.
Perhaps that also contained a defence of his other work in the
thirties and forties, which I didn't know about.

Later, still playing back the newsreel, I saw that, almost
as an aspect of this defence of the things he had chosen not
to do, there was with Foster Morris a final disapproval even
of those writers—like Graham Greene—whom he appeared
to admire.

And then—how could I have missed it at the time?—I
saw that though in his letter he had said that he had loved my
book, and though no one could have been more courteous as
a host, there had run right through our lunch a constant
indirect criticism of what I had written.

The book itself he had mentioned only as we were leaving
the club. He said, "You have written a very funny book.
What I like about it is that I can look through its surface and
see some of the things I saw all those years ago. You know,
the way you can train yourself to see through the surface of
a trout stream, the sky, the clouds, the reflections."

A writer's simile: perhaps he had prepared it, perhaps he
had used it before. It struck a false note. But at the moment
I thought it was his way of taking up something I had written
in my letter. It was only some days later that I saw that, when
it was added to the other things he had said, about farce and
sentimentality, and the need to be serious about what was

serious and wretched in the world, he was really putting me in my place.

AND I DIDN'T actually mind. After four years I had come to the end of the way of writing I had arrived at as a result of the letter from Foster Morris: the language discipline (increasingly a constriction), the comedy. Together they had given me confidence; but they had also given me a writing character I had begun to grow out of. With confidence I had begun to see that the comedy that had become my writing tone, the ability to make two or three jokes to the page, the jokeyness that was my double inheritance from my Trinidad background, however good, however illuminating, was also a way of making peace with a hard world; was on the other side of hysteria. This was true of the colonial society I was writing about; it was also true of my own position in London, which was full of uncertainty.

Unwilled, this anxiety or hysteria, the deeper root of comedy, had become my subject. Both my language and writing personality had changed as a result. This had happened in the actual writing of a book I had been working on for about a year (the time of six-week books had gone) when I went to have lunch with Foster Morris.

I was absolutely secure in this new book, and for the first time, since I had begun truly to write, felt the need for no one's approval. I was weeks away from the end of the first draft, and was full of what I was carrying. I often wanted to say, as Foster Morris was talking (as I thought) about the problems of tone and tact in writing, "Yes, yes, I know exactly what you mean." Once or twice I nearly told him about the new book I was close to finishing—so different from the street book I had sent him, and much closer to the kind of book of which he seemed to approve. I was held back only by the superstition that came to me just then that to talk about unfinished work was to run the risk of never finishing it.

It was a good instinct. A little over two years later—after the book had been revised and handed in, and I had travelled abroad, and was deep in a new work about those travels—I sent him an early copy of the book I had been full of at our lunch. I reminded him in a letter of what he had said about farce and sentimentality and seriousness. And just as I had made an offering to him of the street book, so now I made an offering to him of this larger work.

His reply was swift. It began: "I have looked at your new book. You have passed a stool. It is far prettier than Alan Sillitoe's and those of recent young eminences . . ."

I stopped reading, though his letter, typewritten, was long, as long as the one he had written six years before. I stopped reading, unwilling to allow any further word to fix itself on my consciousness, just as I might have stopped reading a poison-pen letter, one of those that came in small brown envelopes and were written on lined paper in a narrow cramped hand.

I felt a fool to have sent the book to him. That was all. I felt no disappointment, no doubt, no rage; only something like relief, relief that I could set this disciple-guru relationship aside.

But his letter had to be acknowledged. I wrote to his suburban address, saying that I was sorry he felt as he did, but that the book was still new enough for him to sell to Gaston. Gaston was a bookseller in Chancery Lane. He dealt mainly with libraries, and was a kind of patron of book reviewers. The basis of this reputation in the late fifties was that from known reviewers he bought any new book, regardless of its subject, publisher or saleability, for half the published price.

It seemed a light enough reply, what I wrote about Gaston, but Foster Morris didn't like it. Like Lebrun in Trinidad in 1937, I had touched a nerve. He wrote to say that he was getting by; he didn't need Gaston. That, I thought, was the end of it. But two weeks later he wrote again. He had bought a ticket for a big dinner of some literary association. Now he found he couldn't go, and he didn't like the idea of wasting the ticket. Would I like it? If I did, I should telephone him at a particular number at a certain time.

I telephoned. I said I would like to go to the dinner. I did so to let him know that I was indifferent to his abuse. On the telephone we talked only of the literary group. He said, in his beautiful, old-fashioned voice, that it was going to be very dull, full of suburban lion-hunters, but it might amuse me. It was as though his letter had been an aberration; that we were as we had been at the lunch. Then right at the end, before he put the phone down, he said, "I don't like the idea of you being out of pocket."

The dinner card came, creased, smudged, as though it had been for some time in the fluff of a jacket pocket.

Three or four days before the dinner I recognized the hand of Foster Morris in an anonymous review of my book. He had gone out of his way to make signals to me, to show his own knowledge of the background, his own attitude to the background. The review was full of abuse of the people I wrote about. To attempt comedy or profundity or universality about such people was absurd, the reviewer said; they were people of the estate barracks, living off the smell of an oil rag, sunk in superstition, without an intellectual life, without nobility or potential. This was the abuse of colonial days, the opposite of the attitude (and originality) of *The Shadowed Livery*. It took me back to the bad moment in the BBC lobby when he had asked me about the white-nigger man.

I treated this review as I had treated his earlier letter. I didn't read it to the end. But I went to the dinner. I went because I had said I would go; also, a little, for the experience.

But I went mainly because I didn't want him to think I was cast down by what he said about my book.

So I went with his card and sat in the place marked with his name. The occasion was as dull as he had said it would be. I sat next to a middle-aged woman who was there because she had written a textbook of some sort. She was disappointed in me, too. This woman was obsessed with her family; that was where her mind and heart were, rather than at the dinner. We didn't make much connected conversation. When I stood up to go I saw that I had sat all evening with my trouser zip undone.

That was how my brush with Foster Morris ended. Then I realized that I hadn't needed to go to the dinner at all.

AN ANTHOLOGY (aimed at schools and universities) of contemporary criticism of the great nineteenth-century European novels, a Patrick Hamilton–like novel about Gerard's Cross that didn't get into paperback and sank, a scattering of small reviews—this was all that I noted about Foster Morris over the next five or six years. He was in his sixties now; there were fewer reminders of him. He became part of the past for me.

At the end of 1967 I went to Antibes to interview Graham Greene for a London paper. The meetings with the writer were spread over two days. At one stage Greene talked of writers he had followed but who had then stopped writing or faded away. There were three such writers. Two were young; I had reviewed their work; they had tried to write Graham Greene novels.

The third writer was Foster Morris. Just after the war he had published a novel that Greene thought was much better than his own *England Made Me,* published a few years before the war. The Foster Morris book was there on the shelves in Greene's flat, part of his great collection.

He took the book down and read without talking for a minute or two, with the expression of a man who was finding that memory had played him false. He said, as though addressing Foster Morris rather than me, "You see, you see." And he read out a sentence from the Morris book: "The Easter drizzle persisted like remorse."

"Actually," he said later, "he was a prodigy. At Oxford we thought him among the best. He was at Oxford when he was writing *Seedtime*."

The famous book was on the shelves. Greene took it down and showed it to me. Its yellow cloth binding had faded now to a very pale primrose.

"The title seems tame now, but I loved it. It was full of meaning, full of ironies. It was from the Wordsworth line in *The Prelude,* 'Fair seed-time had my soul.'

"It was a running-away book. I cannot tell you how original and good it felt to us at the time. Foster ran away from his school for almost a whole term when he was sixteen. He used all his school money and survived quite well. He ran away as a protest against the school and his family. His family ran a small engineering firm in the Midlands. *Seedtime* was about that running away, the people he met, the poverty he saw, his sexual awakening.

"Foster made the notes during the two months, but he didn't write the book until he was at Oxford. He was an adult when he wrote, but still very young, and I suppose that gave the book some of its quality. It was precocious and knowing, and technically quite skilled, yet you have to say that it was also innocent. It was full of echoes that Foster didn't know about. It felt very original, but of course running away is one of the great themes of literature. Huckleberry Finn, David Copperfield running away to Betsey Trotwood, Smike running away from Squeers, De Quincey. Foster said the only name that came to him, half-way through, was W. H. Davies, the super-tramp man. In some ways his book anticipated Orwell and that American book, *Catcher in the Rye.*

"It sold eight thousand copies, a prodigious number in those days. It was famous for ten years—Connolly's limit, you know. They keep on trying to revive it, but it doesn't work now. The sexual awakening bit is silly, and the protest parts are very old-fashioned, a little bit like *The Way of All Flesh*. That's the trouble with precocious things. They really belong to the earlier generation.

"You might say Foster never recovered from that success. He floundered. If he hadn't had that family firm to fall back on, he might have had to take a job, like the rest of us. But he had that little income. It wasn't a great deal, but it was there. So he kept on at the writing. He was always looking for another piece of luck, that happy landing on a subject. He tried his hand at many other things. He did the Forster personal relationships, though no one knows what that means; he did the Marxist thing; he tried to do the Catholic thing. He tried to do the Auden and Isherwood travel book, but I always thought that Trinidad book was a lazy piece of work. Then he wrote that novel after the war, and I thought he had found his feet. I was wrong."

HE WAS precocious, as Greene had said. A precocious writer doesn't have much experience to work on; his talent isn't challenged. The quickness of such a writer lies in assuming the manner and sensibility of his elders. Foster Morris's runaway adolescent experience and his "rebellious" style as an undergraduate had disguised his essential mimicry, and later made it hard for him to find himself. The contemporaries who admired him soon began to outpace him. For the rest of his writing life he was a man always saying goodbye to people. It couldn't have been easy for him.

It was strange that a man so much in search of his own voice should have been the one to help me find mine. But perhaps it wasn't strange. He would have seen at once, when he looked at my manuscript, where my difficulty lay, how I had chopped and changed between various modes. In that first, long letter he would have been like a man half talking to himself.

More than twenty years after that strange literary dinner, when he was very old, he appeared to make some amends. A book of mine had been published when I was out of England, travelling. When I came back some months later I found that the publisher was using a favourable quotation from a Foster Morris review.

It left me cold. I never thought to look for the review itself; and it is only now that I wonder whether I shouldn't have taken notice of the old man's gesture. I think, though, that my instinct was correct. To meet Foster Morris again would have been to repeat the lunch I had had with him, to expose myself to his courtesy and beautiful old-fashioned voice (not unlike Greene's), and to find, below that, even in old age, I am sure, the intellectual uncertainty of the unful-filled writer, with his disapproval of all the people he had said goodbye to.

IN THE late thirties (when my memories of them begin) the cruise ships, from Europe and the United States (and the United States cruise ships continued for some time after the war), would dock in Port of Spain in the morning. My father, or some other journalist from the *Trinidad Guardian*, would go aboard with a photographer to do something about the more famous passengers. Sometimes they could be very fa-mous: Lily Pons, Oliver Hardy, Annabella, the wife of Ty-rone Power. The photographs and the stories would come out in the next day's paper. By that time the ship would have left, so the visit of these great people from the great world would have been like something one had missed, a blessing in the night.

I never thought then that we were at a great turn in

history, and that one day I would be able to look from the other side, as it were, at these visits. I never thought I would be able one day to understand what Foster Morris had come out of, and to follow him in all his uncertainties as a writer out to Trinidad.

His book was incomplete but not bad. In its direct presentation of subject people as whole, belonging to themselves, it was even original, and it can be fitted into the great chain of changing outside vision of that part of the world. That chain might begin in 1564 with John Hawkins's precise and fresh accounts of aboriginal life (down to the taste of the potato: somewhere between a parsnip and a carrot); might go on to Sir Walter Raleigh in 1595 miraculously rescuing, and naming, the tortured and half-dead Amerindian chiefs of Cumucurapo who had been dispossessed by the Spaniards; might then lead through the high spirits and cruelties of the early nineteenth-century naval novels of Captain Marryat; to the Victorians, Trollope, Kingsley, Froude. *The Shadowed Livery* has a definite place between the decadent imperial cruise books and the books of post-colonial writers like James Pope-Hennessy and Patrick Leigh Fermor. Over four centuries the vision constantly changes; it is a fair record of one side of a civilization.

CHAPTER 5

On the Run

I

AT OUR lunch in his South Kensington club in 1959 Foster Morris had spoken of Lebrun, the Trinidadian-Panamanian communist of the 1930s, as one of the most dangerous men around Butler, the oil strike leader.

That was news to me. Lebrun wasn't one of the names I had heard about. But then I didn't know much about the strike. I was five when it happened; it was some years before I could begin to understand about it.

Lebrun's name I got to know only in 1947, when I was in the sixth form at Queen's Royal College, a full ten years after the strike. And then it was a name connected with a book he had written. A name—like Owen Rutter and Foster Morris—with a local connection, and with the glamour of print.

This book of Lebrun's was on a bottom shelf of our sixth-form library: two or three rows of glass-cased shelves above a cupboard. The shelves to the left held the school's small lending stock: popular books (Sabatini, Sapper, John Buchan, the William books) expensively re-bound and gilt-stamped (in England, we were told: that was where the dies were) with the college arms and motto: unyielding, shiny leather spines providing an elegant front for cheap paper furred and worn with handling, with the print itself a quarter rubbed off.

Lebrun's book was on a shelf next to that, below text-books and dictionaries. The purple-brown binding had grown so dark that the name on the spine was almost illegible.

The book was about Spanish-American revolutionaries before Bolívar. I never read it, and knew no one who had. Thirty years later people were to write about it in radical journals as one of the first books of the Caribbean revolution; but people doing research in university libraries, where every-thing is accessible, sometimes see progressions that didn't exist at the time. There would have been very few copies of Lebrun's book in Trinidad. There were none in the shops or the Central Library. The only copy I knew about was on the library shelf at school, and it was just there, unread, hardly known, its dark spine illegible.

Still, it was a book, published in London. It gave an aura to the man. It suggested a life of unusual texture. I asked a boy a year ahead of me—he had won a scholarship and was going to Cambridge—about Lebrun.

He said, "Oh, he's a revolutionary. He's on the run some-where in the United States."

That was dramatic, the exotic black man, Trinidadian-Panamanian, on the run. But I didn't believe it. I could under-stand, from the films, how a John Garfield character could be on the run. But I didn't understand it about Lebrun. I suppose—I was fifteen—I didn't believe in his character as a revolutionary; didn't believe such a character was possible for a black man from Trinidad and Panama; and didn't see how such a man could be thought dangerous enough to be hunted down.

Eight years later I saw him for the first time. He was among the speakers on the bandstand in Woodford Square, outside the Red House, part of the new politics that had come to the island while I had been in England. Almost twenty years had passed since the Butler strike, and Lebrun was now in his fifties, slender, fine-featured. Words poured fluently out of him. He spoke in complete sentences. The working people of the West Indies, he said, had been engaged for centuries in the mass production of sugar. This meant that they were among the earliest industrial workers in the world: the fact of slavery shouldn't be allowed to conceal this truth. So the people of the West Indies were readier than most for revolution. He had waited for twenty-five years for this moment. He had never lost hope that the moment would come, that the people could be marshalled for political action.

He talked—I heard him more than once during the few weeks I spent in Trinidad at that time—as though the whole movement was an expression of his will and his ideas, as though he had brought it into being.

Yet he was not one of the people trying to get into the new politics. He had no local base. He was not one of the men to whom power came. After the elections he disappeared, as he had disappeared after the Butler oilfield strike.

That was all that I knew of Lebrun when Foster Morris talked of him three years later. For both of us he was a man from the past. What we didn't know was that Lebrun—the sexual taunter in the oil-lamp shadows of the little Trinidad country house in 1937, as yet unknown as writer or agitator, the man to whom Foster Morris as a London writer might have shown patronage—was going to be another person to whom Foster Morris was going to say goodbye.

In extreme old age Lebrun fetched up in England, and in a world greatly changed, where black men were an important subject, he was "discovered" as one of the prophets of black revolution, a man whose name didn't appear in the history books, but who for years had worked patiently, had been

behind the liberation movements of Africa and the Caribbean.
So a kind of fulfilment came to him. It was very much the
idea of himself he had had, and had promoted, for much of
his life. It had anchored him, had been a kind of livelihood,
that idea. But it had also got him into trouble, with the very
people whose cause he thought he served.

ONCE HE was declared to be an undesirable immigrant by
the chief minister of one of the smaller West Indian islands.
In the long run this didn't do Lebrun's reputation any harm,
but at the time—this was at the start of decolonization, and
this chief minister was one of the lesser men of the region—
it was a humiliation: the old black revolutionary barred from
the revolution he claimed as his own.

Not long after, I went to this island. I sent in my name
to the chief minister's office—as a courtesy, and an insurance
against trouble. To my surprise, the chief minister asked me
to have lunch with him at Government House. He wanted
to talk about Lebrun.

He said, "Let him come here and try to walk the streets."

Street-corner talk in Government House. Lebrun wasn't
at all a street-corner man, but as a revolutionary—even in the
Butler days—he had always thought that the strength and
roughness of the crowd were things he might call on. Now
they were being used against him.

The new politics had thrown up people like the chief
minister in almost every territory. Most had started as trade-
union organizers; and many of them, like Butler in Trinidad,
had a religious side.

This man now lived in Government House. It was a
modest house, but it was the best in the small island. The
uniformed sentry, the local abstract paintings, the heavy locally made furniture—it was all there, the inherited pomp, as
in other territories. But the chief minister was already bored.

He had already got to the limit of what he could do with power. Power had already begun to press him down into himselt, and he now lived very simply, as though it was a needless strain to do otherwise. He didn't make many speeches now. He seldom went out. The person closest to him was a middle-aged black woman called Miss Dith, a woman of the people, someone you wouldn't notice on the street. She was said to be his spiritual adviser, his housekeeper, his cook, his protection against poison.

For the lunch Miss Dith had prepared shredded saltfish in a tomato sauce, sliced fried plantains, rice. You couldn't get simpler food on the island. She brought out the dishes herself. The food was cold. The tablecloth was stained.

Once the man who was now chief minister would have been flattered by Lebrun's attentions. He would have loved the big, technical-sounding words Lebrun would have used to describe the simple movement he had got going. He would have loved Lebrun's introductions to more prominent leaders in other islands. But Lebrun had other ideas about what power might be used for, and the chief minister wanted no part of that. The chief minister didn't want to undo the world he knew; he didn't want to lose touch with the power he had risen to.

He said of Lebrun, "The man want to take you over."

Lebrun was an impresario of revolution. That was the role he had fallen into; it had become his livelihood. He had no base of his own, no popular following. He always had to attach himself to other leaders, simpler people more directly in touch with the simple people who had given them power, and with a simpler idea of that power.

It had always been like that. It had been like that for Lebrun even in the days of Butler. Butler hadn't achieved power—he had emerged in colonial days, when such power was not to be had. But in his own eyes Butler had achieved something that wasn't far short of that power: he had achieved the headmanship or chieftaincy of his particular group. And then, after the excitement of the strike and the marches and the Charlie King affair, he had become bored. He was interned during the war. That might have suited him. His political activity afterwards never amounted to much. He became a member of the legislative council, but he preferred to spend his time in England, far away from his followers— doing no one knew what, perhaps doing nothing, perhaps just letting the days pass. Leadership and action no longer had any meaning for him. All that mattered—as it mattered to the chief minister who had roughed up Lebrun—was his chieftaincy, his position; that was what he was keen to protect.

So that contradiction between the complicated ideas of Lebrun and the simple politics he encouraged was always there; and couldn't but be apparent to him. Foster Morris said he was the most dangerous man around Butler. And I suppose what he meant was that in another situation, at another time, Butler or someone like him might want to do more than win a chieftaincy, might want to turn the world upside down, and Lebrun would have been there to show him how.

In the meantime he was a man still on the run, though often now from old associates; never living with the consequences of what he encouraged as a revolutionary. Others had to endure that: like certain middle-class brown people in that island where Miss Dith read the cards and kept in touch with the spirits and cooked for the chief minister. There were dozens of ways in which these brown people could be tormented. And they were; not as part of any programme of action on the chief minister's part, but simply because this tormenting of people was an aspect of chieftaincy.

"THE MAN want to take you over," the chief minister had said over the stained tablecloth in Government House. And

I knew what he meant, because Lebrun had tried to do something like that to me. This was at the time of my break with Foster Morris.

He wrote an article about my books in one of the Russian "thick magazines." He sent me the magazine, together with a translation (or the original) of his article, and a card. He gave a London address; from this I assumed he was still "on the run."

The article filled many pages of the thick magazine. No one had ever written at such length about my books. To tell the truth, I didn't think the books I had so far published deserved it. I thought of myself as still a beginner whose big books were to come. I knew that there were people who disapproved of my comedy, some of them because they felt I was letting my side down, and I thought that Lebrun in this Russian magazine would be severe with me.

He wasn't. His method was original. He ignored the comedy, over which I had taken so much trouble—such care in the mounting of so many scenes, such judgement in the matter of language and tone. He looked through all of that to the material itself—the people, the background—and he considered that with complete seriousness. He said I was writing about people impoverished in every way, people on whom history had played a cruel trick. My characters thought they were free men, in charge of their own destinies; they weren't; the colonial setting mocked the delusions of the characters, their ambitions, their belief in perfectibility, their jealousies. The books, light as they were, were subversive, the article said, and remarkable for that reason.

It was a version of what Foster Morris had said, in elaborate metaphor, about my first book, as we were leaving his South Kensington club. As with a trout stream, he had said, you had to train yourself to look through the surface reflections to what lay below.

I had said nothing to that, though I had thought the comment misplaced, and of no value to me, because it was denying me—who relished it so much—the gift of comedy (the discovery of which was still linked in my mind with getting started as a writer).

Lebrun's article, on the other hand, though different only in angle and emphasis from Foster Morris's comment, was like a revelation to me. I knew immediately what he meant about the helplessness of my characters; I realized I had always known it; I had grown up with that knowledge in my bones.

It was as though, from moving at ground level, where so much was obscured, I had been taken up some way, not only to be shown the petty pattern of fields and roads and small settlements, but also, as an aspect of that high view, had been granted a vision of history speeded up, had seen, as I might have seen the opening and dying of a flower, the destruction and shifting about of peoples, had seen all the strands that had gone into the creation of the agricultural colony, and had understood what simple purposes—after such activity—that colony served.

The article seemed to me a miraculous piece of writing. It stuck closely to what I had actually written, but was about so much more. Reading the article, I thought I understood why as a child I felt that history had been burnt away in the place where I was born. I found myself constantly thinking, "Yes, yes. That's true. It was like that."

The revelation of Lebrun's article became a lasting part of my way of looking. I suppose I was affected as I was, not only because it was the first article about my work, but also because I had never read that kind of political literary criticism before. I was glad that I hadn't. Because if I had, I mightn't have been able to write what I had written. Like Foster Morris and others, I would have known too much before I had begun to write, and there would have been less to discover with the actual writing. The problems of voice and tone and naturalness would have been that much harder; it would have been harder for me to get started.

I wrote to Lebrun to acknowledge his marvellous article, and a short time later there came an invitation to dinner, to meet Lebrun, from a common West Indian acquaintance. The acquaintance worked in a large insurance company. He was in his early thirties, a few years older than me. He did occasional scripts for the magazine programmes of the BBC Caribbean Service; that was how we had met. He came from one of the smaller islands, and I would have said he was a mulatto. He said he was Lebanese. His wife was like him, but with an accent more of the islands.

They lived in a squashed mansion block flat in Maida Vale. It must have been rented furnished. There was a lot of fat upholstered furniture of the 1930s, a feeling of old dirt, of smells and dust ready to rise. The dim ceiling light in the sitting room was made dimmer by a frosted-glass saucer-shaped shade that hung on little chains and was full of dead moths and other insects.

I thought when I arrived that the come-down-in-the-world atmosphere suited the occasion. Lebrun had lost his access to other chief ministers, and was generally out of things in the Caribbean; there were many little towns where he couldn't walk the streets. And I thought that this was going to be a melancholy little dinner in London for sentimental people who wanted to show solidarity with the old man.

In fact, if I had thought about it, I would have seen that Lebrun, old and displaced as he was, was now at the start of the finest phase of his reputation, the one that would grow and grow until the end. People in most of the territories had lost faith in the first wave of populist politicians. The corruption of these men didn't matter too much; what power had done was to show up their ignorance and unexpected idleness. Lebrun had been rejected by those men. He remained pure and principled, and educated; he could still speak the language of revolution and liberation. This was what many people—like the people who had come to the Maida

Vale flat—still wanted to hear. So it was an air of conspiracy, rather than melancholy, that hung over our dinner. Black liberation was the principal theme. But we were a mixed group; that was part of the civility of the occasion. And Lebrun, when he came, was with a white American woman, of Czech or Polish origin, a good twenty years younger than he. That reputation, as a womanizer, or as a man successful with women, had always been Lebrun's. Lebrun was now past sixty. He was slender and fine-featured; he took care of himself. Close to, he was delicate, smooth-skinned, with a touch of copper in his dark complexion that spoke of some unusual—perhaps Amerindian—ancestry.

It was understood that we had come to hear him talk. And everything that occurred between his arrival and his settling down to talk—the general greetings, the brisk and colloquial exchanges with his Lebanese hosts to establish how well he knew them, his "don't-mention-it" attitude to my acknowledgement of his article in the Russian magazine—everything was like an orchestra tuning up, to background chatter, for the evening's big event.

Soon enough—while our hosts went to their little kitchen and cooking smells came out to cling to the old curtains and the fat upholstered furniture—Lebrun was launched.

He was born to talk. It was as though everything he saw and thought and read was automatically processed into talk material. And it was all immensely intelligent and gripping. He talked about music and the influence on composers of the instruments of their time. He talked about military matters.

I had met no one like that from our region, no one who had given so much time to reading and thought, no one who had organized so much information in this appetizing way. I thought his political reputation simplified the man. And his language was extraordinary. What I had noticed in Woodford Square was still there: his spoken sentences, however involved, were complete: they could have been taken down and sent to the printers. I thought his spoken language was like Ruskin's on the printed page, in its fluency and elaborateness, the words wonderfully chosen, often unexpected, bubbling up from some ever-running spring of sensibility. The thought-connections—as with Ruskin—were not always clear; but you assumed they were there. As with the poetry of Blake (or, within a smaller compass, Auden), you held on, believing there was a worked-out argument.

It was rhetoric, of course. And, of course, it was loaded in his favour. He couldn't be interrupted; like royalty, he raised all the topics; and he would have been a master of the topics he raised. But even with that I don't think that I am pitching the comparisons too high. I thought him a prodigy. I was moved by the fact that such a man came from something like my own background. I began to understand his great reputation among middle-class black people. How, considering when he was born, had he become the man he was? How had he preserved his soul through all the discouragements of the colonial time?

He had a sense of his audience. He appeared to understand the questions in my mind, and no doubt in the minds of others. Late in the evening he began to talk about himself.

He said, "My mother had an uncle who was a coachman for an English family in Barbados. I'm going back a long way now. I'm going back a hundred years. The thing about being a black man in this Caribbean–Central American region is that you have quite an ancestry here, if you want to claim it. At some stage the English family went to London. I don't know whether they went for good or whether they went for a short time. They took their black coachman with them.

"In London this coachman became friendly with a black man who worked as a servant in the Tichborne house. A famous family, connected with a famous law case. An uneducated Australian appeared one day and said he was the Tichborne heir. Lady Tichborne, for some strange reason of her own, said the man, who could hardly read or write, was her long lost son. A great Victorian scandal. The best account of the affair is by Lord Maugham, who used to be Lord Chancellor, and on the evidence of this Tichborne book was a much better writer than his novelist brother.

"The black man who worked for the Tichbornes was married to one of the servant women of the house. This had a powerful effect on my mother's uncle. He used to be in and out of the house. You must imagine him going down the steps to the basement. He said whenever he went the servants gave him tea and cake. The women petted him. He pined for that when he came back to Barbados. When he was very old he was still talking about the black man in the big house in London who had married the white woman and nobody minded, and he was still talking about the white servants who always made him welcome and gave him tea and cake. He would say of the servants, 'They always much me up.' Meaning they had made much of him.

"I heard such a lot about this when I was a child that I developed a fantasy about a big house in England, and white people giving me tea and cake too. The house in my fantasy was like a big estate house. It wasn't like your big house in Belgravia or South Kensington. And years later that fantasy house came back and got in the way when I began reading the English novelists. It still does, a little bit.

"My mother's uncle, the old coachman, and a very proud man, used to say, 'It had no trouble in those days. Black people and white people was one.' And that was what I grew up believing too, that in the old days things were better. When I was old enough to understand what the old coachman had taught me, I was ashamed. I tried to forget. From various things I deduce that the old man was born in 1840. This was six years after the abolition of slavery. This means that his mother had been a slave, and all the older people around him.

It also means something else. The slave trade was abolished in 1807. So when my mother's uncle was ten or twelve there would have been people of sixty-five or seventy in Barbados who had been brought over from Africa. And still the old man thought that things were better in the old days, and had got me to believe it.

"I was tormented by this memory, until I arrived at my own political resolution, and saw it for what it was."

"Political resolution"—it was his indirect way of referring to his Marxism; it was as though to speak the word itself would have been too crude.

"But even after I had arrived at my political resolution I couldn't bring myself to talk of this memory. And then I did so in Trinidad, during the Butler strike. I was at a public meeting, before the big march on Port of Spain that so terrified the colonial government. I was saying something quite simple. Something like: the time had come for black people to take their destiny into their own hands. Just then the memory of the old coachman came to me, and I began to tell the crowd about the white servants and the tea and cake. I could feel them listening in a new way. They had never heard anything like that before from a black man on a public platform. But the biggest effect was on me. As soon as I began to talk about what my mother's uncle had got me to believe as a child, that in the old days white people and black people were one, as soon as I did that—in five seconds the shame I had carried for twenty years dropped from me."

He paused. There was a silence. As though everyone was being given time to examine himself.

Then Lebrun said, "And every black man has a memory like that. Every educated black man is eaten away quietly by a memory like that."

The food was brought out into the dim sitting room. Our hosts were Lebanese, but the food was West Indian, in honour of the occasion. Not the Asian-Mediterranean or French-creole style of a cosmopolitan place like Trinidad; but the rough African food of the smaller islands. The central dish was an oily yellowish mound of what looked like boiled and pounded green bananas.

Lebrun made a big show of being excited by this dish. "Ah," he said. "Coo-coo. It is the last thing one expected in London. We must give it our full attention."

Somebody else said, "At home we call it foo-foo."

Lebrun said, "Coo-coo or foo-foo, it is the serious business of the evening."

A heavy glistening mound was placed on my own plate. I probed it: boiled yams and green bananas and possibly other tubers mashed together with peppers, the whole mixture slimy from the yams and—the Lebanese touch—olive oil. Below the pepper it had almost no taste, except one of a tart rawness (from the green bananas), and I thought it awful, the texture, the slipperiness. I didn't think I would be able to keep it down. I let it be on my plate. No one noticed.

While Lebrun ate, and his dutiful woman friend ate, and the smell of meat and oil became high in the squashed sitting room with the old upholstered chairs, and people asked the Lebanese where they had got the yams and green bananas from, I (feeling that I was betraying them all, and separating myself from the good mood of the evening) remembered my aunt twenty years before, fanning her coalpot on the concrete back steps of our house in Port of Spain, and talking about Grenadians boiling their "pitch-oil tin" of ground provisions once a week.

Soon, through his mouthfuls of the coo-coo or the foo-foo, Lebrun began to talk again.

He said, "Perhaps the most extraordinary discussion of the century was the one between Lenin and the Indian delegate, Roy, at the Second Congress of the Comintern in 1920."

I felt that this was an offering to me.

"A re-interpretation of Marx, with special reference to the struggles of non-European peoples in the twentieth century. There is a certain racial view of Marx that we all know about. It was encouraged by the journalism he did about the Indian Mutiny for the American papers. Pieces done to order, unconsidered in parts, clearly not the whole truth. A re-interpretation was necessary, and the work was done all of forty years ago. Some people can forget that. When Gandhi and Nehru and Mountbatten and the others have become footnotes in the history of Asia, people will look back and see that meeting between Lenin and Roy, just three years after the revolution, as one of the crucial events of the century."

THERE WAS no moment of break with Lebrun, as there had been with Foster Morris. For me the illumination of his article in the Russian magazine remained; but we both soon got to recognize—what I feel sure we always knew—that the relationship between us was forced. We shared a background and in all kinds of unspoken ways we could understand one another; but we were on different tracks.

A great embarrassment occurred just a few weeks after our dinner.

Lebrun's woman friend—intelligent, easy of manner, accepting, curiously calm—lived in New York. I hardly knew the city and had met very few Americans. I couldn't set the woman in a background, couldn't separate what might have been background and background manner from the person. I liked what I saw, though. I liked her especially—she was ten or twelve years older than I—for her calm; that gave her a kind of attractiveness.

It happened that I had to go to New York. I had a commission of sorts: to provide a story idea, for a possible film (really an impossible film): the kind of futility and self-betrayal a young man can be easily lured into. Near the end of the Maida Vale dinner, when things were more informal, I mentioned this trip to Lebrun and his friend. They were interested. They mentioned names to one another. Then Lebrun said he would send me a list of people I should meet in New York.

He did what he said (I always found him punctilious in that way). And so a few weeks later, on a Sunday afternoon, having been let out as on parole from the expensive hotel where my film work was like a torment, I found myself being driven around Manhattan, having the famous sights pointed out to me, by a couple who were overwhelming me with their friendship, and more than friendship: involving me with something like love as Lebrun's fellow countryman and London friend.

After the sightseeing there was to be a dinner. They had invited some people to meet me; Lebrun, they said, had written to various people about me. The dinner was going to be very nice, the lady said. They had prepared some special dishes; they had prepared gefilte fish.

She asked, turning around to me from the front seat of the car, "Have you had gefilte fish?" (A memory here, connected with this movement, that she was wearing a fur coat.)

She looked happy to hear that I hadn't.

I knew almost nothing of New York, and couldn't place these people, couldn't assess the suburb and the house to which we drove when our sightseeing in Manhattan was over. I couldn't assess the people who began to arrive, quite early, as I thought, for the dinner and the special dish the lady had gone straight to her kitchen to see about.

They remain vague, but I know they were nice people, intelligent, friendly people. Some were near neighbours. Others had come from some distance for this Sunday dinner. They were all anxious to show friendship to me; but I knew they were showing friendship to Lebrun.

I had accepted Lebrun's introductions, but I had never really believed in the value of his international contacts. Even with the regard I had grown to have for him, I thought of him as a talker more than anything else. I saw him as a gifted black man compelled by the circumstances of his time, from fairly early on, to live on his wits. His Russian connection, the article in the Russian magazine, his appearance at the Maida Vale dinner with the attractive Polish or Czech woman—all of that, though real enough, I saw as attributes of the now old black man living as by second nature on his wits.

He belonged to the first generation of educated black men in the region. For a number of them—men as old as the century—there was no honourable place at home in their colony or in the big countries. They were in-between people, too early, without status; they tried to make their way. They came and went; they talked big in one place—the United States, England, the West Indies, Panama, Belize—about the things they were doing somewhere else. Some of them became eccentric or unbalanced; some attached themselves to the Back-to-Africa movement (though Africa was itself at that time colonized); some became fraudsters.

When I came to England in 1950 there were still extravagant black figures from that generation about on the streets of London: men in pin-stripe suits and bowlers, with absurd accents. Sometimes they greeted me; they were prompted to do so by solitude, but they also wished to find someone to boast to. One wet winter evening one of these men, met in a Regent Street bus queue, straight away took out his wallet and began to show me photographs of his house and his English wife. They were shipwrecked men. They had lost touch with themselves and now, near the end, were seeing the fantasies they had lived on washed away by the arrival of new immigrants from Jamaica and the other islands, working men in Harlem-style zoot suits and broad-brimmed felt hats.

Lebrun, with all his gifts, I saw as part of that older generation. He too came and went, and was spoken of (like many others) as a man of mystery. But my feeling always was (considering my own arrangements) that the hidden, foreign segments of Lebrun's life would have been quite tame and full of small financial alarms. In that way I thought he would have been a little like Butler, the 1937 strike leader, who, after the war and internment, went to live, very quietly, in London, cutting himself off from the demands (though not the subsidy) of his followers and his political party, the British Empire Workers and Citizens Home Rule Party. I thought that Lebrun's time abroad would have had that element of quietness and rest.

So, just as I had been overwhelmed by Lebrun's article in the Russian magazine, never expecting such penetration from him, now in this New York suburban house I was thrown into some confusion by this evidence of Lebrun's international life, which was far more elegant than anything I had expected. It was far more elegant than anything I had known.

They knew a lot about the politics and the personalities of the islands; and they knew about this from Lebrun's side, as it were. They satirized the local politicians who were Lebrun's enemies; they described one as a gangster, another as a witch-doctor.

One woman had travelled in the islands, visiting places I didn't know. It was impossible, she said, to be in those islands without having an idea of their history, and some sense of their future. What had she seen? She couldn't really tell me. She refused to speak as a tourist; that refusal was like part of her self-esteem. And I felt that, just as (considering the island she had spoken of, the one with the witchdoctor) all the forests that had been there at the discovery had been scraped away for the sugar-cane fields, so she had stripped the people she had seen of all their too easily seen attributes, to get down to some ideal structure that existed in her head.

I remembered the effect on me of Lebrun's article in the Russian magazine: it had appeared to take me above road-level and show me the pattern of things from above. I felt that Lebrun had done the same for this group, that everything in that woman's way of looking would have come from her own interpretation of what Lebrun had said.

I remembered how out of tune Lebrun had been in Wood-ford Square in Port of Spain during the great emotional assemblies of 1956. The meetings were billed as educational; the square was described as a university. People hadn't of course gone to learn anything; they had gone to take part in a kind of racial sacrament. Lebrun had appeared to be participating in that when he talked about having waited all the years of the century for this great occasion, and never having doubts that the moment would come. But then he had gone off on a track of his own. He had begun to talk about history and the production of sugar.

Windmills and tall factory chimneys were a feature of the landscape of the islands, he had said; they had been for more than two centuries. The large-scale production of sugar had always been an industrial process. Sugar-cane was a perishable crop. It had to be cut at a certain time and it had to be processed within a certain time; in the making of sugar many things could go wrong. This meant that the black people of the islands were among the earliest industrial workers in the world, obeying the discipline of a complex manufacturing process. For this reason they escaped standard racial categorization; they were not like the peasantry of Africa and Asia and large areas of Europe. They were a very old industrial proletariat, and the history of slavery had shown them to be always a revolutionary people. Now they were destined to be in the forefront of the revolution in the New World.

People hadn't understood what he had said, but he had spoken with passion and fluency, and this had made it appear to be part of the great movement of the square; and he had been applauded. (And the photograph of him on the Victorian bandstand in the square, addressing the crowd below the trees, had been used on the cover of the two or three books of his speeches that had been published in Czechoslovakia or East Berlin.)

This was the view of the region he had offered. This was the currency—this news of the coming revolution, his place within that revolution—with which, as it were, he had paid his way among revolutionaries abroad.

When I had heard him talk in the square in 1956—not absolutely knowing about his Russian sympathies, knowing about him only vaguely as a far-off black revolutionary of the region—I had been as puzzled as anyone by his stress on the industrial nature of slavery in the Caribbean. Later I thought of it as ideology for ideology's sake, a man on the periphery over-staking his claim.

Now, in the New York house, catching fragments of his views and rhetoric and even his voice in what was being said to me, I saw this stress as part of the "political resolution" he had talked about at the Maida Vale dinner. He had said that that resolution had enabled him to lay aside the shame he had grown to feel because of his mother's uncle, the old coachman, who looked back to a time nearer slavery as the good time, when white people and black people were one.

The confession had been impressive: every black man, he had said, had some tormenting secret like that. Yet the words, "political resolution," had appeared to conceal something. And now I felt—with shame, grief, sympathy, admiration, recognizing something of myself in his struggle—that, as much as the uneducated old coachman of ninety years before, and the middle-aged black man in bowler and pin-stripe suit stepping out of the bus queue in Regent Street in 1950 to show me photographs of his house and English wife, Lebrun had always needed to find some way of dealing with the past. With his fine mind, and his love of knowledge, his need might even have been greater.

The ideology he had found (and his interpretation of it) enabled him to do more than most. There was a type of revolutionary (or merely protest) writing which found it easier to move imaginatively in the time of slavery, with its fixed structures, its clear enemy, its clear morality. This kind of writing saw the period of slavery as a time of almost continuous guerrilla war; it relished that drama, but was unable to deal with the period after the abolition of slavery, which by comparison was flat, directionless, without moral issues. Lebrun's political resolution was very far from this sensationalism. It enabled him, not to embrace the period of slavery, but to acknowledge it without pain, and, presenting it in his own way, to make a claim for its universality, and even its precedence.

"'THE MAN want to take you over," the chief minister had said, over the stained tablecloth in Government House. And I began to feel something of that in the house in New York. I was using Lebrun's introductions and I suppose it was to be expected that they should think I was a revolutionary too. But after a while I couldn't help noticing that I was being regarded as part of Lebrun's revolution. They all knew about the article in the Russian magazine. And somehow my work ceased to be strictly mine; it was as it were contained in Lebrun's vision of the region. I began to feel that in their vision I was incidental to my own work: I was an expression of Lebrun's will. I didn't like the assumption but didn't know how to speak against it. I had allowed them to talk and never spoken up; I had allowed them to go too far.

I could see that they were willing to make room for me, as once no doubt they had made room for Lebrun. No words about this were spoken, but I could sense that I was being invited to shed my racial or cultural burdens and to be part of their brotherhood. And they were so nice and attractive, and the house was so pleasant, and the thought of the film work in the hotel was so disagreeable, it would have been marvellous, it would have been less trouble, if I could have pretended to be a convert. And I had a sense that years before, in much harder times, Lebrun might have made such a deal, would have shed one smarting skin and felt himself reborn in another.

Few of us are without the feeling that we are incomplete. But my feelings of incompleteness were not like Lebrun's. In the things I felt myself incomplete Lebrun was—as I thought—abundantly served: physical attractiveness, love, sexual fulfilment. But there were other yearnings that no shedding of skin could have assuaged: my own earned security, a wish for my writing gift to last and grow, a dream of working at yet unknown books, accumulations of fruitful days, achievement. These yearnings could be assuaged only in the self I knew.

No other group would ever again make me an invitation so wholehearted or so seductive. But to yield was to cease to be myself, to trust to the unknown. And like the chief minister, I became very frightened.

We went to a smaller room for the dinner. The walls were of plain brick, rose-coloured, pale, seemingly dusted over, very attractive. Eventually the gefilte fish, which had been promised since the afternoon, came. I didn't like the way it looked, and have no memory of it. The idea of something pounded to paste, then spiced or oiled, worked on by fingers, brought to mind thoughts of hand lotions and other things. I became fearful of smelling it. I couldn't eat it. With the coo-coo or the foo-foo in the Maida Vale flat I had been able to hide what I did to the things on my plate. That couldn't be done here: everyone knew that the gefilte fish had been specially prepared for Lebrun's friend from London.

Manners never frayed. Conversation revived. But the embarrassment that began in the dining room lasted until I was taken back to the Manhattan hotel.

. . .

THE ART collectors we know about and envy are the successful ones, like those who a hundred years ago bought Van Gogh and early Cézanne for very little. The people we don't know about from that period are the people who—perhaps with equal passion—collected works by contemporaries who have faded. I once asked a London dealer about such collectors. Did they get to know at a certain moment that they had been wrong? The dealer was unexpectedly vehement. Bad collectors, he said, were a type: they believed in themselves more than in the art they paid for.

I wonder whether that was also true of Lebrun's New York patrons, or whether they had to find other ways over the next few years of acknowledging that the news he had been giving them was wrong, that the special revolution he had promised in the islands wasn't going to happen.

The politics of the islands never really changed. The leaders who had come to power at the end of the colonial time— like the chief minister who had ordered Lebrun off his little island—remained in power. It didn't matter that many of them were bored and didn't do much. They were all in their different ways racial leaders, and the first successful ones. They were very local, and for that reason special, each man embodying in his territory the idea of black redemption. In the almost mystical relationship between these very local men and their followers there was no room for Lebrun.

He was now old and very poor, a revolutionary without a revolution, occasionally flourishing (as his enemies reported) on the bounty of women admirers from the past, but at other times living a hard bohemian life, lodging in other people's houses or apartments in the Caribbean and Central America, in England and Europe, and always moving on. I grew to feel that at some stage he had given up, lost faith in his cause—though nothing was said, and though, earning his keep, he continued to write communist-slanted articles in small-circulation left-wing magazines.

Lebrun and I never met after that evening in the Maida Vale flat; but I saw him a few times on television when he was very old, and because of that I have the feeling I witnessed his ageing and physical decay. We kept up the courtesies after the New York embarrassment. We exchanged letters; sometimes he sent me magazines containing articles he had written in which he referred to my work. Those references became fewer; finally they stopped.

In 1973 he sent me his last book, *The Second Struggle: Speeches and Writings 1962–1972*. It was printed in East Germany, and the cover carried the 1956 photograph of him in Woodford Square in Port of Spain, standing at a microphone on the bandstand, before the crowd. He had inscribed the book to me as to "a fellow humanist." And he had added, "To understand that is at any rate to make a beginning." A touch of the old charm, the way with words. It didn't mean anything, but I was moved to see his shaky hand.

It was a dreadful book. It had nothing of the brilliance and the underground emotions of his article in the Russian magazine. In spite of the cover photograph I doubted whether many of the pieces had been speeches. There was an undercurrent of defeat and rancour. There was little subtlety, no sly humour. In certain articles he used stock communist words— "opportunists," "petit-bourgeois nationalists," "reformists," "Blanquists"—almost in a personal way, to denounce his Caribbean enemies, the successful politicians, the men in Government House.

The decline (which might have been partly due to age) was more noticeable in the hack work he had chosen to reprint, the pieces in which, as a colonial, he compared non-European communist countries with imperialist client states—Kazakhstan, for instance, with the Philippines or Pakistan, Cuba with Brazil or Venezuela. Official facts and figures for the communist country, of rising industrial production, of rising numbers at school and universities; and then a simple expository account (like something taken from a simple encyclopaedia) of the backwardness of the Philippines or Brazil or Iran, population figures and areas in square kilometres always given, where feudal landlords owned much of the country and almost no one went to school; the whole essay locked together with a couple of academic-looking tables and a quotation (excessively documented) from an unknown "professor" or "doctor." Did he believe in those articles? Or were they written by a man who knew that such articles only filled space in official magazines?

Thinking now of his decay, into which he had been led by his cause, the cause that had appeared years before to rescue him from racial nonentity, thinking of that and his poverty, his dependence on others, for lodging and livelihood, I thought how strange it was that he had turned out to be like the people he had written about in his very first book, the one that had lain unread at the bottom shelf of the cupboard in the sixth form at Queen's Royal College in Port of Spain.

HE HAD written in that book about some of the Spanish-American or Venezuelan revolutionaries before Bolívar, and he had concentrated on those with Trinidad connections.

For some years after it had been detached from Venezuela and the Spanish empire and had become a British territory, Trinidad was used as a base by revolutionaries on the mainland, across the Gulf of Paria.

One embittered Spanish official, a refugee in Trinidad, had plotted with an associate on the mainland to start a slave revolt in Venezuela. A hopeless idea: Trinidad was still full of Venezuelans and a number of them were Spanish agents. And then this plot, like so many Caribbean slave plots, was betrayed to the authorities by a slave. The rebels were hanged and quartered, and the quarters of the hanged were displayed on the highway over the mountains between La Guaira on the coast and the inland valley of Caracas. This attempt at revolution never really became famous: everything happened too fast.

Miranda was better known. He had left Venezuela early and had travelled about Europe and the United States. He gave himself the title of Count and got to know important people; in revolutionary France he even became a general. In exile he began to improve on the country he had come from. The blacks and mulattoes of the slave estates receded; the people of Venezuela became Incas, the original rulers of the continent, nature's gentlemen, as noble as anything the eighteenth-century philosophers dreamed of. These were the people Miranda represented; all they needed was freedom. In middle age, finally, he came to Trinidad, his base, to start his revolution across the Gulf. He had money, a ship, arms, all he had said he needed. He also had the prospectuses of the London merchants who had subsidized him for years; he had promised to scatter these about Venezuela, after he had liberated it. He didn't liberate Venezuela; he released a kind of anarchy, and was destroyed by the colonial pettiness he had run away from half a lifetime before. It had always been there, waiting for him.

In order to write this book Lebrun had had to do some original work in the Venezuelan archives. His purpose in writing the book in the 1930s had been to prove his old point about the revolutionary nature of the islands; to give himself and his ideas a great past, to link the revolutionary stir of the 1930s to the stir caused in the region by the French Revolution; to lift the islands from the end-of-empire smallness in which they had been becalmed since the abolition of slavery, and to attach them once again to the great historical processes of the continent. He wished, above all, to make the point that revolutions do not simply happen: they have to be prepared for, the people have to be educated, there has to be a revolutionary political party.

All that labour, and I doubt whether a dozen people in Trinidad or Venezuela had read his book. No one at school had read it. I hadn't read it; I had handled it only as a book, a wonderful object.

I read it one afternoon in the London Library not long after I had looked at *The Second Struggle*. I would have been the first person for ten years perhaps to take it from its shelf.

What a spirit was locked in its pages! Always there, waiting to speak to me. In Trinidad in 1948 I wonder how much I would have been able to make of it. Not a great deal. I would have been then too much part of that end-of-empire smallness Lebrun had talked about. I would have been as baffled by it as I was when I was told that the writer was a revolutionary and on the run somewhere in the United States. I needed the passage of time, distance, experience, to understand what he had written.

I was aware of the room in which I was reading, in London—how changed from the London in which the book had been published and, as the printed sticker said, presented to the London Library "by the publishers." It wasn't only that I had changed since I had seen the book at school. The world had changed; my presence in the London Library was an aspect of that change.

Thinking of the ironies in Lebrun's life, that at the end he should have been like the people he had written about in his first book, and feeling almost superstitiously that there was a circularity in human lives, I began to wonder where in my own writings I had marked out regions of the spirit to which I was to return. Just as Lebrun, who had sought to submerge his racial feelings in the universality of his political beliefs, had had that dream removed and in old age had been returned unprotected to heaven knows what private alarms.

I thought of his capacity for talk. That gift had opened doors for him all his life. But there was hysteria there, as well, the hysteria of the islands, expressed most usually in self-satire, jokeyness, fantasy, religious excess, sudden spasms of cruelty. I thought of the burning of Charlie King at the time of the strike in Trinidad, and the almost religious, sacrificial regard for the victim ever afterwards. I thought of the taunting of Foster Morris in the old wooden house with the distorted shadows cast by oil lamps. I thought of the black man in the bowler who had stepped out of the bus queue in Regent Street to show me photographs of his wife and house. How could one enter the emotions of a black man as old as the century?

PRIVATE ALARMS, perhaps. But the world had changed. Lebrun wasn't being returned to his beginnings. The Caribbean was independent. Africa was independent. He had been around for a long time; he was known. And now, near the end, his underground reputation began to alter. At one time he had been the man of principle, the man of the true revolution; the various politicians of the Caribbean had been the men who had sold out. Now, with subtle addition, he became the man of true African or black redemption, the man of principle there, the man who had held out against all kinds of enticements to give up the cause, unlike the false black leaders.

So now he stepped in and out of his two characters, now the man of the revolutionary cause, now the man of racial redemption, the man always of principle. He appeared, in this new personality, to be going against the whole life of revolution he had lived; against the "political resolution" he had come to years before, the universality in which he had shed the burdens of race and shame; against the admiration of his New York supporters; against, even, the inscription to me, as to a fellow humanist, in the copy of *The Second Struggle*.

His name didn't appear in books about Africa or the Caribbean; writers and publishers didn't want to offend the rulers. This added to his prestige; he could be presented on the radio or the television, in the programmes on which he was called to give his opinion about this and that, as the hidden black prophet of the century. He looked the part; he was very old now, almost saintly, the man without possessions.

He never spoke against a black racial regime. He presented Asian dispossession in Amin's Uganda and Nyerere's Tanzania as an aspect of class warfare. Guyana in South America he defended in a curious way: since the days of slavery, he said on one radio programme, the Caribbean could be considered as black people's territory. He put this racial statement in a vast, categorizing way—very much in the manner of the old Lebrun—on a television programme. He said, "The day the first African slave was landed, the region became black territory. If they had known that was going to happen, they might have thought twice."

It was as though at the very end of his life he had found the role he had been working towards since the beginning. He was the black spokesman of the century, offering not the gross semi-mystical redemption of the politician of the islands, but something higher and more universal, something which had elements of historical inevitability: a little like the view he had offered me in his article on my books in the Russian magazine in 1960.

In his new role he began to make African pilgrimages. In the 1920s and 1930s a number of educated people of Lebrun's generation had joined the Back-to-Africa movement. As a revolutionary he had disapproved; he had thought the movement sentimental and escapist. He acknowledged that, but he said the world had changed.

He went to Africa as a famous black man. He was welcomed by the leaders; his reputation began to feed on itself. He was said to be advising. He went to all kinds of tyrannies; to countries of murderous tribal wars; to collapsed economies. But when he came back he spoke on the television and radio as though he had been granted a vision of something more ideal, an Africa stripped of all that was incidental and passing: like the vision his New York supporters had been given years before, of latent pure revolution, in the West Indian islands.

He never tried to stay in the places he had visited. He always came back to his base, in England, Europe, Canada. He had learned his lesson from the West Indian islands in the 1950s and 1960s, and wished to threaten no one.

It was a kind of fulfilment for him. It was not to be begrudged. I thought his vision of Africa a harmless fantasy. Then I had a letter from a friend, a writer, in a French-African territory.

Paul wrote, "A funny thing. A black American poet passed through. A grand old man, a proper GOM. The USIS asked me to chair the meeting. But I didn't want to see the old soak drink. And then your friend Lebrun came, on his own. Looking very grand and wise. The Brits did a little show for him. He began to lecture us about the way Africa had been politicized, in defiance of Marx. That was surprising to me. I thought the man was a communist. Then something happened. He couldn't bear the sight of the young French *coopérants*, prancing about in Africa, as he thought, and he didn't like the sight of the African women of the university with their white boy friends. He began to threaten everybody, in a quiet way. He went wild, and then he calmed down."

The man with the New York friends, in the old days, and the New York manner, the hard-won political resolution. The old man wild in free Africa, expressing old hurt.

II

NOT LONG after, with no thoughts of Lebrun in my head, and simply to satisfy an old urge, I went myself to French-speaking West Africa for the first time.

And there the French language developed a whole new set of associations for me.

The earliest association the language had had for me—as a child in Trinidad, and not long after I had come to Port of Spain—had been with prisoners escaping in open boats from the prison colony on Devil's Island off French Guiana. Sometimes their boats drifted on to Trinidad. They were allowed to stay for three days, I believe. They were photographed and interviewed by the *Trinidad Guardian* and the *Evening News*; the local people gave food and water and other gifts; and then they were sent on their way again.

At about the same time there was my first-year study of French at Queen's Royal College. Queen's Royal was a famous island college. To go there from an intermediate school was not only to make a big academic jump, but also to be more grown up. The study of French was like part of the excitement and elegance of the place.

A lot of what I felt about the French language was given me by my teacher. He was a young man, but with the neatness and formality of someone older. Before he sat down at the master's table he always greeted the class: "Good morning, boys." The handkerchief he took out to pat his forehead and mouth and neck on a hot day always remained folded. He came from a well known black family. They were professional, cultured people. That represented a considerable effort, in our colonial setting: there were not many like them.

This teacher loved the French language and French ways, and I heard that he and other members of his family used to spend time in Martinique, the French West Indian island to the north. (This would have been before the war; during the war the French islands were Vichy and out of bounds.) They went for the language, the foreignness, the stylishness, the cafés where you could ask the waiter for pen and paper and write letters at your table. In Trinidad (where the restaurants were Chinese and rough and disreputable-feeling, with tables in separate cubicles) we didn't have these metropolitan touches. They also went for the racial freedom. I heard it said by many people that in Martinique and Guadeloupe a black man of culture was treated as an equal.

All of this was associated with the language. I transferred it even to the pre-war *Siepmann's French Reader* that we used, with French texts on the left-hand pages and, on the right-hand pages, lovely full-page pen drawings of French scenes—streets, gardens, fields—by H. M. Brock.

These were among the ideas and French associations that I took to Martinique—nearly twenty years after *Siepmann*—when I was travelling for my first travel book. And in less than a week all the stored fantasy connected with the French language, from that early time, fell away. I found a little island that seemed to have been scraped clean of its original vegetation (Trinidad had large tracts of primal forest in the northern hills, and primal swamps), scraped clean and cropped and cropped: small views from the narrow winding roads, but not cosy views, a little island showing its serf past, over-cultivated, socially and racially over-regulated, even obsessed, small, constricted, pressing down on everyone, unconscious cruelty in everyone's speech. This was a place you wanted to get away from.

My French teacher's pre-war holidays in Martinique spoke now less of the attractions of the island than of the hardness of the world at that time for black people.

IN THE country where I was in former French West Africa the people I got to know were expatriates. The Africans were in their own country and lived their own lives. The advertisements of the rich city were in French and the traffic signs on the highways suggested France; but the Africans also had their own language, their own families, clans, *ethnies,* religious practices, their own totems and household gods, their own instinctive reverences. You could meet Africans and talk about the economy and the presidential succession; but afterwards they could retreat to areas of the spirit where you couldn't follow them.

It was curiously exciting, the thought of that complete and very old other life out there. But for friendship, for dinner companions, for people with whom you drove out to the beach on Sundays, you depended on the expatriates. They were mainly French and Americans. There were also some French West Indian women, in their thirties or forties, from Martinique and Guadeloupe. These women had gone from their islands to Paris. There they had formed the African connections that had brought them here. Now for a variety of reasons they were unattached.

I had never thought that French West Indian women might be a type or a special group. Now I saw that they were different from the black or brown West Indian women I knew: their world-picture was different. The French West Indian women were set apart by the very language that had attracted my French teacher to Martinique and the French islands in the 1930s and 1940s. In those days my teacher had sought to escape not so much from the English language as from its hard racial associations. In the French language of Martinique he could find a whole new idea of himself.

Now it worked the other way. The French language restricted the people of Martinique and Guadeloupe to a special French-speaking world. It shut them off from the other islands and the rest of the continent. Their thoughts were of Paris; legally they were full citizens of France. But the Paris they went to was not the city of light. It was the black immigrant world of that city, which was like a constricted version of home; and from there some of the women went to Africa, following the attachments they had made in their version of Paris. Strange zigzag, in part reversing the journey of the slavers of a hundred and fifty years before; now, though, not returning these women to what was theirs, but sending

unprotected women of the New World to what was very far
away and strange.

In West Africa I had got to know Phyllis. She was in her
thirties or early forties, from Guadeloupe, brown rather than
black, speaking a clear, delicate-sounding French. She had
married an African in Paris. That marriage, like the marriage
of many other *antillaises* to Africans, had broken down almost
as soon as she had come to Africa with her husband. It was
to the neighbouring country that she had come out. When
her marriage had failed she had left that country and come to
this one—the French language and the structure of French-
speaking Africa had given her at least that room for manoeuvre. She had found a secretarial-librarian's job in one of the
embassies, and was more than able to look after herself.

She was part of the expatriate group I moved in. I saw her
everywhere, at every dinner party, on every Sunday beach
excursion (her hair straightened out by the sea, drying to salt
on her freshly burnt skin), at every cultural occasion which
the foreign embassies laid on, officially for the local African
audience, but in reality for the expatriate community. She
knew many people, was stylish and self-possessed, was out-
going and generous; but she appeared to have no partner or
special friend.

Such energy in going out! It was disquieting, after a time.
I felt she didn't like going back to her flat, and this made me
feel she didn't like being in the Africa she had found herself
in. I wondered whether she hadn't thought of going back to
Guadeloupe. I asked her one day. She said she hated the
island; it was so small; the people were so small-minded,
content with so little. The only other place she could think
of—and it was the only other thing she had known—was the
version of Paris she had lived in. And she didn't want to go
back to Paris. So she stayed where she was, and went out.

I discovered also that there was a certain fluidity to her
character. She could adapt her behaviour to the company.

She might appear to agree when people complained about African behaviour (accepting invitations to formal dinners and then not turning up, not coming to cultural evenings at the embassies). But then on another day, when we were alone, she might say, "Why should an African want to leave his house and come to a room and sit with all these foreigners and hear someone play the violin? If they would just think about it, they would see it is a foolish thing to ask people to do. The life that Africans have among themselves is so beautiful—they should be trying to find out about that, but they don't want to know."

She began to talk one day about Lebrun's visit to French-speaking West Africa. He was someone we had in common. She thought of him as a fellow *antillais*. She was critical; she hadn't committed herself until she felt she knew me. I had heard a lot from various people, but in an imprecise way, about his behaviour. I had heard about his rage.

Phyllis said, "Something happened here, in the capital, when he came. Something happened to him. He wasn't happy here. He came with his daughter. She was almost white. Did you know that? She wasn't like him physically. She was very big. She was like a wall, like that door. I think there was some unhappiness there. She lived with her mother. This trip with Lebrun was like a holiday for her."

"How old was this daughter?"

"Twenty-four, twenty-five."

Perhaps then her mother had been the calm, attractive woman, Polish or Czech, I had seen with Lebrun in the Maida Vale flat, the woman whose friends I had been sent to in New York later.

I said, "I believe I met her mother."

"She left him. That's the story here. She became bored with his communism, and she had the money. The people in the movement begged her to go back for the sake of the movement."

"Was there somebody else?"

"Obviously there was somebody else. She is a woman. Lebrun went crazy."

"The other man was black or white?"

"Lebrun didn't know for a long time."

"Which would he have minded more?"

"That was the thing. I don't think Lebrun knew what would have hurt him more. He became very racial-minded when he was here. He insulted quite a few white people for no reason at all. There was something here he didn't like. What was it? He never absolutely said. It's a rich city. You see that. It's not what you think of when you think of an African city. It's not only rich, but elegant. I don't think he actually liked that. All the cars, all the shops, all the auto-routes. I suppose it made him feel poor and unwanted. He made his objections political, or tried to. He talked about blacks selling out, about capitalism and imperialism. But do you know what I feel? I feel he expected people to be as excited about his white daughter as he was. He didn't know Africans. They are strong people. And they are cruel. There was a lampoon in the university paper after he made that famous and shameful scene about French men with their black girl friends. A cartoon. The white daughter saying to the old black man in English, 'Daddy, why don't we leave these Negroes and go home?' "

It was cruel and unfair. The students of the university here—a new university, with landscaped grounds and paved roads and red-brick halls of residence: most of the students the first in their families to get higher education, and all with government grants—the students here couldn't possibly imagine the discouragements Lebrun had had to live through in the world outside.

And it was strange that Phyllis, in spite of her own history, her unhappy African marriage, her blank life in Africa, her dependence on expatriates for society, should have taken

the African side in this judgement of Lebrun. But that was
her way. She didn't like it when visitors were at all supercil-
ious about Africa; she liked it much less when the visitors
were black, from the United States or the West Indies. It was
as though she wished to make it clear that she was standing
by her decision to come out to Africa.

One day I asked her about her marriage.

She said, "I used to go to this club in Paris. It was for
blacks. A cellar, really. And there was this ugly little African
fellow. And I mean little. He was small and black and soft,
with a lot of gold. Gold watch, gold rings, gold pen. The
gold used to reflect on his skin. He courted me hard. He said
he loved my name, Phyllis. And my voice. Then he began
to ask me to marry him. He said his family was very rich.
They were like chiefs, he said. They had lots of land, lots of
servants, lots of slaves."

I said, "He said that about the slaves?"

"I thought he was lying. But I didn't mind. I liked him
for it, in fact. I thought he was just trying very hard to
impress me, and I liked him for trying. This went on for
some time. And then I agreed to marry him. Do you want
to know why? Will you believe me? I agreed because I didn't
like him, because I found him repulsive, in fact. That ugly
face and that soft body and that very smooth skin reflecting
the gold. I thought it would be good for me, to marry a man
I couldn't possibly love. I felt I was making a deal with God,
giving up love and pleasure. I felt I couldn't go wrong. I used
to talk to myself in my room. I used to say, 'Phyllis, you
have to forget about love and beauty. You have to forget
your old ways. They haven't got you anywhere, my girl.
They have just got you to this room in Paris. You have to
think about your life and future. That is where true happiness
lies.'

"So I went to my little chief and said yes, and tried to
find happiness in his happiness. The days afterwards in Paris

were the best. I felt I had done the right thing, made my deal with God. And I was courted more than ever. After some months, when my little chief had finished his studies, we came out to Africa. And there it all crashed. He hadn't told his family about his marriage, and they ignored me. Literally. They didn't talk to me. They even in my presence began to talk to him about the need for him to get married."

I said to Phyllis, "But how could you go so calmly to that country? Surely you knew it was a tyranny?"

"I didn't believe it. I didn't believe what I read in the papers. I felt they were lying. I thought there was another truth. You see the way we can tie ourselves up. And I was more concerned with my own adventure. I was nervous, you know. I was more frightened of Africa than any European woman would have been. I have known European women who have married Africans. It's different for them. There's the element of pleasure, excitement, even vanity. If it doesn't work, it doesn't work, and that's that. For me it was different. I had staked too much on it. I had talked too much to myself."

"Did you feel protected by your little chief?"

"In the beginning. He took me around everywhere with him. And he didn't exaggerate. They had a lot of land, and they had a lot of servants and slaves. You didn't buy the slaves. They were just there in the villages, certain groups, certain families. They were there to look after the other people. Everybody knew about them, so there was no question of them running away.

"Something happened not long after we arrived. We went to my little chief's village. There was some ceremony of welcome, and at the end the little chief's feet were washed in blood. Let me tell you about my feelings. I was excited and proud. I loved the ritual. I felt it was very old. I felt it came from the beginning of time. It wasn't how I had thought of Africa when I was in Guadeloupe. I felt these rituals gave me a place in the world.

"Later I heard that a few days before that ceremony a child had been kidnapped from one of the slave villages. I put two and two together. You normally use animal blood in that foot-washing ritual, but the highest honour, the one that does most good to everybody, is when you do it with human blood. So look at that. Look at how far I had gone, so quickly. I was stunned, of course. But it didn't do away with my feeling for the beauty of the ritual. My little chief had tried to impress me with his money. But it was the ritual side of his chief's life that became more and more important to me.

"It was important to my little chief too. As he fell back into his old ways, he thought less of the beauty of my name, Phyllis, and of the beauty of my Guadeloupe French accent. The time came when he wanted to be rid of me. He wanted to do what his family wanted him to do, to marry a suitable woman of his tribe. He began to be violent, the little chief. He began to beat me, the soft little fellow with the gold. I remembered the foot-washing ceremony. And I didn't have to be told now that I was in a country without law. The day actually came—it was as though someone were working magic on me—when I felt that if I stayed one more night in the country I would go mad. That was when I went to the airport and took a plane here. And to think that when I went against all my instincts and married him I thought I was making a deal with God.

"He's very much on my mind now, if you want to know. I'll tell you about something that happened about a month before you came here. The telephone rang very early one morning. In fact, when I woke up it felt like the middle of the night. It was a man's voice on the phone, a French voice. The line wasn't good. I thought it was a nuisance call. It does happen here. The voices are usually French. It makes me feel far from home, and very alone.

"I should have put the phone down right away, but luckily I didn't. The call was from the police in Santos Dumont,

and not from a man giving a bogus name. Santos-Dumont
was an early aviator, and the French gave the name to a
frontier post they established in the north. There are a certain
number of French officers in the police here, and you have
seen the French army barracks just outside the town.

"The officer spoke to me as though I was a member of
the embassy, rather than a locally employed secretary. I didn't
put him right. He was very polite; I didn't want to spoil that.
He said he had with him in the police station someone from
across the frontier. He gave the name of the little chief. He
put him on the telephone. It was the little chief all right. His
voice was squeaky with terror. He said things had gone very
badly on the other side of the frontier. The president there
had suddenly turned against him and all the rest of the *cheferie*.
Somebody had told him the day before that he was to be
arrested in the morning. He decided to run. He had been
driving since the previous afternoon.

"'Thank God for the Mercedes,' he said, as though we
were still together, and I still used the Mercedes. He had
driven for hours on bad roads and dusty tracks and the car
hadn't broken down. In the middle of all of his trouble he
was still proud of his car.

"He wasn't absolutely out of danger. He could have been
handed back. You know that over the frontier they are very
Maoist and anti-French, and they don't lose a chance of making propaganda in other African countries against the government here. However, I spoke to our ambassador, and he
made a few telephone calls. He knew my story. The embassy
more or less took the little chief under their protection. I
drove up that afternoon to Santos Dumont with someone
from the embassy to pick up the little chief.

"He was staying in a police building in a sealed room
with an air-conditioning unit. It was very cold in the room.
He was in a dirty peasant's cloth and without his gold. Nothing shining on his skin. It was his idea of a disguise. The
terror was still in his eyes.

"'Me, me,' he kept on saying. 'A man of the *cheferie*—
they were going to put me on the *diète noire*.' You know
about that famous black diet, don't you? They put you in a
cell without food or water and leave you to die. It's what the
president does to his enemies. I had heard about it when I
was there. But I will tell you that it was another one of the
things I heard about and didn't believe in. I saw now, for the
first time, that my little chief had always known about it.
And I was shocked by that.

"Through the sealed window you could see the flat, hot
countryside. Very strange. The trees, even when they were
far away, didn't bunch together. They were just standing one
by one, like poles. The dust was like mist. It was the famous
desertification people came to see and write reports about. It
was what he had been driving through all night, and the
Mercedes hadn't broken down.

"He never asked me about myself. He never asked me
how I had come to the strange country myself, or got my
job or how I'd managed all these years. He never thanked me
for taking his telephone call or arranging his asylum or driving down to see him. He expected me to treat him well. He
was a chief, you see. He was full of his own sufferings and
betrayal and his bravery in doing the long night drive. All
the way up to the capital he complained like a child. He said
his family had always supported the president. They had sent
him to school and looked after him and his family. They had
stood by him when the president had kicked out the French
and there had been all that trouble. And then the president's
mind had been poisoned against the *cheferie*. Everyone knew
who had done that. It was Lebrun, the *antillais*. Lebrun had
bewitched the president. He had flattered him and turned his
head. It was Lebrun, Lebrun—the little chief was obsessed
with him."

I had heard many things about Lebrun's trip to French
West Africa. But I hadn't heard before that he had had any
local political influence.

Phyllis said, "It is what people say. He was very angry when he left here, and I suppose when he went across the border they would have received him with open arms. They did a lot of anti-French propaganda with him."

I said to Phyllis, "You said the little chief was on your mind."

"With the help of the embassy we've been getting some of his money out from the country. We've arranged his papers, and he's getting restless now. He's forgotten some of his terror. He is talking of going to Paris. He's got a lot of money there. And these past few days I've been thinking, 'Yes, he'll go to Paris now, and he'll pick up some other woman and dazzle her with his chief's talk and it'll begin all over again.'"

THE TIME came for me to move on. The next stage of my journey was the dictatorship next door. This was the country Phyllis had come out to, the country that had kicked the French out, with all their aid and *coopérants,* and had, as some people said, gone back to bush.

So, without premeditation, I was following in the footsteps of Lebrun. Phyllis had names for me in the other country. There was someone there she especially wanted me to meet. This person, she said, would give me an idea of the true Africa, the Africa that the newspapers didn't write about.

The day before I left she came to the hotel to say goodbye. We sat out on the terrace. A tourist feature had been made of the lagoon, which in the old days was famous for its mosquitoes and disease.

She said things she had said often before, about Africa, about the false ideas brought by black people from the West Indies and the United States. She was killing time, I could see. And then, just before she left, she did what she had come to do: she opened her handbag and gave me an envelope with

banknotes. The money was for the man she wanted me to
see. Life was hard for people over there, she said.
It was a roundabout journey. Political stresses had made
a direct flight between the two neighbouring countries impossible. A plane to a neutral country to the north; a breakdown,
a long wait at night in an open shed at the edge of an airfield,
local police lounging with the passengers; traders in dingy
gowns sitting on sacks of cheap rubber shoes and other goods;
and then the shaky final trip to the dictatorship.
There were many policemen at the airport. It wasn't a
busy place. The arrival of this small plane was the big event
of the morning, and the eyes of the idle officials glittered at
the thought of the money to be made from the few people
who had come in. It was a shed of an airport hall, with old,
blown-up photographs of what must have been local scenes,
relic of an earlier time of tourist promotion. I would have
had trouble getting Phyllis's money for her friend through—
everything had to be declared, and some people were searched
by customs officers trembling with excitement. But the man
in front of me was detained so long—he was even taken off
at one stage to a cubicle—that I was waved through by a
senior officer anxious to close down the desks for the morning
and go home.
The climate was similar to the climate of the other place.
But, strangely, the light and heat that were part of the life
and excitement and crowd of the other place here felt, right
away, like tropical or African torpor. The newish airport
highway, unmaintained, and cracked in many places, ran
through bare red earth. No villages were to be seen, only big
boards with sayings of the president's, and large signs, facing
the highway, as though they were meant only for visitors:
INCREASE PRODUCTION.
It was strange to think of Lebrun coming here with his
daughter; and, in extreme old age, after having gone back on
so many of his old views, being received with honour,

and finding a kind of revolutionary fulfilment. INCREASE PRODUCTION—it was like coming across a little bit of the raw material, part of the facts and figures and tables, of one of Lebrun's old communist articles, in which this kind of "production" was better than the other sort of wealth.

The hotel, one of an international chain, was not very full. The air-conditioning was fierce, and the room I had was damp and musty, with a touch of rust on some bits of unprotected metal. I felt it hadn't been occupied for some time. Everything was very expensive; the exchange rate was absurd. The bar and lounge and other public rooms were full of plain-clothes policemen in dark glasses, as though, in this already desolate place, their principal function was to catch out visitors.

I eventually got Phyllis's friend on the telephone. He exclaimed when I gave Phyllis's name. But then he became nervous; he became even more nervous when he heard where I was staying. He said he would telephone me back.

The hotel was silent. No one raised his voice. And I felt something of that stillness when some days later I went to an embassy lunch. The embassy building was really a government building of the colonial time; and the lunch to which I had been invited—a last-minute guest—was something of a local occasion.

In colonial days the head of the up-country Christian missions paid an annual official visit to the capital, and was received in some style by the governor. The lunch was an adaptation, or relic, of that colonial ceremony. There wasn't a governor now: there was the ambassador of the former colonial power. And what had been the governor's house was now the ambassador's residence. As for the mission stations—the very words came from the turn of the century—they had gone through many transformations even in colonial times. The main station had become a medical centre, a hospital, a general training centre, a polytechnic. Its missionary associations—which had become more ecumenical—were now underplayed, and the representative who came for the ceremony in the capital was, officially, the principal of the polytechnic. This year, for the first time, the principal was a black man; he was said to be a Baptist. This was the special little drama of the lunch.

We, the early arrivals, sat downstairs, in the loggia, amid the bougainvillaea. Everything had been swept and dusted that morning, but already everything, including the bougainvillaea, was dusty from the desertification. The sand was in the air. It fell fine all the time; it was something you felt below your shoes.

We were waiting for the principal. He was in the building, but he had arrived late, just an hour or so before, and he was upstairs getting ready. There had been some trouble earlier that morning, many kilometres away, with the rope-pulled ferry over some dwindling river. That had delayed him.

When thirty minutes or so later he came down the steps to the patio—from the room he had been given, the room the principal (and, before him, the chief missionary) had always been given—the smell of talcum powder preceded him. He was a big man, brown more than black, with a big, strongly modelled face with great ridges of cheekbones, a big, strong body, and big feet in big shoes. He was in an old and thin dark suit, sepia in patches from sunlight and wear and dry-cleaning fluid. He had been shaving; a dull white bloom—like the desert sand on the bougainvillaea—lay over the chin and cheeks he had been shaving very close.

He talked about the ferry and the bad road and the delay that morning. His words gave me a picture: the flat barge with the old Peugeot car, the shallow river issuing out of swamp, the morning heat-mist, the ferryman pulling on the slack rope or cable looped across the river, the principal standing tall and upright, and then the barge running aground.

The principal said, "Bad roads, primitive ferry. But these are the sacrifices we have to make for the next generation."

A guest said, not wishing bad things to be said about Africa, "There are wonderful roads over the frontier."

But that was like bad manners. The principal looked affronted. I thought there was something about his voice and manner and accent.

I said, "Has anyone told you, Principal? You have a West Indian accent."

He said, with a curious gesture, in which I at once recognized the gestures of many people I knew in my childhood, "I am West Indian."

His father had studied in London in the 1920s. He had become attracted to the Back-to-Africa views of Marcus Garvey and others; and he had done what many people had talked about but few had actually done. He had come out to West Africa, and had lived there until he died. All these years, this life in Africa!

Our hostess asked, "You would say that's one reason why the Christian vocation came to you?"

The principal said, "I don't know. We were Baptists in my family, but the reason why I wanted to go into the church was that when I was at school it seemed the only thing to do. I wanted to be like the men who taught me. The same is true for some black Roman Catholics I know. People of my background. I know an old West Indian man here who became a Roman Catholic priest. I asked him the same question you asked me. Just a few months ago. This old man said to me, 'What else was there for me? The monastery was the only safe place I could see. And I thought it was nice. I thought they would send me to Ireland.' That's true for me too. It may be a vocation. I don't know. I am a Baptist and a believer. But without colonialism I wouldn't have had the vocation. I would have been another kind of believer. Let me say that too."

Somebody said, "You're talking like your president."

The principal threw his big shoulders back and made a gesture with his open palms. And it was clear then that he was charged up, that he had come ready to speak for the regime, and ready to take on the criticisms of everyone at the table.

It wasn't what we were expecting. We were expecting something quieter and more indirect, something that acknowledged the civility of the occasion, not something that imposed the silence of the hotel and the streets on us.

Someone said, "Do they still talk about the chiefs where you are?"

The principal said, "If they do, I haven't heard it. Lebrun was right. The president was a prisoner of the *cheferie*. They were getting in the way of all his reforms. But the president didn't know what would happen if he tried to take them on. Lebrun said very simply, 'Take an axe to the root.' Do it decisively, and they'll all run. No more slavery, no more ritual murders, no more killing of wives and servants when a big chief dies. All the superstitions of feudalism wiped out in one blow. All the things that give Africa a bad name. 'Take an axe to the root.' I remember how the women and slaves used to run just before a big chief died. Everybody knew about it, but nobody talked about it. And that was exactly how the chiefs ran when the president brought in the people's courts." He made a West Indian gesture, to suggest flight, brushing one open palm glancingly off the other. "You were telling me about the good roads and the Lacoste shops and the lovely houses and the beach restaurants with cabarets and *bananes flambés* on the other side of the frontier. But the chiefs are still ruling there. The French are doing the job for them, but it is all for the chiefs. When something happens and the French go away, all of that feudal life will still just be there, waiting to terrorize people. Not here. You have the bad ferry, but you don't have the chiefs now. The chiefs here used to say that they spoke for the people. All right. So let them be tried by the people's courts. That was the president's idea."

I wanted to hear more about the people's courts.

The principal said, "Highest form of democracy." And he fitted a West Indian gesture to his words: he raised his open palms just above the edge of the table and threw his shoulders far back—as though to make room for the significance of his words. It was like a choreographed movement: a backward sway suddenly arrested: the most elegant of the movements he had been making at the lunch table.

The gift of speech, the beautiful, timed gestures of hands and upper body, the easy dominance of the lunch table: this took me back. It took me back to Lebrun talking in the cramped Lebanese flat in Maida Vale. And I wondered whether Lebrun's visit here some months before hadn't revived certain rhythms of speech in the principal.

But perhaps not. Perhaps this gift of speech and movement went back further, had another parentage. I went back in memory to the solicitors' clerks in the Red House in Port of Spain, searching for property titles in the big bound books of the Registrar-General's Department. They sat at the mahogany desks in the high jalousied rooms of the Italianate building and they gossiped and gestured in their conspiratorial fashion, like people with secrets. Make-believe, but just a few years later there were to be the meetings in the Victorian colonial square across the street, where ideas of racial redemption were offered as a kind of sacrament. The passions of that sacrament were proving to be unassuageable, and were now beyond control.

This French West African colonial building where I was now, listening to the principal—long table in the arcaded loggia, tablecloth, glasses, flowers, the fine sand and dust gathering slowly on walls and plants and on the tiled floor—was like the one on the other side of the Atlantic where the clerks had gossiped in their spacious search room: Italianate too, thick walls, with tall jalousied windows hinged at the top, propped open at the bottom just a little way to let in air and light and to give a view of the gardens outside, but to keep out the hot morning sun. Both buildings had been put up at about the same time, just after the turn of the century, at the zenith of empire.

The principal had grown up in Africa. But he had grown up with his father's story and all the passions, from the other side of the ocean, of the Back-to-Africa movement. In the West Indies his body movements and the rhythms of his speech would have been considered African or black. Here, though, they made him recognizably a man apart.

At the lunch table he continued to talk, holding the attention of all and imposing silence on all: like a theatrical figure with his size and his faded dark suit, the white razor-bloom on his cheeks and chin, and the dusting of talcum powder around his collar: rocking with his big body from the waist up, and making gestures, at times like a dancer's, with his open palms.

"The president hasn't put his hand on anybody, whatever the propagandists say from across the frontier. It's all been done by the people's courts. They are the guardians of the country. Every street and every city block and every village has its own people's court. That's where the chiefs were tried. By their own people, the people who allegedly loved them. You can't get a higher form of democracy than that."

And then the principal began to look down at the table, began to go silent, gave up his body dance; and something began to happen to his face. It began to change. Like some actors who, at the end of a performance, continue for some time to have their face set in the role they have just taken, and then, almost visibly, begin to return to themselves, so the principal began to alter. He was like a man beginning to understand the nature of the embassy lunch, beginning to understand the dignity he represented; beginning to understand how old attitudes of survival had led him away from that dignity.

He went silent. He looked down at the tablecloth without seeming to see anything. He made no dancer's movement, no gesture with his palms.

He was supposed to stay some days at the embassy, as his predecessors had done. But the principal didn't stay. He left in the Peugeot soon after the lunch, and I heard later from my embassy hosts that he never came back. So with the first black principal a little colonial tradition fell away.

MY MEETING with Phyllis's friend took place in a café in the main square. It wasn't easy to arrange. Twice he cried off; and he never wanted to come to the hotel. "Those people there don't like me," he said. So when at last we met it was in the old French colonial square. It was run-down, ghostly, with buildings no longer serving the purposes for which they had been built. The café, done in red, with folding red-painted metal chairs at metal tables, was between dingy shops with goods from the communist countries, things like tinned fruit from Vietnam.

In spite of the parked police vans, the area was dangerous with aggressive beggars and cripples and men, still young, who had been deliberately deformed as children. The first time I had gone there I had been mugged, near the news-stand with old newspapers from the communist countries. This had happened in the middle of the morning, coffee time, café-dawdling time. The French colonial square encouraged these ideas, but this was a ghost square: little traffic, no dawdlers. The muggers were a gang of youths and children, apparently beggars, appearing from nowhere, the children suddenly surrounding me and throwing themselves at my feet, turning up to me—as in a famine film clip—pleading, starving, pared-down African faces, plucking at the same time now at my shoe laces, now at my trousers, and appearing to mimic the gestures of hunger and eating, as they had been trained to do by the beggar-master, going through their routine very fast, to confuse the foreign victim and distract his attention from the bigger and more skilled pickpockets. But these criminals in the square were the only local people I had seen who behaved like free people. They moved about a lot, and they moved fast, whether whole or crippled, the crippled on wheeled boards, like wider skate-boards, or in little box carts, like home-made toys. They shouted and spoke loudly among themselves, as though they didn't have to be as quiet as everybody else.

Their apparent leader was a young man both of whose legs had been cut off at mid-thigh. Flat round wooden pads two or three inches thick had been strapped on to the base of his stumps; these pads, more or less the diameter of his stumps, were further cushioned or shod with black discs of rubber or leather. When he walked, these thick stumps were all movement; but each step was small, a child's step, and the torso above the busy stumps moved very slowly. The malevolence in the face of this half-destroyed man, his contempt for the world, was unsettling; and I wondered whether some religious or magical idea, of the dictator's, about the powers of deformity wasn't behind this licensed display in the square.

Phyllis's friend was waiting, as he had promised, in the café with the red-painted metal tables and chairs. He was at a corner table and was reading the local paper. He was a handsome, sinewy man, in his forties, in features and physique and skin-colour more West Indian than African.

I felt, as soon as we began to talk, that there was something Phyllis had left out in her story of her married life here with the little chief. I felt she had liked this man very much and wanted, even at this distance and after all this time, to show him off to me. And there was a touch of vanity in him too, at being recognized as the man Phyllis had liked.

When he heard that Phyllis had given me some money

for him he lost control of his smile. It became a grimace; and he made a curious series of dismissing sounds. I felt he had had subsidies like this from women before. I felt it was a way of life he knew. And that expression—tight, unsmiling, unreliable—stayed on his face when I told him that Phyllis had said he would give me an idea of the true Africa.

He spoke of wise men he knew, both in the town and the villages, and the magical tricks they would perform for me, if he asked them. These men would disappear in front of my eyes. They would go through solid walls. They would slash their hands and blood would pour from the wounds; and then they would so heal the wounds that no scar would show. They would perform staggering feats of telepathy, entering houses and minds in many continents.

It wasn't at all what I was expecting. I had thought, from what she had said, that Phyllis had developed some feeling for the antiquity of tribal ritual; and some idea as a result, stronger than any she had had as an *antillaise,* of her grip on the world. I might have read too much in what she said. This man was like the con-man of African hotel lounges, offering hippy-style magic to travellers. Perhaps she had known very little of Africa when she had become involved with this man. Perhaps memory had added to him. Perhaps she had become profounder in the other country. Or perhaps this man had answered so many of her needs here—comforter, lover, as-trologer, magician—that she had not really been able to judge him.

I wanted to leave the man. But, after this talk of magic, he wanted to stick to me. He came out to the square with me and—strong, elegant, easy in his movements, very attrac-tive—he began to walk back with me to the hotel. The beg-gars saw us and squawked at us; some of them raced up aggressively in their carts; the man with the padded stumps drove them away.

Phyllis's friend said as we walked, as though he wanted

to live up to what Phyllis had said about him, "You get only
the bad news about Africa in the European papers. The wars
and the famines. But I will tell you. There are seven sacred
spots in Africa. All the forces of the continent are concentrated on those seven spots. There is a holy man in each one
of those spots. Every month these holy men meet and arrange
the destiny of Africa."

What was the implication of that? That we were on one
of the seven spots, and that he was one of the holy men?

I asked, "How do these seven men meet?"

He made a gesture, making a circular sweep above his
head with his index finger. "Telepathically."

Was this magic African? Or was it part of a fantasy of
Africa from across the ocean, a hippy-style fantasy about the
powers of old cultures, something that had made its way
back here and was now being offered as African to travellers,
strangers and solitaries who needed this kind of magic?

Soon, I knew, I would be hearing from this man about
the extra-terrestrial beings who had landed on a certain part
of West Africa. And, indeed, he was beginning on that when
we got to the entry to the hotel. He was frightened of the
policemen there. He didn't follow me in.

WE ALL inhabit "constructs" of a world. Ancient peoples
had their own. Our grandparents had their own; we cannot
absolutely enter into their constructs. Every culture has its
own: men are infinitely malleable. And perhaps Phyllis, with
the fluidity of character which her African life had given her,
enabling her to be many things to many people (critical of
Africans, critical of Europeans, critical of West Indians and
black Americans, critical of one group by reference to another), perhaps Phyllis, with her initial French-speaking limitations (Guadeloupe, Paris, West Africa), had established her
own further construct of the world. Perhaps in that fluidity,

in that shiftingness, she had found freedom. Perhaps, as the years went on, she would recede more and more from her own background; perhaps logic would leave her. As much as the principal's father's Back-to-Africa escape (or struggle) had determined the principal's twin natures, so Phyllis's construct had been determined by her marriage to her little chief and, before that, by her flight from the French West Indies (so liberating to the black man who was the first to teach me French). She couldn't go back to what she had left behind; she couldn't absolutely undo anything she had done; that was part of her woman's nature.

It was otherwise for Lebrun. He had always been on the run, a revolutionary without a base, always a failure in one way, in another way fortunate, never having to live with the consequences of his action, always being free to move on.

Perhaps he never knew the consequences of his words in the French West African dictatorship, when for the first time he found a ruler of a state who was ready to be his disciple, because the advice so matched the ruler's own needs.

When the dictatorship collapsed and the desolate country was opened up, no one thought of calling him to account. He was not associated with desolation. He was, rather, the man who had held fast both to ideas of revolution and African redemption; and had not been rewarded for his pains. In the mess of Africa and the Caribbean he was oddly pure.

He was now very old, and famous among people who were interested in colonial and post-colonial history. But the people who wrote occasional profiles of him couldn't really understand him. They had grown up in another world, and were simpler than he was. The profile-writers and the television interviewers, who promoted him with self-conscious virtue, were serving a cause that had long ago been won. They risked nothing at all. They had no means of understanding or assessing a man who had been born early in the century into a very hard world, whose intellectual growth had at every stage been accompanied by a growing rawness of sensibility, and whose political resolutions, expressing the wish not to go mad, had been in the nature of spiritual struggles, occurring in the depth of his being.

They came with their interview files, and they asked all the questions that had been asked before. They asked especially about his mother's uncle, the coachman of the English family who had gone from Barbados to London, and had found friends among the servants of the Tichborne house, who gave him tea and cake. Lebrun told the story again and again. Towards the end of his life, he sometimes forgot the point of the story. He had the old coachman say that in the old days black people and white people were one, and then he, Lebrun, searched for the thing that he knew followed but could no longer find. For the interviewer or the television producer it was enough, a text for today; not understanding that Lebrun's anguish had begun there, with the old coachman taking him far back, almost to the times of slavery, as to the good times. But perhaps, too, in extreme old age, he had become a child again, looking only for peace.

CHAPTER 6

A Parcel of Papers, a Roll of Tobacco, a Tortoise: An Unwritten Story

PERHAPS A PLAY or a screen play, or a mixture of both—
that is how it came to me, an unrealizable impulse, a long
time ago: the first set being a view in section of the upper
decks of a Jacobean ship, the *Destiny*. The time, 1618. The
setting, a South American river, grey when still, muddy
when rippled. It is almost dawn. The sky is silver. The two-
tiered set is in semi-gloom; but the tropical light is coming
fast. The pre-dawn silence is broken by the sound of a heavy
splash. A man has jumped overboard. After a while there are
shouts from the decks of the ship, and the sound of running
feet.

At the same time the light begins to show a thin and very
old man in Jacobean undress in the captain's quarters. This is
Sir Walter Raleigh. He is sixty-four. He has been ill for many
months; he has only eight months or so to live.

He has been a free man for just under two years. For
thirteen years before that, he had been a prisoner in the Tower
of London, because of some trouble with the king. He has
been released in order to go and find the gold mines of El
Dorado in Guiana in South America. He has always said that
these mines exist somewhere on the banks of the Orinoco,
and he has always said he knows exactly where the mines are.

Twenty-two years before, he had raided the Spanish island of Trinidad, which guarded the entrance to the Orinoco and El Dorado, and he had captured the Spanish conquistador, Berrio, the so-called governor of the province of El Dorado. He claimed to have plundered all the old conquistador's knowledge about the golden territories. And he also claimed to have won over all the Indians of the region to his side. He has been let out to prove his point now, and he has accepted conditions that are like those of a game. If he finds gold, everything will be forgiven. He will be executed if he doesn't find gold, or if he disturbs the Spaniards. Guiana is Spanish territory.

And now—in this land which in his mind and writings existed as a kind of Arcadia where he could be king of the Indians, ruler of a golden empire—he is a man under siege. The Indians avoid him. He cannot get the food he once wrote about, the sweet fresh-water fish from the fresh-water pools in the Pitch Lake. The Spaniards on Trinidad, few, but the advantage is with them, watch him. They have their muskets. They don't fire recklessly. They wait, they take careful aim at forty paces, no more. He regularly loses one man, two men, when little parties go ashore to get pitch, good for caulking ships, or oysters, or food, or water. Food is running short for him.

As the weeks pass, and no news comes from the south, from that tributary of the Orinoco up which he has sent half of his gold-mine expedition, he feels bereft. The skiff he sent afterwards up the river to get news—with a captured Indian as pilot—hasn't returned. The conviction grows on him that knowledge of what has happened up river has spread around these Indian villages. The Indians all speak Spanish now. They have no reason to ignore the Spaniards for the sake of Raleigh. Raleigh has stayed away for twenty-two years, after all. And again it was to get news, as much as to get fresh food, the fish from the pools in the hard asphalt of the Pitch

Lake, La Brea, and the delicate, "fat" flesh of the "pheasants" of the country, that he allowed the second of the three Indians he captured—secret Spanish-speakers, and possibly in league with the Spaniards in Trinidad and on the mainland—to go ashore, leaving his friend behind as a hostage.

A soldier knocks on his cabin door and comes in and says that Martin, the third Indian, has escaped.

"Well, well," the old man says. "Who was on watch?"

"Piggott."

"I feel I should put Piggott alone in a skiff and send him up to the Orinoco."

"We can lower a boat and try to get him back. The Indian."

"I don't see what good that will do."

"It won't be easy, but we can try."

"Of course it won't be easy. By the time you lower your boat and put on your armour he will be in the woods. Once he's got a tree between you and him, that's that. You couldn't keep him on the ship. You certainly won't be able to catch him in the woods."

"We were going to hang him today, because his friend didn't come back from the village. The men didn't like that. They feel now that everything they do will rebound on them. They've had too much bad luck already."

"That reminds me. Go and tell the surgeon to come. I must have my draught. Why aren't you wearing your breast-plate? I gave those instructions. We should be ready at all times. Metal is hot, but a poisoned arrow will be much hotter."

"I was putting it on when the Indian jumped overboard."

"What scum."

"I'll go and call the surgeon."

"These mariners and soldiers. Their friends and families sent them to sea on purpose. Wanting them only to drown or disappear. Sometimes I think the people they gave me were born only to eat rations. They stole my last apples. I was keeping a few in that sand barrel. They found out and stole them. I went to a lot of trouble to pack them in good clean white sand before we left England."

The sky gets brighter. A hot day, already. The surgeon comes to the cabin, to give the old man his draught. They talk about Martin, the Indian who has escaped. They agree that it is better for the man not to have been hanged. The threat was made only to encourage the other Indian to come back, before they sent him—as they thought—to his village to trade English goods for food and perhaps news. Clearly, though, the man didn't mind sacrificing the friend or fellow tribesman he'd left behind on the ship.

"Your draught," the surgeon says.

"There is a balsam that can be collected in those woods," the old man says. "In 1595 I got quite a bit from Wannawanare's people. This time I had just got about a little nutful when I went ashore. The sweetest thing you ever smelled. Like angelica. For twenty years that smell has been with me. But then they opened up on us."

"You have to forget about things like that now. We won't be allowed to land."

"And the oysters. Little ones growing on the roots of the mangrove below water. You could hack away a piece of mangrove root and bring away a dozen oysters, all alive. Sweet oysters, sweeter than anything you ever tasted. And the rain water in the hollows of the Pitch Lake. You can taste the tar in it, but that is part of the sweetness of the water."

"You torment yourself, and other people, by talking of those things. Sweet things. How many of them you promised us when we were coming out! You talked a lot about a cassava liquor."

"I remembered it from 1595. Right here. On this Guiana coast. The Indian women chewed the cassava and spat it out into a vessel. In England women are the brewers, and so they

are here too. Or were. I don't know what happens now. I
haven't gone to their villages. The chewing of the cassava
was woman's work, because long ago they found out that
woman's saliva caused cassava to ferment fast. You wouldn't
imagine it when you saw a group of them sitting flat on the
ground and chewing and spitting into a hollowed-out piece
of tree trunk, and giggling when they saw you looking at
what they were doing. The first time I saw Moriquito's
women doing it, it looked so strange, I stopped and asked,
and they all roared with laughter, and I thought they were
joking. But when it was ready it made the clearest and the
sweetest liquor you ever tasted. Sweeter than any nut, finer
than any ale. On drinking occasions the chiefs took their
leisure in their hammocks, swinging from side to side in the
shade of trees in their villages. Because it's cool there, in
the woods, not as hot and sweaty as it is here on the ship in
the Gulf. And the women served this nectar to their chiefs,
filling tiny cupfuls at a time with little ladles. Such women.
Plump, and as fine as any well-bred woman in England.
White skins, regular features, black hair."

"That was what you told us almost as soon as we left the
Canaries, to give us courage for the crossing, after the trouble
we had with the Spaniards there, and after that captain deserted with his ship."

"What scum. All that fighting aboard the ships even before we had left England. What scum. When that man deserted, I was half with him, to tell you the truth. But there
was no place for me to go. I had to stay with the expedition.
I had begged for it for so long, and when it came it was
like something with its own life, quite separate from me.
Something to which I simply attached myself. And then the
sickness—all those men sick and dying in our new ship. All
those friends. I haven't even begun to grieve for them. I am
frightened to be left alone with grief now. I feel it will take
me over. My own cook, Francis—he died. The gold expert

I had, a man who was the best gold refiner in London, Fowler—he too died. They all died. The ship began to stink with sick people who couldn't move and the corpses I had to bury."

"And you kept everybody's spirits up by talking to them about this paradise on this side of the ocean. Not only gold, but fresh water and fresh food, and the friendly beautiful people, waiting for you to be their king."

"I was ill, too. Fever. Three shirts a day, three shirts a night. All wringing wet. And there were days of calm when we didn't make above six leagues, and the sun hung above us in the sky and in the afternoon the sea seemed to blaze with the glitter. I wasn't well. The expedition had its own life. I just surrendered to it and it dragged me through one day after another. I wasn't willing anything. I was in no position to do anything like that."

"Ten ships full of sick and dead people. And when we arrived we saw a Dutch ship, very calmly trading. Hatchets and knives and bits of metal, for tobacco and salt and hides. And we were full of sick and dead men looking for gold. Aren't you amazed that the men who were still able-bodied didn't mutiny, and ask where you had led them? You were supposed to have led them to a mysterious part of the world that none in England or Spain or the Indies knew about. And when we got to this place Captain Janson was trading, and you had yourself carried ashore in your shirt, to breathe clean air, to recover, and then to bury your dead. And all the while the little Indian canoes were going out to the Dutchman. The people who were going to be your subjects. They speak Spanish and Dutch. They don't speak English. They haven't come to you.

"Why did you tell so many people that you could be king of the Indies? You made them expect so much when they came here. They had suffered so much on the journey. We had suffered so much, all of us. I thought the chiefs would come out to meet you and honour you. The fresh, sweet water, the little cupfuls of liquor, those women, the fresh food. The deer and the fish and the oysters. Nothing happened. We lived on what we had. Your lieutenant Keymis sent an interpreter to the nearest village to ask for your two Indian servants. Servants. Not chiefs. But the people you took away to England in 1595, to show them off."

"Also to learn the language from them."

"We waited for two weeks. The man you called Leonard never came."

"He was never in good health. He must have died. I sent him back ten or twelve years ago. He wanted to die at home."

"After two weeks a canoe came with a sick old man dressed up in old English clothes. A barefoot old Indian scarecrow in English rags. With the few teeth in his head blackened with the tobacco they use here to quell hunger when they go on a journey. Broken pieces of cassava bread lying about the canoe, and black tobacco rolls, and the rest of his food carefully wrapped up in a leaf. We thought we were going to witness the meeting of two chieftains. Fine clothes, feathers, an Indian standard. We witnessed the meeting of two old men. And you couldn't talk to Harry, because he had forgotten his English."

"I was surprised by that. He spent fourteen years with me. I was hoping he would have married someone in England. But he became homesick. He had an Indian bandeau, cotton, blue and white. When the homesickness really came on him, he would tie that around his forehead and he would sit facing the wall. He often did that in the Tower. He wouldn't talk or move or close his eyes. He could do that for a whole day, until the homesickness left him. It was terrible to see. I sent him back here with William Harcourt. That was nine years ago. He wanted to take back a lot of English clothes. He liked clothes."

"The men were close to mutiny that day. I don't think

you know how close. And that day or the next you sat in this cabin and wrote to your wife that your name lived among the Indians, and that you could be their king. That was one of the letters a ship went back with."

"I didn't know my letters were being read."

"It would have been negligent for them not to be. This big expedition, all these deaths. All this potential for trouble when we want peace. We have to know what you intend. And you know that your letters are copied and passed around in England to your supporters."

"I knew there was a spy with me. I wasn't sure who he was. All the weeks before the sickness I tried to work it out. I didn't think it was you. I thought it was John Talbot, my friend from the Tower. Then he died from the sickness, and I thought there wasn't a spy any more. He was one of the men we had to bury here. A good man, I always thought. A scholar, too. Eleven years with me in the Tower. He wanted to get out. I couldn't blame him for that. I didn't mind him being the spy."

"He's been useful to us, in fact."

"My examination has begun?"

"It was high time. We've been here two months. We've lost so many men. On all expeditions you lose people, but we've lost too many. Food is running short. You've sent five ships and four hundred men up the river. We have no means of knowing what has happened. That Indian you seized and sent up in the boat hasn't returned, and I don't think he will. All the other Indians we see keep well clear of us. On the Trinidad side of the Gulf the Spaniards are watching with their muskets to prevent us from landing. We have no means of knowing what has happened on the other side, on the river, at that settlement of San Thomé. We know that the Spanish governor went there from Trinidad, no doubt to fortify the place. This governor's a new man. He was specially sent out from Spain. He is not one of the old colonial crew. He's a nobleman, a relation of the Spanish ambassador in London. We have no means of knowing what's happened to your lieutenant Keymis or your son. Or the five ships you sent, and the four hundred men. Clearly something has happened. You can tell it. You can feel it in the air. In a little while we are likely to find out, but then neither you nor I may be in a position to sit and talk."

"Don't you want pen, paper? Aren't you going to write anything down?"

"Not at this stage. Though I always prefer to work with a written statement. Unless you write things down, you miss a lot. Certain things that people say can reveal their meaning only if you can read them again and again. The words physically have to be in front of your eyes. It's the only way you can discover things. Simple things, to start with. Like: 'But I don't understand that sentence.' Or: 'How did we get from there to there?' Especially with someone like you, very skilled with words. But in fact both you and Laurence Keymis have made quite detailed statements many years ago. You both wrote books about Guiana and El Dorado and your discoveries. Richard Hakluyt reprinted them in his own compilation. It was something that John Talbot, your Tower friend, put us on to. He said, 'It's all there. Study those books from twenty-two years ago. Dissect them.'

"I tried reading them in England before the journey, but I found it hard. I got lost with all the strange Indian and Spanish names, of people and places and tribes. You gave too many names: I must tell you that made me suspicious.

"There was no question of reading on the journey, especially after the sickness. I've begun to read only since we've been in the Gulf, and really only since Keymis and your son went off to look for the gold mine of El Dorado. We've had a lot of time since then, a lot of empty days. Sunlight from six to six. Even so I have to read your book again and again. It's a slippery piece of work, if I can use that word. You slip about, you lose your footing. It's nice and easy and clear and brilliant for a number of pages, and then suddenly you feel you've not been paying attention. You feel you've missed something. So you go back. You've missed nothing. It's just that something's gone wrong with the writing. This happens many times. So even if you're a careful reader you lose the drift of the narrative. It's not easy, noticing first of all that the writing has changed and then finding exactly where. But those are precisely the places you have to identify. Because those are the places where the writer decides to add things or to hide things.

"One of the more extraordinary things in your book occurs in the 'Advertisement,' a kind of preface which you print between the letter of dedication and the book itself. It's very bold, very effective, to place something so important in that half-way-house place, where people don't read all that carefully. You say you wrote the Advertisement in reply to people who all those years ago, when you went back to England, said you were lying about El Dorado, that you'd found nothing, that the so-called 'ore' you brought back was really sand and that the piece of Guiana gold you showed was something you had bought beforehand in North Africa. The tone of the Advertisement was manly and honest. You stated very clearly what your detractors said. And then in a very open way you appeared to give an explanation. You said that you'd sent forty of your men to look for gold ore. They brought back sand. Not all the same sand. Men chose different colours. You told them it was sand they'd brought back, but the men for various reasons insisted on keeping it and bringing it back to England, and you allowed them to do so.

"But there is no mention of this sand-collecting episode in the book itself. I am not able to say when your men were ordered to go and collect this ore. It seems from this that if your enemies or other people hadn't said you were lying and had brought back sand from Trinidad and Guiana, we would never have known about the forty men who at your orders went and looked for golden sand and brought it back to the ships.

"So in London, when people began to ridicule and doubt, you produced the piece of North African gold and said it was from Guiana, from some mountain of gold and diamonds beside a turbulent river. You weren't going to be proved a fool. A traitor, a pirate, someone in league with the king of Spain—better any of that than to be a fool, a clown. After Drake and Hawkins, to be a clown privateer and explorer— that would have been worse than death.

"We do things for all kinds of reasons. Some of these reasons can appear quite trivial. And it may be that one of the reasons—just one, perhaps—at the bottom of this venture—so chivalric now, at the limit of the world, so heroic, so doomed to failure, an old man's nobility—bringing us all here, at the cost of so many lives—it may be that one of the original reasons for this might have been your wish all those years ago to prove that you weren't a fool, that you hadn't brought home a cargo of sand as a cargo of gold.

"When you showed the North African gold, people asked why you hadn't brought back more from this fabled land of El Dorado. Of course you didn't have the money to buy more. But you say in your Advertisement rather sharply that no one has the right to ask you for more. You go on to say that you didn't have the time or the tools or the men when you were on the river of El Dorado. The gold had to be hacked away from very hard rock. And people accepted that, though you had prepared for the expedition for years, and had so many men and ships. You had captured the Spanish conquistador who had been on the El Dorado quest and you had picked his brains, and you had gone to look for the mines. It was strange then that, after all of this, you didn't have the tools, you didn't have the time. You say the river tide was running so fast you couldn't stay too long on the banks, and you were far from your ships and you had left them unprotected.

"So all you took back to England was a lot of marcasite sand. I will tell you something else that made the sand business so shameful. Some Frenchmen had done the same thing and had been laughed at. And then, weeks before you, a young English nobleman had done the same thing too. Sir Robert Dudley, the Earl of Leicester's son. He had gone to Trinidad. He had asked Indians on the Gulf beach about a gold mine. Just like that. As soon as he arrived. Not knowing the language or anything. And he thought the Indians had made signs to say yes, there was a gold mine just a short way up the beach. They went in full armour and saw the glittering marcasite in the sand. For three days Dudley's men loaded up with sand. The Spaniards saw, but didn't trouble them. And then young Dudley left, because you were coming, and he was nervous of being found by you in your El Dorado patch.

"This happened literally just a few weeks before you came to the Gulf, and killed all the Spaniards. While you were exploring the Guiana estuaries Dudley was taking his marcasite back to England. Captain Wyatt wrote up this adventure in very high romantic language. It has been circulated in manuscript. Hakluyt didn't want to print it. When Dudley was told he had brought back sand, he pretended he had known all along, and had brought the sand back on a whim.

"That was more or less what you said when you went back with your own load of Trinidad sand. You didn't know about young Dudley's adventure. You'd found nothing else. Your book doesn't say you found anything. You had talked to one or two chiefs, that was all. But you had found nothing. In spite of the title of your book, *The Discovery of the Large, Rich, and Beautiful Empire of Guiana*. A difficult book, not easy to read.

"I think a deliberately difficult book. It's only here that I understand why the book is so difficult. It's a deliberate mixture of old-fashioned fantasy and modern truth. Everything you write about this side of the Gulf, the eastern side, the Trinidad side, everything is correct and very clear, every name, every tribe, every little Indian port. Real knowledge, real enquiry. On the river side, it's a different story. When you get down to the main Orinoco, you write about a strange land of diamond mountains and meadows and deer and birds. It's beautiful, but only like a painting. The book's like the work of two different men.

"I think that when you began to travel in Guiana up that river, when you saw what a foolish old man the old Spanish conquistador was, when you saw the poverty of the tribes, you knew that there was no El Dorado. And you hated travelling on the river. I can understand from your writing how hard that kind of travel is. The sun, the airlessness, the constant running aground, the excrement and the food and the cooking all mixed up on the galley, people getting wet and dry and then wet again, the smell of many sweaty men in a small space.

"You were differently dieted, you said. However much you wanted to be like Hawkins or Drake, you couldn't do the kind of thing they had done. You never wanted to get too far from your ships and your cabin. But you had killed too many people, you had talked too long about El Dorado, and when you went back to England you didn't want to appear foolish, with the sand. So you had to stick to the El Dorado story.

"Unless you had given up on El Dorado when you were on the river, it doesn't make sense what you did. You left one man with the Indians to go to the city of gold. One man, in the middle of the forest. The Indian chief asked you to leave fifty men, to protect them against the Spaniards. You said no. You left one man. After all that journey and preparation, all those years of reconnoitring. The man you left was a servant, Captain Gifford's servant, Francis Sparrow. Francis Sparrow, one of the meaner sort you always rail about, was the man who was going to discover El Dorado for you. "And to show to people in England where you had been you took the son of the chief Topiawari. You left a boy in exchange. A sixteen-year-old boy, Hugh Goodwin. I don't know how you could do that. If people had read your book more carefully they would have taxed you with that. Keymis found out the following year what happened to that poor boy. Keymis wrote about it, and we found out from the Spanish reports as well. Before you had even got back into the Gulf that boy had been killed. The Indians told the Spaniards that the boy went out walking in the forest in his English clothes, and a tiger was so maddened by the sight of the clothes that it fell on him and killed him. Sometimes I think it sounds good, sometimes it sounds a mocking Spanish story, sometimes I think it sounds a foolish story. Who knows? Perhaps the Spaniards killed him, perhaps the Indians did. Think of this boy close to tears walking in the forest, in his best clothes, with such goods as he had taken off the ship. Walking in solitude away from the village, after the ships had begun to drift downstream, a hundred miles a day.

"It was harder for Francis Sparrow. He never went looking for El Dorado and the city of Manoa. The Spaniards captured him a few days after you had set him down. The Indians must have informed on him. From the Spanish reports we know he spent seven years in Spanish jails, and you know the terrible things that happen to Protestant people in Spanish jails, even here in the Indies, where the Inquisition also exists.

"You had given up on El Dorado, and after all the hard deaths I think of these two boys left behind in the forest, four hundred miles up river, as special sacrifices of yours. All that we know of them are their names. You never paid too much attention to people like that, the labourers and rowers on the ships.

"And look where it's brought you back. Look where it's got us all, waiting in this muddy Gulf for news of your son, and news of your lieutenant Keymis. From time to time during the day the Spaniards in Trinidad will fire off a shot, to let us know they are watching. Just before the sun goes down the Indians will light fires on the shore. Their canoes will paddle by and no one will come to us.

"Yet the day after you arrived you wrote to your wife that you could still be king of the Indies. We will talk about that later. I will come later and give you a second draught, when it's cool. I have to read and think some more, picking my way through your slippery words. Look how the sun shines through your green silk curtains. They've already begun to fade."

WHEN THE sun went down—it never became really cool on the water, at the south of the Gulf, almost in the river estuary—the old man said to the surgeon, "You asked why I wrote as I did to my wife. She will get that letter in some months. By the time she reads it all this may be over. It didn't matter what I wrote her. And at one time it was true: I could have been king of the Indians."

"A long time ago. In 1595. Twenty-three years ago."

"I rescued all the Trinidad Indian little kings or chiefs from the Spaniards. I was the first man here ever to punish the Spaniards for what they had done. I killed the Spaniards in Port of Spain and broke open the jail in their town inland and set the kings free, and their people burned the Spanish town. But when I wrote my book and gave the names of the kings there were people in England who said that I was making the names up. Wannawanare, Carroari, Maquarima, Tarroopanama, Aterima. I still know the names. And then— luckily, not for me so much as for the kings—a Spanish ship was captured taking duplicates of reports to Spain, and some of the names were there. The Spaniards founded Port of Spain on Wannawanare's land. In the report they sent to Spain they said he agreed to handing over his land and his people. The man I saw was naked and tortured and half dead in that little jail room. I can still see their faces turned to one side against the wall, the five wasted kings, all on one chain, their bodies burnt in places with hot bacon fat. They would have just stayed there and died if we hadn't freed them. And if duplicates of the Spanish reports from Trinidad hadn't been captured, with the names of some of those kings, saying they had agreed to the Spaniards' taking over their land and their people—if that hadn't happened, nobody would have believed that those kings existed, and that they had gone through this torment in the closed cell."

The surgeon said, "The Spaniards are like that. They record everything, and get it attested by notaries, and they send duplicates and triplicates by different ships to Spain. Very little gets lost. It's a great help to us. We often have the two sides of a story."

The old man said, "It's terrible to think that people mightn't have known about those men, or believed what I wrote about them."

"Everything you write about the Trinidad side of the Gulf is true. It's remarkable. Every tribe, every village, every river is as you say. And you did rescue Wannawanare and the others. But you went away, and, as you know, the Spaniards came back. They sent a very big expedition to the Gulf some months later. I don't think anyone knows what happened to Wannawanare and his people, and all the others, after you left. The Spaniards had a lot of scores to settle. The Indians you had helped didn't stand a chance. Those two boys you left on the river didn't stand a chance. When you sent Keymis the following year to reconnoitre on his own, he had to move very carefully. He couldn't even land on Trinidad. He heard later that the Spaniards were resettling the Indian tribes on both sides of the Gulf. You know what that means. Keymis didn't mention Wannawanare. Strange—of Keymis, I mean.

"For a few weeks in 1595, when you had all those ships and men, I suppose it would have been possible for you to be the king of the Indians. But you were fooling those people. When Keymis went out the next year, an Indian chief came to the river mouth to meet him with twelve or twenty canoes provisioned for war. The chief asked Keymis where the rest of your fleet was. Keymis spoke the lie he had prepared. He said he hadn't come to fight the Spaniards. You had killed all the Spaniards the previous year, and if you had sent a bigger force now the Indians would have thought that you wanted to invade their territory. After Keymis had said that twice, word spread among the tribes, and no one came to see Keymis. All the Indians on the river could think of was hiding from the Spaniards and trying to make peace with them.

"You stirred people up, here in this Gulf, and you went away. You stayed away for twenty-three years. You left a lot of people to face the consequences. The Spaniards had a lot of scores to settle. And you can't blame them. Those Spaniards you killed at Port of Spain—some people would say you behaved dishonourably. Those men had been on the island for some years and were almost destitute. They came aboard your ships to try to buy linen from your men. You encouraged them, you talked to them about Virginia. You said that was where you were going. You gave them wine, which they hadn't had for years. You entertained them for days. As soon as the rest of your fleet came into the Gulf, and you felt sure of your strength, you fell on those Spaniards and killed them."

The old man said, "It was what they had done to some of the people I had sent the year before. They invited them to leave the ships and go hunting in the woods. They had Indians and dogs. When our men were close to the shore they fired on them and killed them."

"All right. You settled that score, but you left these others for the Spaniards to settle. And they didn't forget. Spaniards are like that. Fourteen years after, a friend of yours, Hall, a

London merchant, sent two ships to the Gulf to trade. To pick up tobacco, mainly. This foreign trading in a Spanish colony is illegal, but the Spanish governor didn't mind breaking his country's laws. He got the men on the London ships to talk. He found out that Hall, the owner of the ships, was a friend of yours. One day, when thirty-six men from the ships were ashore at Port of Spain, they were all seized and roped up. They were tied back to back, and the throats of all thirty-six were cut. Right away. On the black sand of that Port of Spain shore. The man who did that was the son of the old Spanish governor, the old conquistador you had captured and led about in 1595. It was bad luck on the thirty-six men, but the old conquistador's son owed you that.

"This was part of what you left behind. The Gulf had always been a place of blood and revenge, of Indian dispossessions and resettlement. Even before the Spanish time. The man-eating Caribs were moving down. There were dreadful wars. You added to that. But you went away and wrote a book about an untouched paradise on the rivers, a place to which you alone had access, where the Indians lived in beautiful meadows and didn't know the value of the gold and diamonds by which they were surrounded, and where you alone had the secret to Indian hearts.

"I am trying to find out how you arrived at that book, at that version of your adventure.

"You had heard, like the rest of the civilized world, about El Dorado. You knew about this old conquistador who had been made governor of the provinces of Trinidad and Guiana and El Dorado, and had spent his fortune looking for the golden city. You assembled a force. You came and captured the old governor. You had forty men dig sand—just in case—and load up the ships. You went exploring with the old governor. You thought him foolish. You found nothing. You're an intelligent man. You lost much of your faith in El Dorado. You believed so little in El Dorado that you left only one man, a servant, to look for it. Just in case.

"You began to try to get a ransom for the old Spanish conquistador, the governor of Trinidad. That isn't in your book, but it's in the Spanish reports. None of the neighbouring Spanish officials would pay up. In fact, they all wanted the old man dead, so that they could claim his province and get whatever gold was going.

"So, at this stage, for all your trouble, and after all that killing, you had only sand. And this is where the Negro tells us something."

The old man said, "I had no Negroes with me in 1595."

"I know. You came straight from England with your force. I am thinking about the Negro who suddenly appears in your book when you are on the Guiana river, and see the meadows and fields and flowers near the falls. The river is full of crocodiles, thousands, you say. And the Negro—who would know about crocodiles—jumps in from the galley— for a swim, you say—and is immediately eaten alive. And that's that. There's nothing more about crocodiles or Negroes in your book. I have thought a lot about that vanishing Negro of yours, and I'm certain you borrowed him from John Hawkins's account of his voyage to Guinea in West Africa and the West Indies in 1564. In Guinea Hawkins saw a Negro who was snatched by a crocodile and pulled under as he was filling water at the river's edge. That's a better story.

"Just as you were taking back Topiawari's son to England to show people that you had really been to Guiana, so, as you were writing about foreign adventures, you wanted to let people know that you had seen what other famous adventurers had seen. There is a little more, connected with that Negro. Hawkins was a slaver and privateer, a sacker of Spanish cities. I feel that when you left the Gulf, with only the sand to show for your pains, your thoughts were turning to sacking a city. Hawkins was in your head. You thought you would do what he had done.

"Outside the Gulf, not far to the west, just below the salt-pans of the Araya Peninsula, is the town of Cumaná. It is the oldest Spanish town in this part of the world. You thought you would capture that, as you had captured Port of Spain. But the Spanish governor there had heard about you, and he was waiting, with his musketeers and his Indian archers with their poisoned arrows. The land sloped up from the sea to the town. It was sandy, open, full of low, prickly cactus. Your men were massacred as they came off the boats. There is nothing of this in your book, but the Spanish reports say that forty of your men died there. They were important men. The Spanish reports give the names. They couldn't have made them up. The men who died from musket or sabre wounds on the Cumaná shore were the lucky ones.

"Terrible things happened to the people who were hit by the poisoned arrows of the Indians. They went mad with thirst. Their bowels burst, their bodies blackened. The smell was awful in the ships. You asked the old Spanish conquistador you were dragging around with you about an antidote. He said he didn't know. So he had his revenge at last. It didn't matter how much you abused him for being unlearned and incurious: he said he didn't know.

"In your book you don't talk about the attack on Cumaná, of course. But you talk in a very concrete and passionate way about the effects of the poisoned arrows; you slip it in as a necessary digression—to use your words—in the Guiana section. You mention the antidote you heard about from someone you said was a Guianian; but what this person said suggests he was a Spaniard, a renegade you mention in another context, someone lower down the coast from Cumaná, always ready to trade with foreigners. Some Spaniards, this man said, had been cured with garlic juice; the golden rule was to take no liquids before the wound was dressed. Twenty-seven men died in the ships from the arrows: this was the figure given by the old conquistador to the Spanish enquiry. He was let off the ship at this stage, the old conquistador, perhaps exchanged for two English prisoners.

"Twenty-seven people died on the ships, but you did what you could to spare yourself the smell and the suffering. There were two Dutch ships at anchor off the Araya Peninsula, no doubt loading up with contraband salt, with the connivance of that man who told you about the antidote. You spent the hours of daylight and heat with them, when the smell of the dying men in your own ship would have been very high. At night you came back to your cabin, with the green hangings. Just like this one. Later you buried your dead—just as you did this time, when you reached the Gulf.

"That journey of 1595 had begun with murder; it had ended with a massacre of your people and the stench of death in the ships. And all you had to show for it was sand. As for all the deaths, you didn't have to explain—people always die on expeditions.

"Perhaps if you hadn't taken back the sand and been mocked for it, you might have written nothing. Or you might have written a little account of your exploration of the Gulf and the river. But you had to prove that you were not a fool, that you had found something more important than gold or booty. You had found a new empire for England, an empire of willing Indian subjects. So you wrote your difficult book, mixing up fantasy and history with your own real explorations. Everything on this side of the Gulf was real, everything on that side was fantasy. That made it easy for you to write, but by this means you also created a book that no one could ever disentangle and very few would read. The story was in the title; that was as far as most people would get. *The Discovery of the Large, Rich, and Beautiful Empire of Guiana, with a Relation of the Great and Golden City of Manoa (which the Spaniards call El Dorado) and Other Countries, with their Rivers adjoining. Performed in the year 1595 by Sir Walter Raleigh Knight.*

"The book was offered as proof, if anyone chose to go through it. But the more important proof was your own behaviour. You insisted that El Dorado existed. You had your Indian servants. You sent Keymis the next year to Guiana. You sent people to keep in touch. The only thing that gives you away is that you yourself never wanted to go back. You sent Keymis. You sent other people later. But you never went back yourself. And even now, at the end of your life, you haven't wanted to go up the river. You arrived this time as you left twenty-three years ago, with the stench of death in your ship. You have buried your dead. But you have preferred to stay out here in the Gulf. You don't really want to know. You are hoping for luck. Or perhaps you are hoping for nothing at all. There was never any El Dorado in Guiana. The Spaniards stopped looking many years ago. The French have stopped looking. The Dutch never looked. They always came only to trade, to get tobacco and salt. Neither you nor Keymis saw anything on the river. You both thought only that where so many had looked for El Dorado, El Dorado existed. Keymis in his book said El Dorado had to exist, if only as a sign of God's providence: to give England an empire as Spain had been given one. And now we wait for news of Keymis and your son and the others."

THE SHIPS and canoes that went down to the main river from the Gulf went down one branch; the ones that came up from the river to the Gulf used another, some way to the east, where the current was not so strong. Up to fifty years before only the Indians were masters of these waters; now that trick of the estuary was known to all. Normally now the canoes ignored the *Destiny* and its sentinel ship. But one day there came a canoe or launch.

Imagine the wide southern Gulf at sunrise: the flat many-channelled estuary to the west and south, the long barrier arm of the low, sandy peninsula of south-western Trinidad to the east: the morning sky high, the water reasonably calm, river water from the continent mingling with the Atlantic in froth-edged bands of colour: mud, various shades of olive, grey. Almost mid-way between the estuary and the peninsula is a high, broken rock formation which now has a Spanish name, Soldado, The Soldier. Only pelicans and the birds now called frigate birds live there; they have done that for centuries, perhaps tens of centuries. They nest there, and when the time comes they settle down to die, not far away from where they have nested, with the same kind of deliberation, folding their legs neatly below them. Guano and bones fill every crevice and cushion every ledge of the broken grey rock, and create a kind of earth where vegetation grows.

At night the water is more turbulent than at sunrise, and the weak lights of the rocking *Destiny*, lying within the Gulf, and its sentinel ship, lying south of The Soldier, can be seen from far.

In the middle of the day the sky is blue, the birds circle above The Soldier, mere glitter replaces the colours of the choppy water and blurs far-off objects.

So the small vessel, coming up one afternoon from the eastern channel, bobbing up and down, appears and disappears in the glitter. A canoe? Indian canoes steer clear of the *Destiny* now. This vessel comes steadily on. The sentinel ship signals. The vessel coming up is one of the expedition's launches. The captain of the *Destiny* fixes his glass on the approaching shape, its outlines dissolving and re-forming in the white glitter. The deck of the ship is hot below the thin leather soles of the soldiers, watchful now, sweating in their hot breast armour.

In the captain's glass a launch defines itself at last. Not an Indian canoe. An English launch: its sails can be seen: the oars of the rowers are at rest. Some armed soldiers are with them. And a gentleman, a man in splendid clothes, sitting on one of the benches. Not English clothes. Spanish clothes.

It can only be the Spanish governor. Is he a captive? Has

some act of war therefore occurred? Or is he coming to parley, to offer a deal, nobleman to nobleman?

In the general's cabin, hot in the afternoon, with the smell of the sea and the estuary mingling with the smell of sickness, and the small bleached curtains glowing in the light, the old man bestirs himself and begins to dress, to receive the governor. The surgeon helps him. A clean shirt for the general: it smells of the brackish water in which it has been washed. Then the two men go out together to the light on the deck.

The launch gets nearer.

"Is it Palomeque?" the old man asks.

"It's an Indian," the surgeon says. "They've dressed him up in Spanish clothes. The governor's, or some other nobleman's. The clothes are far too big for him."

The old man falls silent. The sails slacken, the launch pulls alongside. The Indian looks up, all face in the too-big clothes. A soldier from the launch climbs half-way up the ship's ladder. A second soldier passes him things from the launch.

The man on the ladder says, "For the admiral. Captain Keymis's compliments. A basket of oranges and lemons." He passes the fruit, already shrivelling, to a musketeer on the deck. "A roll of tobacco. A parcel of papers."

The surgeon takes the papers and glances at them. He says, "Spanish papers."

"A tortoise," the man on the ladder says, as that creature, its shell warm from the sun, its lower part cool from the bilge water where it's been resting, is passed up. "And Don José himself."

This is the Indian. He is pushed up the ladder. The clothes are the clothes of a man a foot taller, and they are not as fine as they appeared from a distance. They are flecked with mud and stained in places with old blood and bilge water; sweat stains under the arms show purple on the blue silk. The Indian

is uncertain. He fixes frightened eyes on the old man with
the white beard.

W E S T A Y with those Indian eyes. When we next consider
them they are calmer, even self-possessed. Let us stand back
a step or two. We see then that the possessor of those eyes is
now wearing English Jacobean clothes that fit. He is sitting
at a heavy dark table in a high, bare room. It is cool in the
room, though it is sunny outside. The solid walls are un-
evenly plastered and the sloping projections catch the dust
here and there.

A year has passed. In spite of Don José's English clothes,
we are in New Granada, back in the New World and South
America, and Don José is giving evidence to a priest, Fray
Simón, who is writing a history of the Spanish New World.

Fray Simón is reading back from his notes.

" 'And witness says that after these gifts were handed
over, the surgeon asked for news. A letter was handed over
to the general. And when the letter was half read, the general,
whose name at that time witness thought to be Milor Guateral, looked at the deck and the sea and the sky, and then at
the birds flying above the rock known as The Soldier, and
then he looked at the deck again and began to cry silently, in
the presence of all, for the death of his son.' And so?"

Don José says, "The surgeon came forward to support
the old man, and the old man allowed himself to be held."

E Y E S A L O N E now, we will go down the fast-flowing channel from the Gulf to the main river. The water and the banks
are all that we will see. We are travelling at the speed of the
ships, and we are seeing (without interference, with the help
of this camera's eye) the once aboriginal waters down which
Captain Keymis's four ships passed a full year before, with

four hundred heavily armed men, among them a section of pike commanded by the old man's son. Big forest birds fly ahead. The white sky yellows, then glows red; the muddy water turns violet in the fading light. Night falls on the river and the banks; the bush begins to sing. We slow down. The expedition has drawn near to the Spanish settlement.

Here we begin to fit pictures to the words of Don José. The narrative is now his.

"When the people of San Thomé heard that the English were coming they were frightened. When they heard that all those ships had anchored outside the river they began to take away their goods from their rancherías to the island in the middle of the river."

"Rancherías?" Fray Simón said. "Shacks, huts? Do you mean that? Were they living in huts?"

"Only the governor lived in a house, and everything was in that house. The jail, the Royal Treasury, everything. The Treasury was full of people's goods. The governor, Don Palmita, was a very hard man."

"Palomeque. Pa-lo-me-que."

"The governor took people's goods when they broke the law. The people didn't have money to pay the fines. Don Palomeque didn't like people trading with the foreigners."

"Don Diego. Don Diego Palomeque."

"Don Diego said this kind of trading was against the king's laws, and he was determined to put an end to it. So he took people's goods. He was no respecter of persons. In the Treasury in his house in San Thomé there was a lot of silver plate belonging to the wife of the previous governor. I mention this because I used to work for the family. In fact, the previous governor was my father. Don Fernando Berrio. You can look at my face and see that I am Spanish."

Fray Simón said, "Not especially."

"I am just telling you what people say. My mother was an Indian woman, of course. People didn't like this new governor, Don Diego, and if he didn't have those soldiers from Puerto Rico with him, they would have killed him in Trinidad or San Thomé. He was coming and going between the two places and, even with the soldiers, there were many places on the river where he could have had an accident. I am not giving away any secrets if I say that some people were happy to hear that the English were coming. One Indian servant actually said so in Don Diego's hearing. The governor had the foolish man whipped in the open ground we called the plaza and then had him chained up in the jail in the governor's house. This happened about four days before the English came.

"The next day news was brought of the size of the English force. People said four hundred men, five hundred, seven hundred men were coming. At nightfall all the vecinos or people of the little town left their rancherías and took all the food they had and went to the island in the river. My people did that too. They left me behind just in case something happened when the English came and I was in a position to recover the silver plate from the governor's house. The next evening, or the evening after that, the soldiers from Puerto Rico deserted. There were about fifty of them. More than enough to frighten the vecinos of San Thomé, but not enough to face the English. They went to the island where the townspeople had gone.

"There were only twelve people in the town the next morning. I counted them. There was the chained Indian in the governor's house. There was myself. There were three Indian servant women. Two Negroes, left by their owners to fend for themselves. A crippled priest, and a Portuguese boy. There was the governor, and there were two captains with him, Captain Monje and Captain Erenetta."

Fray Simón said, "Arias Nieto. That was the name that came out at the official enquiry."

"The governor, Don Diego, behaved like a man. I have

to say it. There were only the three of them who were soldiers, and he behaved as though they were three hundred. He
was a big, stout man, the biggest Spaniard I had seen. I had
never seen him do any manual work. Now he showed how
much he could do. He and the two captains worked from
first light to fortify the redoubt the soldiers from Puerto Rico
had begun to create around some rocks just outside the plaza.
He and the captains dug. They got the two Negroes to dig
with them, and they made me dig with them as well. So there
were six of us digging. Six men can dig a lot in a day. They
had about a dozen muskets and they were preparing three
lines of defence. We cut down branches and created barricades
in front of each musket position. In the outer line the musket
positions were far apart, about forty yards. In the second line
they were closer, and in the last line they were very close,
just inside the plaza. They set up rests for their muskets, and
in some rests they placed primed muskets.

"They didn't have a chance, but they were going to do
all that they could. And they were working with such a will
that it was only in the afternoon, when it was very hot and
quiet, that I began to think that they were really dead men,
that this was the last day of their life. I must tell you I admired
them then, and I began to work with a will like theirs. The
Indian women prepared food for us and brought us water,
and the governor didn't forget the crippled priest. We worked
right through the day. A silent day, a deserted plaza, and we
were all so active. The Portuguese boy acted as scout and
watched the river.

"When there were two hours of daylight left, the governor said they had done as much as they could do. For an hour
or so he and the two others practised running from musket
position to musket position, and withdrawing from one line
to another. Then they ate their last meal, and the fires were
put out. The sun went down, and after the silence of the day
the forest began to roar. We waited. I don't know how long.

I don't think it would have been possible for the whistles or signals of the Portuguese boy to be heard with all that forest noise. And then we heard four musket shots. Just four, very close together. There was nothing more after that. Just the forest. In the morning, when it was silent again, the English soldiers came into the square. They carried very big lances.

"I was in the Berrios' house. The soldiers had no trouble finding me. They found the three Indian women, too, hiding in one of the rancherías. And the Portuguese boy, and the two Negroes. They began to drive us very roughly to the governor's house, shouting at us in English and what they thought was Spanish.

" 'You,' they said to me. '*Castellano*'? I wanted to tell them that my father was the previous governor, but I didn't know how to say that. So I just made signs to say yes. This made them very angry. One of the soldiers unhooked a coil of rope from his belt, and I think they would have hanged me there and then if the Negroes hadn't said, 'No castellano, no castellano. Indio, indio. Indian, Indian.'

"There were many soldiers in the governor's house. In one room, the office, we saw a man with bandages and blood on his torn clothes. He had been wounded by a musket shot. In another room, the one with the Royal Chest, we saw two dead men laid out. We were taken to the main bedroom. There we found the English commander. He was an old man, very tall, as tall as the Spanish governor, but very thin. He had a bad eye. As commander he carried a polished stick about a yard long. He said through an interpreter to the women, 'Some Spanish men died during the night. We want you to tell us who they are.'

"They took us to the redoubt, where we had done so much digging in the red earth the day before. The ground had been scuffed by the English soldiers' feet, but you could still see the branches we had cut and where we had dragged them on the ground. Don Palmita, Erenetta, and Captain

Monje had died at musket positions in the outer line. All that work, and the fight had lasted only a minute. Four musket shots. One man had fired twice. With those four shots they had killed two English soldiers and wounded one. Only one shot had missed. And then all three of them had died. You could see where the big English lances had thrown aside the branches. I don't think they were expecting the English to come so far up the river with those lances. Erenetta and Captain Monje still had their clothes, but they had already stripped the clothes off Don Palmita. He was naked and dirty and the blood was black on him and there was a gash from the top of his head down to his teeth.

"I told the commander who the dead men were. He changed colour when he heard that the naked man was the governor. The women were crying at the sight of the dead men, and when the English commander asked them to bury the dead men they said they didn't know how to bury people. I don't know what rule the commander was following. I don't know why he wanted the women to bury the dead men. He didn't ask me. He didn't ask the Negroes. When the women said they didn't know how to bury dead men, he looked as though he didn't know what to do. Then he said to the women through the interpreter, 'All right, all right. Cook for us. If you cook for us, nothing will happen to you. What can you cook for us?' The women said they had only maize, and there wasn't much of that because the vecinos had stripped the fields and taken most of the maize to the island.

"They cooked the maize, boiling it with some herbs, and the commander asked me and the other Indian, the one chained up in the house, to eat with them in the governor's house. They treated us with a lot of honour. I wasn't expecting that. The man who had been chained they called Señor Don Pedro. It wasn't his name. It was like a joke with them.

"All the time there were those two dead bodies in the

Treasury room. One of them was the son of the English general. And outside were those three other bodies. When people die they should disappear. A dead body is like a weight on the earth, a weight on the soul. Later that day, when everyone was less tired, some of the English soldiers went out to the dead men, tried to compose their limbs, tied the bodies together and buried them in one of the holes we had dug the day before. That felt better. The crippled priest said some prayers in his house.

"The next day they buried the two men stretched out in the governor's house. They brought shrouds from the ships and wrapped the bodies in them. They placed the bodies on planks and some men carried the planks round the open bare ground of the plaza, in front of the shacks and the thatched adobe church. The commander walked alone just behind the planks. It looked strange, but again I didn't know what rule they were following. Some of the soldiers marched in formation with their flags pointing down. Others held their big lances in their right hands, the points sloping up, the wooden hafts dragging on the ground behind them. Twice they walked round the plaza. Then the bodies were buried in another hole we had dug the day before, not far from the other.

"After this, the commander began to look for gold. He dug up the ground in every ranchería. Once for a whole morning he had the Portuguese boy whipped back and forth through the settlement. He thought the Portuguese boy knew where the gold was. It might have been because of the boy's accent. Then he left the poor boy alone. Day after day he had the soldiers dig. One night he went out of the settlement. In the morning he came back with some sand. He showed it to me. 'Is this gold, Don José?' He became demented. His bad eye flickered out of control more and more. He went up and down the river. Once he went too near the island and the soldiers from Puerto Rico opened up and killed six of his soldiers.

"Every day now, in little incidents like this, he began to lose men. Every day there were burials, and not always with their rules. Once for many days he went up the river in a launch. He travelled in this way for two hundred miles. He took me with him. He had said before we started that he knew this stretch of the river well, but it soon was clear that the river here was quite new to him. He was terrified that the people on the banks might shoot poisoned arrows. Every time he saw a rock or coloured earth or sand he wanted to know whether it contained gold. But he never wanted to stay too long on the banks because of his fear of the arrows. When we came back to the settlement we found that one of the ships had gone away.

"It was strange. I had hated Don Diego, the governor. Then I grieved for him. Now I began to grieve for the man who had killed Don Diego. He was frightened and unhappy. He held on to his polished stick but he no longer knew what to do. The soldiers were sick and dying. We had no food. His men had no regard for him. He was frightened that more ships might desert. That was when he decided to send me in the launch to the river mouth to meet the general.

"He sat in the bedroom of the governor's house and wrote a letter. He said I was not to tell the general about the death of his son. The general should read it first in his letter. Then he began to put things in the launch. A lot of papers from the Treasury, where the general's dead son had lain for two nights and a day. The oranges and lemons. The only gold things in San Thomé. There were some trees in the settlement. The roll of tobacco. There was tobacco everywhere. That was what people grew to trade with the foreign ships. If only it was food no one would have gone hungry. Then he thought of the tortoise. He would have liked to send the general an armadillo, he said. On the river one day in 1595 he and the general and everybody else had feasted on armadillo. The tortoise wasn't food, but the general was interested in these strange animals. I was to keep the tortoise cool.

"And then, just before I left, the idea came to him to dress me up in the clothes they had stripped off the dead governor. They were pretty clothes, but they were too big for me. That made him laugh. I thought it was a strange time for a joke like that. But he was probably following some rules of his own. It was like the time he and his officers unchained the Indian in the governor's house, dressed him up, and called him Señor Don Pedro, and then wanted him and me to sit and eat boiled maize with them in the governor's house, while the three dead men were unburied outside, and the two dead men were lying in the other room."

EYES ALONE again, we move down river. But now we are looking at what the launch is leaving behind. We are never far from the northern bank, and we are moving fast, at about four or five miles an hour. At a certain stage we leave the main river and turn into a channel that flows north. We slow down. The current no longer drives us. We depend on wind and tack from side to side, until the banks vanish. We are out in the wide Gulf again, and soon we see the heavy brown pelicans and the slender frigate birds flying over The Soldier.

Half-way through these pictures, as we consider water and flat land, green and brown and yellow, we hear the voice of Fray Simón, the historian.

"You are now a well-travelled man. Better travelled than most people in the world. You've been to England. You've seen some of its great cities and great buildings. You've seen things I haven't seen. The spire of Salisbury, the great cathedrals of Winchester and Southwark, the Tower of London that they say Julius Caesar built. You've met important men. You've been to Spain, too. You've been to Toledo and Salamanca. You've been to Seville. You've seen the galleons from the Americas on the river there. And now you're back here, in New Granada, where you were born. Don José in name and deed."

"It was the doing of Sir Guateral, the English general. He could have condemned me with a word."

"Why did he like you?"

"He never said."

"Did he see in you some resemblance to the son he had lost? Was it because you were among the last people to see his son?"

"We never talked about it. He never asked me about his son."

"Did you know the general was going to die in a few months?"

"I didn't know, and I'm glad I didn't know. It would have been too much for me after all that had happened. And I was full of my own grief."

"Because of all the dead men? Or grief because you were being taken away?"

"It had been with me for some weeks. But it was only on the launch that I began to understand what I was feeling. I wasn't a Guiana man. I was from New Granada, and had made that long journey down the river with the Berrios. I always had the hope that I would be able to pick my way back home from Guiana. When the settlement was abandoned, and the vecinos took refuge on the island in the river, I felt the world had changed for me. I felt I had lost touch with things. On the launch this grief grew and grew. Sometimes a child playing in a puddle after rain gets suddenly frightened by the reflected sky. I was like that. I felt I was falling into the sky, falling into the sea. I hardened my heart. And then, from being frightened by that idea of falling into the sky, I began to hold on to it. It was the only comfort I had. The thought of my doom lifted me above people. I thought I would acknowledge no one. Even if people laughed at me, or smiled at me, because of the clothes I was wearing, I wasn't going to smile back."

"Was this the face you showed to the general when you went aboard his ship?"

"Yes."

"You were a lucky man. He had fallen out of love with the Indians. He thought they'd let him down."

"As I said, he could have condemned me with a word."

"It may be your demeanour impressed him. Perhaps he saw his fate in yours."

"He didn't look at me at first. And I was thinking about the birds above the rock they called The Soldier. Then he began to read the letter, and he cried for his son, and the surgeon held him. It was only after this that I felt his eyes fall on me."

"Of course, you were the only thing from Guiana he was taking back to England."

"That was what people said later. At the time I just felt his old man's eyes falling on my face, and I felt at ease with him."

"I was hoping to get something else from you, I must confess. My feeling now is that as an historian I should deal as simply as possible with the moment of news. I should present only the facts."

We consider again the frigate birds floating high over The Soldier, and, lower down, flying in well-spaced lines above the sea glitter, the awkwardly shaped pelicans (like miniature airborne caravels), heavy-bodied, heavy-beaked, with no balancing length of tail.

Over this comes the voice of Fray Simón, reading aloud as he writes his history.

"So their joy at the death in battle of the valiant Don Diego Palomeque de Acuña was well watered by the weeping that began in their ships for the death of their own general's son."

WE FOCUS again on Don José: his confident face, his fine Jacobean tunic. He takes up his narrative again.

"When the general was a little restored, he gave orders that I was to be taken to his cabin and given some of his own clothes. So at once my position on the ship changed. People who had looked at me with irony stopped doing so. Even my name they pronounced in a different way. The general's cabin was small, but the hangings were richer than anything I had seen. The attendant who took me to the cabin opened a chest that was battened down to the floor, took out some clothes, and asked me to choose. The general was closer to my size. It was a relief to get out of the Spanish governor's clothes. They were the fine clothes he had put on for the battle. The blood had turned black on them, and the red San Thomé mud, from that night of the battle, had dried to powder. They gave off the smell of death and the forest, river water and wet old leaves, and, faintly, as if from a long time before, the smell of the sweet root the governor had kept in his own clothes chest to perfume his clothes and keep out insects. I folded the clothes as neatly as I could and placed them on the lid of the chest.

"I dressed in my new clothes, with the help of the attendant, and was wondering about going outside when the general and the surgeon came in. They made me understand that I was to sleep in the cabin. A hammock would be set up for me. I was to be the general's personal servant. The general asked whether I knew about waiting on people, and I told him that I had been in the household of the previous governor of Trinidad and Guiana. I didn't tell him that the governor was my father.

"My first duty was to serve him his dinner. His cook had died on the voyage out, and he ate what the ship's galley provided. It was a maize gruel that day. He hardly touched it. Later he and the surgeon walked, and he played with the tortoise. In the cabin in the evening we didn't talk. He didn't want to be alone. He wanted my company, but he wanted me to stay a stranger. At some time in the night he got out of his cotton hammock. He wanted to eat something. He ate a stewed prune, from a barrel he had brought out from

England. I didn't like the way the prune or the barrel looked, after he had taken out the cover, and I thought the smell very unpleasant. He said it was the only thing he could eat easily, after his sickness on the voyage, and he had very few left. He said the last few apples he had brought out from England had been stolen by the men. He looked very thin in his shirt. It was pitiful to see him.

"He was old and sick and thin, but he could be very rough with people, especially with people who served him. He wanted them to know that he didn't think much of them; he could be a shouter. For some reason he wasn't like that with me, and this gave me some standing among the English on the ship. I have to say that I had never in my life been shown anything like that regard, not in New Granada, not in San Thomé when I was with the Berrios. At the same time I saw that this good fortune of mine wasn't going to last, that the position of the general here in the Gulf was almost like the position of his commander on the river.

"He was a doomed man. Everyone knew it. The surgeon, the mariners, the soldiers, the men who cooked his meals in the galley. He had lost many men, many friends, many noblemen. He had lost his son. And he had Spanish blood on his hands. He shouldn't have allowed that to happen. He had promised the English king there would be no fighting with the Spaniards. That battle at San Thomé shouldn't have taken place. I understood about that later. What I understood at the time was that he had not found gold, and that as soon as he went back to England he would be arrested by orders of the English king, and after that he would be executed.

"That was his future, yet in the meantime he was the general. He had ships and men at his disposal. He could order men to do what he wanted. He could shout at the mariners and the serving people. And of course it was still possible that if he found gold everything would be reversed. He would live and be honoured. If he could find the gold that he had made people believe only he knew how to find. But the gold didn't exist. To the people of San Thomé it was a joke when we heard that the English were coming to seize our gold mines.

"I don't think anyone on the *Destiny* or the other ships believed in the gold either. And yet they were all there in the Gulf, under the orders of the general whose life was more or less over. They were waiting, doing nothing. Like the general. Some of them found it hard. A few days after I arrived, a couple of the general's ships slipped away, heading north up the Gulf to the Dragon's Mouth and the Caribbean Sea. The general appeared not to notice.

"The surgeon came to the cabin three or four times a day. The general talked a lot to him. In fact, he was the only one the general talked to. He talked about attacking Trinidad and holding Port of Spain to ransom. He had done it twenty-three years before, he said, and he could do it again. This time he would ask the Spaniards for twenty thousand pounds, and he would burn the city, a street a day, until the Spaniards paid. He talked about attacking Cumaná and Puerto Cabello, and then establishing a base in Florida.

"At first I took what he said seriously, and then I saw that he stood no chance at all, had nowhere in the world to hide, that whatever luck he might have the first time or the second time in those ventures he was outlining, the ships from England would come after him again and again. The way the Spanish ships had come again and again to our part of the world. Then I understood that he was talking just to impress the surgeon and even a little to impress me. He would tell me in Spanish what he had been telling the surgeon, and then he would say, almost as though it was a joke, 'What do you think, Don José?'

"When the surgeon left and we were alone in the cabin, the old man would go silent. In daylight and in darkness I could feel him grieving for his son and thinking of his own death. Once or twice he took out a book and sat down to

write in it. But he didn't write anything. They told me later
it was the journal he had kept since he had left England with
his ships and men. Even when he had been very ill he had
written in that book. But he had written nothing in it since
the launch had come from San Thomé with the news.

"He was waiting for his commander from San Thomé.
It was really all we were doing there in the Gulf, waiting for
that defeated man with the bad eye. He talked about it many
times a day, as though it was the one thing that was still clear
to him.

"At last one day, about thirteen or fourteen days after I
had arrived, the commander's ship appeared in the south,
coming up the channel to our left. The sentinel ship signalled,
the mariners and soldiers shouted the news, and people ran
to the deck to wait. Not the general, though. I had been
helping him to get ready to go out for a walk on deck, but
when he heard the news he said he didn't think he was well
enough. He wasn't making it up. His face changed. It seemed
to shrink. It became older, full of creases. He said he would
stay in his cabin. But he wanted me to go out and see what
was happening.

"I went outside. It was just before noon, and the decks
felt hot below the soles of my new shoes. The sky was full
of big moving clouds, and the choppy sea was all glitter. The
ship came up slowly, the light from sea and sky dancing
about it, the shape and colours of its masts and sails coming
and going. The birds from The Soldier floated high above.
When the ship came nearer I saw that it was flying two white
flags. I don't know what that meant.

"The ship anchored a little distance away. A boat was
lowered. Rowers climbed down the rope ladder into the boat.
The commander appeared on the deck of his ship, tall, dressed
in the same clothes I had last seen him in, holding his polished
stick of office. With that stick always in his right hand, he
climbed down the ladder. He was rowed over to us. He was

still the commander of the river force at that moment, but as
soon as he held on to the ship's ladder and began to come up
to the deck that authority left him. And I thought how strange
it was, that just a few weeks ago the English pikemen at San
Thomé were within two or three minutes of hanging me.
The Negroes saved me then, and after that for many weeks
my life depended on this man. Now I was on the general's
ship, and with everyone else was studying every movement
of this condemned man coming up the ladder with his now
useless commander's stick.

"He had grown very thin. We didn't have much to eat
on the ship. He would have had less on the river. His clothes
were dirty. So were his hands. They were discoloured with
old dirt, and full of scratches, some fresh, some healing. I
suppose a campaigning soldier's hands are very rough, but I
had never thought about it until that moment. One eye was
very quiet, almost dead; the other eye, the bad one, was
jumping about madly. He didn't look at me. There was nothing in his face to show that he even recognized me as the man
he had dressed in the Spanish governor's clothes and sent as
a prisoner to the general.

"He went up to the general's cabin. He knew the way.
Everyone looked at him. The surgeon followed him, and I
followed the surgeon. The general's door was open. There
was no reply when the commander knocked, but he went in,
still holding his stick, and bending—a very tall man, a small
doorway—in order not to strike his head. The general was
in his hammock. Since I had left him he had become very ill.
His shirt was wet with sweat. His face was white above the
hollows of his eyes and cheeks. He didn't talk. And yet, as I
had learned, these two old men were very old friends.

"The commander began to talk. The old man didn't reply. The commander talked on. I felt his words didn't matter.
I felt after a time that even the commander wasn't paying
attention to what he was saying. I think that all of us in that

cabin were waiting for an explosion from the sick man in the hammock. And that explosion did come, and it went on for a long time. It was as though the waiting and the disappointments and the grief of many weeks now, and many years before that, had been gathered up into this moment, as though this was the moment that the general had been waiting for, the one clear thing he had felt he had to do, after he had understood his doom.

"The old commander, already bending below the low ceiling, bent lower before the general's words. The commander had ruined everything, the general said. The commander had come out at the general's expense many years before to look for the gold mines, and he had said he had found the gold mines. There were three people in San Thomé who operated gold mines, the general said. He even knew their names. Don José knew their names. Francisco Fashardo owned a mine. Hermano Fruntino owned a mine. Pedro Rodrigo Paraná owned a mine.

"When I heard my name mentioned, I looked up and caught the surgeon's eye. He translated what the general had said into Spanish. I wanted to say that it wasn't true, that there were no gold mines in San Thomé, that none of those names the general had spoken were real, that Paraná was the name of a river, and that *hermano* meant brother. But the surgeon looked hard at me and made a slight gesture with his head, and I knew that I was to say nothing, that we had to bear with the general in his madness, that this madness was all that remained of his life now, that this rage had given the sick man who had lost his son a kind of life.

"The old man raged and raged at the commander that afternoon. The sun shone through the green curtains. The heat was too much for me, and the anger of the old man, and the grief of the tall half-starved man with the bad eye and the very dirty clothes and hands. I went outside, and found everyone quiet and hushed and unhappy. Nothing that had happened was hidden from anyone on the *Destiny* or in the other ships.

"At length the commander left, without his stick, and went to his cabin. It was above the general's. The general called for me, and I found him trembling in his hammock, his face thin and white, his shirt very wet, and he was complaining of feeling cold. He said, 'I am sick, Don José, very sick.' The commander's polished stick was on the lid of the general's clothes chest. We could hear the commander moving about in his cabin overhead, and the general behaved as though every noise, every sign of life from his commander, was an insult.

"Later, just before sunset, the general summoned the commander and went at him again.

"The commander had taken off some of his clothes. His shirt was undone. This time he didn't listen for very long. He said something which I didn't understand, and after that he didn't try to talk. Not long after, he left and went up to his cabin.

"The general was like a man possessed. He got out of his hammock, got out his book, took some sheets of paper from it, and began to write by the light of a candle. It was the first time I had seen him use a candle since I had got on to the ship. There was a sound of a shot from above. The general made a face. It was dark, even with the candle. If it wasn't dark, I would have said that the general smiled when he heard. After the shot the general wrote and wrote, this man who had not written in his journal since I had come to be with him.

"The surgeon came, and he and the general talked. We all three then went to the cabin above, the cabin of the commander. There he was, in the clothes he had arrived in, fully dressed again, on the floor. They were the clothes I had seen on him when he had put me on the launch at San Thomé and sent me to the general, with the gifts of the tortoise and the papers and the roll of tobacco. The commander's face was turned towards the floor. The general turned him over, like a man anxious to see what other men would have preferred not to see. We could see where the shot had torn the shirt and damaged his ribs over his very thin chest. But there was also a knife, a long, thin knife. It had been thrust in between the ribs. What had come first? The knife or the shot? I think the shot.

"The cabin was soon full of people. The general wanted everyone to see, and no one liked what he had seen. I was told later that they didn't like the idea of a man putting an end to his own life. It was like a judgement the dead man had made on himself. Though among us who are Indians or partly Indian it is better to do away with oneself than to live with dishonour.

"For hours that night, like a man inspired, like a man drawing energy from some unknown source or soul, the general wrote. The next day the commander was buried, without ceremony, his body tied in a shroud, for the sake of decency, rather than for religion, and thrown out into the Gulf, he who had walked according to the rules behind the shrouded corpses of the general's son and the other dead English nobleman at San Thomé.

"That was the end. There was nothing more to do there. The captains of the other ships came to the general and asked what they were to do. He said that he was a doomed man, very sick and very old, a man who had lost his son, a man who had been betrayed by everyone, even his oldest friend, and that they should leave him, because he brought misfortune to all who followed him. When the captains did as he said, and left us, and there was nothing in the Gulf where we had been used to seeing their ships, the general complained about their ingratitude. He complained to me and the surgeon and to other people. But not with any great passion. He didn't believe what he said. He was a tired-out man, drained of feelings, trying to play with feelings.

"It was the end. And in spite of all that the general said

he could do, he decided quite simply, when the time came, to head for home, and his doom at the hands of his king.

"When the poor commander—a very frightened man, as I now understood—had dressed me for a joke in Don Palmita's very big clothes at San Thomé, and had sent me down river in the launch, I had found a picture, in my head, for my own doom. I had felt I was falling into the sea, falling into the sky. I had focussed on that picture and found a comfort in it, because the doom it contained was so complete that it took away meaning from grief and the life of men and the world itself.

"Now, a few days after leaving the Gulf, leaving emptiness where our own ship had been, I found that the world had become like that picture in my head. Just a few days after leaving so many things that were familiar to me, familiar not only from the journeys I had made with the Berrios, but also from what I had heard from so many people: the rock called The Soldier, where the strong-winged pelicans settled down to die; the lake of pitch on the island of Iere, which the Spaniards had called Trinidad; the high solitary hill of Anaparima, a marker for all who travelled in the Gulf; Guanaganare's territory of Conquerabo or Cumucurapo, where my father's father had founded the City of the Spaniards; the high island of Chacachacare and the other islands and islets in the Dragon's Mouth. Familiar places, with clouds and sky and wind and sea as they had always been, but all now in a world changed forever, for me and for everybody else.

"A few days out of that, I was in the world of my old dream, an infinity of water and sky. But there was no terror for me. The ship was its own little world. The shipboard days had their rhythm. The old man was calm in his cabin. He did a certain amount of writing; he talked to the surgeon; he spent a fair amount of time teaching me English. As for emotion: he grieved a lot for the tortoise, which had died: it was too hot on the ship, and there was no fresh green for the creature. With that kind of activity and emotion—teaching me English, worrying about the tortoise—the old man could trust himself. But for the most part he was like a man who had ceased to feel, separated from the rest of us, as I thought, putting myself in his place, by his idea of his own doom.

"His regard for me never faded. More than once the surgeon told me what other people were to tell me. I was an Indian from Guiana and his servant: ordinary enough on the other side of the ocean, but now every day more precious as a human being. When we got to England people would look at me and think better of the old man. I would be like a remnant or proof of the kingdom of gold in his head. So I was part of the vanity that remained to him, part of his idea of the world going on beyond the emptiness of the sea.

"The day came at last when we landed and put that emptiness behind us. Everyone was relieved. Everyone wanted to walk on firm land and drink clean water and eat fresh food. But the old man's authority as general ended as soon as we touched land. As soon as we touched land he was the prisoner of his king. No chains were put on him. No one was waiting to take him away. We went to stay at his house, and there, with all the sorrow, he was still master. But everyone knew that his life was forfeit. Everyone was waiting for the king to act, and the king was in no hurry.

"For days after we landed I felt the ground move below me, as though we were still on the ship. And it was strange that though I was on land again and had that safety, for which I had longed, though the sky pressed low on me and I was once again with small views and small distances, there had come to me something of the mood with which I had travelled down the river from San Thomé to the *Destiny*. It had begun to come on me for a few days before we had arrived at land. It had come to me when I had heard people talking about arriving. I didn't like that idea of arriving. I was nervous about it.

"When we came to the land and travelled to the general's house I was seized by a great melancholy. It overpowered me. It ran through me like a cold fluid. It broke into my sleep. It was at the back of everything I did. It was like a spirit on my shoulder. Just as, on the launch coming down river, the dream of falling into the sea and the sky had lifted me above men, so this grief now cut me off from everything and everyone. I wanted to die. In the room the general's people had given me in his house I tied a cloth around my forehead to feel that tension above my eyes, as though I was a child again, and I turned my face to the wall. I wanted to turn away from all that was around me. I looked at the wall and never closed my eyes. It was like looking at the sky I had seen as a child. I looked hard at that and longed to cease to feel and think.

"Sometimes from far away, as it seemed, I would hear the general and the surgeon calling me, 'Don José, Don José.' If I heard that clearly enough, it would make me think of the general and his own doom, and sometimes after a while the emptiness would leave me. When that happened I would feel my tongue getting furred and my breath getting very bad. It was as though the unhappiness in my head and heart and stomach had turned to that smell inside me.

"At last the messengers from the king came. We left the house and got into a big heavy coach. The surgeon and I travelled with the old man. There was another coach in front, and soldiers on horseback behind. It was warm. The sun came up much earlier than I had known and set much later. In all the villages we passed people were waiting to look at the general. They wanted to look at me too. The soldiers on horseback didn't let them get too close. The surgeon and the general talked a lot sometimes.

"All the time we were getting nearer to the capital and his doom. We came one afternoon to a town where the houses were arranged as in a big square or plaza. The whole of one side of the square was occupied by a very big church with a very tall tower. The old man was in a very playful mood. 'Look, Don José. You will never see anything so tall again. Would you like to go up there?' I thought he was joking, but he said there was a way right to the top, inside the tower. The thought of climbing up so high made me feel giddy, roused me from my own grief a little. This pleased the old man, made him light-headed, I thought.

"We were to stop here for dinner. But when we got out of the coach the old man complained of having a headache. He walked into a post as the soldiers were taking him up to the room where we were to dine. He began to howl with pain, and he had to be supported into the room. He lay down in all his clothes. When food was brought up for him he sent it away. He said his headache was very bad and he felt he was going blind. The soldiers and officials were worried. The surgeon prepared something for him to drink, and immediately after that mixed an ointment for his bruises. All the time the general was groaning. At last he said he wanted to sleep. They took him to another room. They posted a soldier at the door.

"I was helping the old man to undress when he began to vomit. I went outside to get a bowl. That took some time. When I came back I found him half naked, crawling about the floor, chewing at the dried reeds spread there. The ointment the surgeon had applied had caused the bruises to come out in a rash that made me think of the effects of poisoned arrows. I called out to the soldier at the door, and when he saw he began to shout for people to come and help.

"The surgeon looked very serious. He said that the old man would become quite unbalanced if he didn't rest. So the king's officers decided to spend the night where we were. They had the old man's chest brought up to the room. When we were alone I began to unpack what was needed for the night. The old man said, 'Paper, Don José, paper.' He was standing, in his shirt, and smiling at me. I gave him the paper he asked for, and he sat at the table and began to write at

great speed, as he had written that day in the cabin on the
Destiny, after the death of the commander in the room above
us. From time to time as he wrote he looked at me and smiled.
I asked him what he was writing about. He said, 'About the
gold mines of San Thomé. What else?'
"He wrote until it was dark. He filled many pages. He
said, 'My wrist is hurting, Don José. I must stop.' When it
was dark the surgeon came. He was in his travelling cloak.
The two men smiled at each other. From below his cloak the
surgeon brought out, wrapped in cloth, pieces of the dinner
the old man had refused earlier. The old man gave the surgeon
the letter or the document he had been writing. The surgeon
folded the sheets and put them in a pocket.
    "The old man said, 'Don José must eat with us.' He lit a
rushlight, and we ate off the wooden platters that were in the
room. The old man was in a good mood. I had never seen
him in such a good mood. It was like the time in San Thomé
when the commander had insisted that the imprisoned Indian
in the dead governor's house and I should sit and eat boiled
maize with them, with the two dead men lying in the next
room, and the three dead men lying outside in the sun in the
trenches they had dug the day before.
    "The old man's mood lifted my spirits. But I felt at the
same time that death was close to all of us.
    "His own death came quite soon, when we got to the
capital. The prison was on the river. He wanted me to put
on my best clothes to witness what they did to him. And I
did. I could hardly bear to go back to the room afterwards.
I turned my face to the wall and looked at the sky in it.
    "There was an English nobleman who wanted me to join
his household. The old man had known of this and had liked
the idea. But my grief was too great. After getting to feel for
the Berrios, and then that afternoon for Don Palmita, and
afterwards for the English commander, and then for the old
man, moving on in a chain of death from one man to his

enemy; after the journey in the great ocean; I felt I would die if I couldn't get back to the beginning, to the first world I knew.

"The English behaved well. They could have kept me and made me wear feathers. But they told the Spanish ambassador. He was a relation of Don Palmita. The ambassador made arrangements to send me to Spain. Before I left they gave me English clothes, including some of the old man's that I had already worn. In Spain I went to the great city of Seville, where the galleons filled the river, and from there I travelled in one of the galleons to Cartagena. And now I am here."

FRAY SIMÓN said, "You've crossed the ocean twice. You are back here in New Granada, in the very town where you were born. You didn't get lost. The ships always knew where they were going. When you consider the great fear you used to have of the oceans, what do you think now?"

"I've thought a lot about that. And I think, Father, that the difference between us, who are Indians, or half Indians, and people like the Spaniards and the English and the Dutch and the French, people who know how to go where they are going, I think that for them the world is a safer place."

CHAPTER 7

A New Man

WHEN I BEGAN to write of it, the Trinidad landscape that was present to me was the landscape I had known as a child and felt myself part of—the western parts of Port of Spain; the forested hills to the north-west; the sugar-cane plains to the south, with the neat fields coming right up to the huts and houses and bare yards of villages lining the narrow and very black asphalt roads; the coconut estates on the muddy Atlantic coast, where the tall grey coconut trunks made a constant criss-crossing pattern as you drove by: a simple small-island geography.

Later, in London, when I was writing a book of history, I studied for many months the historical documents of the region. The documents (the early ones were copies of Spanish originals stored in Seville) took me back to the discovery. They gave me a sense of a crowded aboriginal Indian island, busy about its own affairs, and almost without relation to what I had known. A sense, rather than a vision: little was convincingly described in those early documents, and few concrete details were given. In my mind's eye I created an imaginary landscape for the aboriginal peoples living—on what was to become my own ground—with ideas I couldn't enter, ideas of time, distance, the past, the natural world, human existence. A different weather seemed to attach to this vanished landscape (like the unnatural weather in an illuminated painted panorama in a museum glasscase), a different sky.

The landscape I had grown up in, and felt myself part of, had been wiped clean of this other past. I had always known that, but I hadn't been able to feel it as something that had really happened. In the first book of *Nelson's West Indian History,* by Captain Daniel of the Trinidad Education Department, a textbook we used at the elementary school in Port of Spain, there was a short early chapter about the Caribs and the Arawaks. Perhaps very little was known about those people; perhaps Captain Daniel didn't have much to play with. I remember nothing of what he wrote—except that the Caribs were fierce and the Arawaks gentle—and have no memory even of the illustrations he used. Because they had ceased to exist, and were not real, the aboriginals of our own island offered less to the imagination than the still living people we read about in *Homes Far Away* in the geography class: Kirghiz in shady black tents on their boundless, empty steppes, Eskimos crawling in and out of their warm ice igloos, Africans in their stockades at night, safe against marauding lions and other wild animals.

The idea of a recent wiped-out past was too big for a child in an elementary school to grasp. Later it became difficult in another way. As soon as you tried to enter that idea, it ramified. And it ramified more and more as your understanding grew: different people living for centuries where we now trod, with our own overwhelming concerns: different people, with their own calendar and reverences and ideas of human association, different houses or huts, different roads or paths, different crops and fields and vegetation (and seasons), different views, speeds, reasons for journeys, different ideas of the ages of man, different ideas of the enemy and fellowship and sanctity and what men owed themselves.

In this way, leaving aside the primary notion of cruelty, the idea of a wiped-out, complete past below one's feet quickly became almost metaphysical. The world appeared to lose some of its substance; reality became fluid. It was more natural to let go, to let the mind spring back to an everyday, ground-level vision that took in only what could be seen.

It was easier in London, separated by many years and some thousands of miles from that ground-level view, and while I read in the British Museum and the Public Record Office, to feel the truth of the other, aboriginal island. From that distance, from that other side, as it were, the landscape of the aboriginal island became fabulous. And it was that landscape—which I wrote about without actually seeing—that I half looked for whenever afterwards I went back to Trinidad.

I found it mainly on the coast, and sometimes in glimpses of the Gulf and the North Coast from certain hills above Port of Spain. I found it inland once, after a highway had been driven through the lower hills of the Central Range. The land here, too broken for fields and roads, would always have been covered by forest or woodland or bush. Now it was stripped, shaved down to a kind of rough grass, and all its ridges and hollows were revealed. It looked unused. It was like another landscape; it was like a bit of the past just revealed and still fresh.

Over land like this, perhaps over this very spot, an Elizabethan nobleman, with thirty soldiers from his ship, all in armour, had gone one night on a long march looking for Indian gold. The hills and ravines and the vegetable debris of the tropical forest—near here, on land now shaved to grass—made marching very hard. To terrorize the Indians, the intruders blew trumpets and fired off their muskets. The Indians ran from their houses; in one village they even left food cooking ("seething") on fires. The soldiers ate the food. They found no gold, though the nobleman thought he saw gold-dross at the bottom of an Indian pot. Later—to complete this New World romance—the soldiers thought they heard Indian war-pipes in the forest. No misadventure befell them, however; and in the morning they marched back to the coast and their ship.

What the food in the Indian village was, whether maize or cassava or potato or meat or fish, how it was seasoned, the pots it seethed in, what the fireplaces were like, and the houses—none of this is known. Captain Wyatt, who wrote an account of the expedition, had no eye for that kind of detail. He had strong literary tastes, and had his own idea of what should be written about. He knew parts of *The Spanish Tragedy,* a new London play, by heart; in the New World, on the Gulf shore of Trinidad, or in the forests, he saw his general and himself and the soldiers (and the Spanish enemy, and the Indians in the forest) as figures in a romance of chivalry.

The expedition itself—which took back loads of marcasite sand to England as "gold ore"—was an absurdity; and Wyatt's account was too inflated. It wasn't published. It was forgotten, and, with it, Wyatt's account of the night march which, remarkably, provides the only witness—the houses, the fires, the cooking pots, the war-pipes in the night—of the still autonomous aboriginal life of the island. When Wyatt's account was at last published, in London in 1899, in a scholarly series, three hundred and four years after the event, the aboriginal Indians had ceased to exist for almost a century; and their grounds had become home for other people.

Three centuries for Wyatt's witness to be disinterred; and seventy years or so after that for the aboriginal land, hidden below bush, to be exposed.

Once exposed, the land quickly altered. People from agricultural villages near and far began to squat on it. Many of these squatters were Indians, Hindus and Muslims, descendants of nineteenth-century immigrants from India. The huts or shacks they put up were on low stilts. The sloping roofs were of corrugated iron; the walls were of hollow clay bricks or timber, sometimes new timber, sometimes old, with irregular patches of old paint. Banana trees grew around these huts. Outside the Hindu houses there were prayer flags or pennants on tall bamboo poles. These were put up after certain religious ceremonies: emblems of piety (sometimes competitive, hut against hut): pleas for good luck. Away from the coast, it was hard to hold on to the idea of the aboriginal and fabulous. What was familiar, the small-island colonial geography one had grown up in, was stronger.

IT WAS different when I crossed the Gulf to Venezuela. Geographically, Trinidad was an outcrop of Venezuela; for three hundred years they had been part of the same province of the Spanish empire. The book of history I had written about Trinidad was also to some extent about Venezuela. When I wrote the book I hadn't been to Venezuela. I did that not long afterwards, and the land I saw then remained touched with fable; no personal memories or associations got in the way.

The Orinoco remained the river of my story. Even in the Araya Peninsula on the Caribbean coast—a desolation of eroded red earth and scrub, where the modern road simply crumbled away to nothing at a certain point (no one had told me, and the Venezuelan driver was also surprised)—I found something of the special atmosphere I had hoped to find.

In the late sixteenth century the salt-pans of Araya were famous, and Dutch and French and English ships were always here, illegally, though with the quiet approval of local Spanish officials. Every kind of Spanish suggestion was made for stopping the trade in Araya salt. One governor wanted to poison the salt-pans, and wrote to the king of Spain to ask for poison. In 1604, to survey these waters and say what might be done, there appeared a Spanish nobleman with a very famous name: the Duke of Medina-Sidonia, entrusted with this minor task (among others) sixteen years after the defeat of the great Spanish Armada, which he had commanded.

Pelicans—only sign of life and community in the desolation—flew in fishing groups not far above the sea. They would have flown in that kind of formation four hundred years before, or a thousand years before. Their awkward, prehistoric shape, their power, their grey-brown colour, which was the colour of the beachless sea, the light, the unstable colours at midday of water and sky and barren earth, all this seemed to take me back to the beginning of things.

In other parts of Venezuela I found tropical woodland like the woodland I had got to know as a child and thought very special.

During the war, for two years or so after my eighth birthday, we moved from the town to the forested hills to the north-west of Port of Spain. This was an area of old cocoa and citrus estates, half derelict after various kinds of plant disease and the long Depression. At that time I thought of myself as a town boy; I didn't like the idea of the country. But this wasn't the kind of country I had known, and I liked it as soon as I saw it: the cool green hills, the narrow valleys, the emptiness, the general feeling of forest and bush.

The bush was full of surprises, found objects, remains of the old estate: avocado and citrus trees, coffee bushes and tonka-bean trees (the tonka bean used for flavouring cocoa) and cocoa trees that in spite of disease and choking bush still bore fruit. Somewhere in the cocoa woods was the old concrete cistern of the estate house. It was useless now, clogged with compacted dirt and sand and dead leaves; but the clear-water spring that had fed the cistern still ran, though in its own rippled channels now, over clean brown sand and between dead leaves. The *samaan* trees that had been planted years before to shade the cocoa trees were now aged, branching giants, themselves overgrown with moss-hung parasites: wild pines, lianas, ferns, vines. When you walked below the trees you could feel a dust, from dried moss and other dead vegetable matter, drifting down. We lived disordered, deprived, and uncomfortable lives; we were like campers in someone else's ruins; and we were glad to go back to the town when the time came. But then I grew to understand that those months in the cocoa wilderness had given me my most intense experience of the beauty of the natural world. They had fixed for me the idea of the perfect tropical landscape.

The place itself soon changed. We ourselves had been there at a moment of change. We had been part of the change, and this change speeded up after we left. The area—which we had known as an area of *'pagnols,* patois-speaking Spanish mulattoes connected with the old estates—began to be settled by poor blacks, many of them illegal immigrants, from the small islands to the north. It became crowded and noisy and confused, like the hillside slums to the east of Port of Spain.

That was what was presented to me—suddenly, completely—when I went there again after my first six years abroad. The tops of the green hills, too steep to be damaged, were as I remembered them; the bush on one side of the road was still there; but on the other side of the road, where there was no bush or woodland, only settlement, I could no longer work out the contours of the land and couldn't tell where old things, even the old estate house, or the formal gardens, or the cistern in the woods, had been. Half the landscape I had cherished was still miraculously there, on one side of the road; but that only added to my memory of what had been erased. I took care after that to stay away. I didn't like even getting near the road (itself much changed) that led to the valley.

And now in Venezuela in many places I found again the vegetation and colours of that Trinidad valley. In Venezuela at that time, with its oil boom and city-property boom, estates and plantations were being neglected; and I was able to rediscover the very atmosphere of the cocoa woods I had known. Once for many miles I drove beside such a cocoa wood. There had been nothing in Trinidad on this scale; and nothing like the smell of vanilla—from the vanilla vine—which was now added to the damp cocoa-wood smell of earth and leaf and mould.

Trinidad was an outcrop of the South American continent. Venezuela was part of the continent, and everything was on a continental scale. The geography that at one time in Trinidad had seemed logical and complete—and had then, because of the growth in population, begun to feel like a constriction—was here immeasurably magnified: the mighty Andes for our little Northern Range, now built up on its lower slopes for many miles, and scaffolded with immigrant shacks around Port of Spain; the empty Venezuelan *llanos*, a country in itself, for our sugar-cane plain, which from certain high points could be taken in at a glance; the wonder of the many-branched Orinoco for the single channel of our narrow Caroni.

Because I had written about it, because for many months Venezuela had existed for me as an imaginary country, created in my mind from the documents I read in London, I felt I had a claim on it. Over a number of journeys I began to think of Venezuela as a kind of restored homeland.

I went on week-long drives along the coast and across the *llanos*. On my second or third journey I went in an open boat on the Orinoco at a point near the estuary. This landscape had existed for so long in my imagination that even now, when I was seeing it for the first time, it seemed to have a half-imagined, formal quality. The river was wide, full, without turbulence. The banks were worn and denuded: no forest. It was the rainy season. The sky was grey and dark grey, with many layers of cloud, but there was almost a dazzle on the water because of the openness. The river surface (though muddy close to, and oily near the bank) was as grey as the sky, and smooth.

The air was heavy: more rain was going to come. It came sooner than I thought—with a roar, and with a noticeable river swell. Big drops spattered on the water as though on concrete, and the boatman turned back to the bank.

It would have been like the rain, constant violent bursts alternating with damp heat, that tormented Raleigh when he was on the river in 1595. In the documents of the region, he is the first man to write in a modern way—or in a way that brings him close to us—of the many small physical discomforts of this kind of exploration. Spaniards before Raleigh had made journeys twenty times as hard on this river, but in their matter-of-fact accounts, plain to the point of being abstract, physical sensation is missing; landscape is missing. The endurance of these earlier men goes with a narrower way of seeing and feeling.

Not far away from here was an abandoned oil camp. It was like a little ghost town. The bush that some years before had been cut down and regulated was now growing fast again (with here and there a vigorous flower shrub from the settlement) over half-stripped derricks, oil pipes, roofless wooden barracks and roofless concrete-pillared bungalows. Concrete-and-metal bases, and a concentrated mess of old oil, dulled to sepia, showed where the pumps had been. For years, while there had been oil to extract, the big metal arms or shoulders of those pumps would have done their measured, creaking see-saw, night and day, with a plunging, sighing sound at the end of each movement.

Oil had turned out to be the true gold of the region. In the beginning, in the 1920s and 1930s, many people from Trinidad were recruited to work as labourers and artisans and clerks in the Venezuelan oilfields. I don't know whether this was because Venezuelans simply didn't want to work in camps in the bush; or whether, after a full century of destructive civil wars, they were without the skills; or whether—as in the Trinidad oilfields, or, earlier in the century, in the building of the Panama Canal—the contracting companies preferred to deal with an immigrant workforce that it could more easily control. But Trinidadians were recruited, and in the oil camps of Venezuela (even with their colonial atmosphere) many of these Trinidadians got their first taste of freedom and money, their first glimpse of possibility.

Until this time Venezuela had a bad reputation in Trinidad, as a South American country of war and poverty, lawlessness, uncertainty, overnight revolutions, dictatorships and sadism. Refugees were constantly coming over; the British laws of the colony offered political asylum. Now, with the oil, Venezuela became a country of opportunity. That was how it was thought of in the 1940s, when I was growing up. But by then Trinidadians were not recruited to work in Venezuela. Venezuela was looking to Europe for its immigrants; there were immigration laws to keep Trinidadians out.

Still, they went. They went illegally. As a boy I used to hear of people going over in this way. With my Port of Spain ideas of our small-scale colonial geography—in which the Gulf of Paria was little more than what I could see of it from the city—I used to think that the people going over illegally would have crossed the few miles to Venezuela at the north of the Gulf, just to the west of Port of Spain. I imagined them getting into their rowing boats at dusk or at night and drifting with the strong currents to the Venezuelan shore.

That was fantasy. But I never asked how the crossing was made, and it was only now, half a life later, and long after I had written my book, and after my own Venezuelan travel, that I began to see that the illegal-immigrant way to Venezuela would have been the old aboriginal way, which in the late sixteenth century became the way used by explorers and traders: down to the far south of the Gulf, and then up the intricate channels of the immense Orinoco estuary—never easy to police.

One afternoon, not long after my short adventure on the Orinoco in an open boat, I came to an estuary town. It had been raining; the main street was sodden, with water in puddles, as though river water had risen up through the earth itself; the air was full of moisture. "The drowned lands of the Orinoco"—the words of an old document came to me. Behind the damp concrete fences flower plants and shrubs and small trees I had known in Trinidad made little jungles around the low houses.

Here and there along this street there came, unexpectedly, through all the damp, the smell of a heavy meat curry. Indians from Trinidad lived here; they were an important part of the local population.

Once aboriginal Indians were masters of these waters. They no longer existed; and that knowledge of currents and tides had passed to their successors. On the south-westernmost point of the long Trinidad peninsula that almost ran into the river estuary there had been an aboriginal port or anchoring place called Curiapan. Curiapan was known to the early Spaniards, and known to Raleigh and others. There was still a fishing village there. But Curiapan no longer existed as a name; the village had a Spanish name, Cedros, the Cedars. Many of the fishermen of Cedros were Asian Indians, descendants of agricultural people from the Gangetic Plain. In less than a hundred years the geography of their new home had remade these Asian Indian people of Cedros, touched them with old aboriginal aptitudes, and given them sea skills which their landlocked ancestors had never had.

I had seen from the air the confusion and the great extent of the waters and the drowned lands of the estuary, and had marvelled at everyone who had come there in the old days, without maps. Because—on the ground, as a traveller—I had approached the estuary from the other side of the Gulf, from the interior of a country that for very long had been for me only an imagined place, I had arrived at a way of looking that contained both the fabulous past and the smaller scale of what I had grown up with.

I had grown up with a small-island geography in my head. But the Gulf I had looked out on as a child was far bigger than the island. The Gulf, with its confused currents, between an island and the estuary of a continental river, had always been part of the fabulous New World. Columbus had found salt water and fresh in it, and—thinking himself only between two islands—had never known why. It had other, and now mysterious, names: Golfo de las Ballenas, the Gulf of Whales, and—like a name that goes back to the beginning— Golfo Triste, the Sad Gulf.

Now I could without disturbance fit Raleigh's 1595 map of the Gulf to what I saw. His map was the wrong way round. South was at the top of the page: it made more sense that way, to a man looking for a way down to the Orinoco. You can look at the map and see what was real and what— from the formality of the shapes: hard in maps absolutely to lie or to invent—he was making up.

USUALLY, WHEN I made these trips to Venezuela, I went first to Trinidad. From there after a few days, in a plane with a more local atmosphere, I did the hour-long flight across the Gulf and over the Venezuelan Caribbean coast to Maiquetía, the airport for Caracas.

It was on one such flight, on a Venezuelan aeroplane, that I met Manuel Sorzano. This was about fifteen years ago.

He had the window seat. I had the aisle seat next to him. Though he had gone aboard only a couple of minutes ahead of me, he looked quite established when I saw him. There were a number of parcels disposed about his feet, in spite of the regulations, and a few more in the locker above. Unusual, this sign that he had been shopping in Trinidad. In those days, of the oil boom, when there was money on both sides of the Gulf, the shopping traffic usually went the other way, to Caracas, with its skyscrapers and glittering commercial centres.

He was a small, elderly brown man, perhaps in his late fifties. His face, carefully shaven, was broad and wrinkled, with a closed expression that held just a hint of aggression. My first quick assessment—while I put away my own things—was that he was an out-and-out Venezuelan, a coastal mestizo, a product of a racial mixture that had started with the Spanish settlement, someone who had known only his own landscape and limited language and his own way of life, and was cut off from everything else.

Later I took in an unexpected touch of style in the old man: his curly hair was plaited and tied at the back into a tight little pigtail about an inch long. It gave him a piratical, eighteenth-century appearance. And I thought, though I hadn't actually noticed it before, that the pigtail might have affected my first reading of his face, and made me see an aggression that perhaps wasn't really there. But no: the pigtail was part of something a little too assertive about the man: below the buttoned cuffs of his shirt I could now see heavy gold or gilt bracelets, of linked big coins.

What was he taking back to Venezuela? I could see some long-playing records, in a plastic shopping bag; and, in a plaited raffia basket, label-less bottles and jars of Trinidad Indian pickles. Those pickles looked home-made. Had I mis-read him, then? Was he, after all, an Asian Indian from Trinidad, with ideas and assumptions I could intuit—and not the Venezuelan stranger I had taken him for? I considered his appearance. He was unusual. He could be one thing or the other: it depended on what you thought he was.

I asked him, "Are you from Trinidad?"

"No. Venezuela." He was firm. But his accent was of Trinidad.

We were now airborne, and in a few minutes were flying low over the Gulf, so much bigger than I had thought thirty or forty years before, a little sea, with for some time no sight of land on either side. The water was of different shades of olive, in wide, distinct, irregular bands, sometimes frothing white or yellow at the edges: Orinoco and Atlantic in eternal conflict, mighty volumes of water pressing against each other.

I asked, "Where in Venezuela do you live?"

"All over. My work take me all over. Presently I am in Ciudad Guayana. But I know all over. Barquisimeto, Tucupita, Maracaibo, Ciudad Bolívar. Even Margarita for a time."

He seemed to love the sound of the place names: it was as though to speak the names was to have a claim on the places.

I said, "Ciudad Bolívar used to be called Angostura. It was where they first made the bitters."

I thought the fact romantic, and thought it would appeal to him. He paid no attention. I let go; I didn't try to think of new things to say.

We had then to fill in disembarkation cards.

He said, "You have to give me a little hand with this. I don't have my glasses."

He took out his passport. It was Venezuelan, reddish brown, and he handled it very carefully (the way I handled my own British passport, always nervous, when I was travelling, of losing it, and doubting whether, if I lost it, I would be able to explain myself to anyone in authority). He passed it to me, and I saw his photograph, and his name, Manuel Sorzano. I knew the name Sorzano from the late eighteenth-century Venezuelan records. It was a good solid Venezuelan name then; but perhaps Venezuela was full of Sorzanos. The occupation of this Sorzano was given as *carpintero*, carpenter.

He took the passport back and put it away. He said he had to get it renewed every year. He did a lot of travelling. The previous year a new passport cost thirty-five bolívares, thirty-five "b's"; this year it was going to cost seventy-five b's. There were two b's to the dollar. He was wrong there; the dollar was worth less than half that; and I thought it strange, in a man who did much travelling and wore heavy gold bracelets, that he didn't know this basic fact about the Venezuelan currency.

Then, as though rewarding me for filling in his disembarkation form and not asking difficult questions, he showed me the new records in the plastic bag. They were of Hindi devotional songs. Some had been done by a Trinidad group, some by a woman singer, Dropati, from Surinam, the former Dutch Guiana.

It was his way of saying that he was an Indian from Trinidad—and at the same time letting me know I wasn't to ask him any more about it. So, once again, his appearance subtly altered; he became what I had been told he was. But though he wasn't the stranger I had thought, he was in some ways still strange, far from me, because of his religious needs, which I didn't have, and his mangled idea (hard to imagine) of the old gods of India, and their due rites.

When the steward offered a snack-tray, Manuel Sorzano refused to have it. He didn't eat meat, he told me, and he didn't drink. I was surprised. I hadn't thought of him as that kind of Hindu. But I didn't really believe him. I thought he had the face of the Trinidad Indian drinking man—the soft, pressed-down lips, the sagging cheeks, the aggressive, watery eyes. But then it occurred to me that he might be doing a penance of some kind; he might have made a religious vow. Perhaps the abstemiousness of which he was making such a show was connected with the funeral rites for someone in his family. Perhaps he had gone back to Trinidad for those rites.

He certainly knew about Trinidad rums. He said he had

been hoping to take back some white rum to Venezuela, but his mind had been "so hot" in the last few days he had forgotten about it. Trinidad white rum was the best thing for a cold.

He said, "You sap a little bit on your head"—he made a delicate sapping gesture with his fingers, and I saw more of his gold-coin bracelet—"and you dab a little bit on your forehead, and the next morning the cold gone."

We had left the Gulf behind. For some time now the Venezuelan Caribbean coast was passing below us, outlined as on a large map, blurred green land, stretches of white or red or brown beach, dark sea, little muddy stains at the mouths of little rivers. Just as space satellites show us a seemingly untouched world, where great cities are mere smudges, so, from the height of this Aeropostal plane, the Spanish Main was still like a new place.

In his earlier life, in Trinidad (his name there not given me, but I thought it would have been a name of the Asian sub-continent), he had had four children. In Venezuela, as Manuel Sorzano, he had nine children, and they all had Venezuelan names.

"It was like choosing names out of a hat. One call Antonio, another one Pedro. The first girl call Dolores. The mother love that name."

Who was the mother of the nine? He said she was an Indian. He meant an Asian Indian. "She talk only Indian."

Hindi had ceased to be a living language in Trinidad or Guyana, and this meant that the mother of Manuel Sorzano's Venezuelan children came from Surinam, the homeland of the Hindi singer Dropati.

Manuel Sorzano said, "I only talk Spanish at home, and the children only talk Spanish."

A new land, a new name, a new identity, a new kind of family life, new languages even (Surinam Hindi would have been different from the Hindi he would have heard in Trinidad)—his life should have been full of stress, but he gave the impression of living as intuitively as he had always done, making his way, surviving, with no idea of being lost or in a void.

But just as it was strange that, with all the travelling he said he did, he didn't know the dollar value of Venezuelan money; so it was strange that, with all his peasant need of what had survived in him, after a century of separation, of the religion of India, and the difficult concept of the deities, and the food and the music, and the reverences, he didn't know that the language the mother of his nine children spoke was Hindi and not "Indian." But perhaps it wasn't strange: living intuitively, he was possessed by what had remained of his ancestral culture. He couldn't stand back from it or assess it; he couldn't acquire external knowledge about it; and it would die with him. He would have no means of passing it on to his children. They had Spanish names and spoke only Venezuelan. These Sorzanos would be quite different; there would be no ambiguities about them; they would be the kind of Venezuelan stranger I had in the beginning taken their father for.

I wanted to look at his gold-coin bracelet. He took it off and showed it to me. The coins were Victorian sovereigns. He opened his shirt and showed me more: he was wearing a heavy gold necklace with a big gold-coin pendant.

He had found gold in Venezuela: a gold hoard. And he had found it years before, not long after he had got to Venezuela, when he was working as a mixture of carpintero and day-labourer, and was one of a gang of twenty-five pulling down an old building in central Caracas. This was part of the great tearing down and rebuilding of old Caracas—rebuilding with motorways—after the oil. In one room, in a hollow in the mud-brick wall, he and two others had found the hoard, many sovereigns like those on his bracelet, and many coins like the one he now wore around his neck. That coin had been cast in 1824. It was big, intended to be historical, a statement of certainty, commemorating an event in 1818, the first Congress of the independent South American state that Simón Bolívar had tried to set up. It wasn't a date I carried in my head: the coin was the first token I had seen of the grandeur of the ambition.

From the date of the English sovereigns it seemed that the hoard would have been hidden some time in the 1860s. So just thirty years or so after the coin had been struck, to mark the end of an old empire, an old order, and to bless the new, the coin had to be hidden away. In Venezuela and elsewhere in South America a century of disorder had followed the destruction of the Spanish empire. In 1869 the English writer Charles Kingsley, a great naturalist, in Trinidad for the winter, reported that there were no ships going up the Orinoco; that only one verminous vessel went from Port of Spain to La Guaira, the port for Caracas; and that after all the years of conflict life and property were still not safe in Caracas.

And just as the buriers of treasure at the time of the break-up of the Roman empire could have had no idea of the twists of history, the further great migrations, that would one day lead people unknown to them, people beyond their imagining, to turn up the treasure they had laid up for brighter days; so those people in old Caracas, at a time of darkness, amassing (almost certainly by plunder) a secret hoard of sovereigns and gold coins, could have had no idea of the twists of history that would lead Manuel Sorzano, whose ancestors in the 1860s had not yet left India, to come upon their gold.

He said, "Is how I buy my own house. I don't have to put up with anybody bossing me around."

I began to wonder whether that piece of luck—his wish to keep it or renew it or not to lose it—wasn't bound up with his abstemiousness now, following perhaps upon some religious vow (marked, it may be, in Trinidad or Venezuela, by prayer flags in a garden).

I passed my thumb again over the coin commemorating the Angostura Congress. It was still so new, the raised letters of its vainglorious legend still sharp.

By a strange coincidence, the year in which it was struck, 1824, was the year in which, in that same Orinoco river town of Angostura, Dr. Siegert first produced his aromatic bitters. Some years afterwards the Venezuelan chaos, sweeping away the promise of the Congress, drove Dr. Siegert and his secret formula across the Gulf to Trinidad. As a British colony, Trinidad provided peace and commercial opportunity; at the same time, as a geographical outcrop of Venezuela, it provided all the tropical herbs and plants and fruits of Dr. Siegert's formula. The town of Angostura in Venezuela was renamed after Bolívar; and now Angostura lived on as a name in the world not because of the Congress which the coin commemorated, but because of the bitters, made elsewhere.

I hefted the necklace again, to feel the weight of the gold, and gave it back to him.

I said, "I would be worried to carry that around."

He made a little bow, and slipped the necklace over his neck with the swift practised gesture of a priest assuming a ritual upper garment. He gave two or three pats over the scattered twists of grey-black hair on his loose-skinned, old man's chest, to settle the coin below his singlet; and he buttoned up his shirt.

"Is only like a souvenir for me. It safer like this than in the bank. If I take it to the bank, they would put me in jail. Is what happen to the two other fellows with me. Negro fellows, not from the islands, but from a place called Barlovento. A lot of old-time plantations there, and a lot of Venezuelan black people."

It was one of the places in Venezuela where I had found

again the vegetation of the little cocoa valley of my childhood. The old plantation barracks and the community of very black people (many of them working in the town now) had been a surprise. But Barlovento—the word meant "windward," and to me was of the Caribbean—was also where one day I had driven for miles beside an unkempt cocoa estate with tall shade trees, through a smell of vanilla.

Manuel Sorzano said, "As soon as those black fellows see the coins, they just want to stuff their pockets and run. I tell them no, they will get catch. At first they listen to me, but then they begin to feel that I want to deny them something. So they just stuff their pockets and run. I stay behind, taking my time. I prise out a few more bricks, looking for a little more, and even finding a little more. Very quiet I start fulling my food-carrier. Three round enamel bowls one on top the other, in a metal frame or cage, with a handle on the top. I full that, the rice and bread and other food keeping the coins very quiet, and I keep my eye on it and went on working in another room, with other fellows, till it was time to knock off. When I leave the site with that food-carrier I was like a man walking on glass, I was so frighten of falling. In the evening I take the coins somewhere else. In the morning I went back to work, very quiet, making no fuss, and that same day we knock down the room where we find the coins. I just keep on doing my work, and sure enough in the afternoon five or six Guardia Nacional men come. They start going through the site like crazy ants. They not saying what they come for, but I know they looking for a room that already knock down. It was because of the black fellows. You wouldn't believe what they do. They feel that all the gold make them important, and they take the coins to one of the biggest banks in Caracas, where everybody wearing suits. Imagine. Black fellows from Barlovento, dress the way they dress, talking with their twang, and going into this big quiet air-condition bank and saying they have gold coins. Of course the people in the bank call the Guardia, and the fellows get lock up and beat up, and they lose everything."

I said, "I hear the Guardia can be rough."

"Well, yes." But then Manuel Sorzano appeared to change sides. "They have a lot of rough people to deal with. And if you want to answer back like a man, you have to take what you get."

A little while later he said, "My son Antonio is in the Guardia. Ever since he small, he want to be in the Guardia."

I said, "The uniform, the gun, the jeep."

"And the accommodation. You mustn't forget that. They can have very nice quarters. Antonio always particular about that kind of thing. I remember an incident that happen some years back. This was in Puerto La Cruz. I was working on a hotel there. I went out in the car with the children and their mother one Saturday afternoon. They was having some kind of fair on the sea road. Suddenly I hear a siren, and this Guardia Nacional jeep start pushing me off the road. When I stop, one of the Guardia men jump in the car with a revolver in his hand. As soon as he see the mother and the children, this man—who was ready to hit me with the butt of the revolver—get very bashful and confused. He say, '*Disculpe, disculpe, señora.* Pardon, pardon, lady.' And he jump out again. For some weeks Antonio make that into a kind of game. Running about the yard and the house, pretending he have a gun and saying, '*Disculpe, disculpe, señora.*' "

We were flying lower now over the coast.

Looking out of the window, showing me his profile with the pigtail, Manuel Sorzano said, after a silence, "The boy a lot in my thoughts these days. He having a little trouble."

"The boy in the Guardia?"

"Yes. Antonio. I don't mean 'trouble' trouble. But it

serious. And is not something where I can help him. Two years or so ago he start living with a young girl. First woman I know him to have. He was very bashful about it, but after a while he wanted me to know, and I went up to see them. This was in a town on the Orinoco. The girl was very young and small, fair-skin Venezuelan type. About fifteen or sixteen, that's what I thought. She was full of respect when I was there and didn't say too much, and I was too shy to look too hard at her, to tell you the truth. When the time come for me to leave them, she come and kiss me on my cheek and I put my hand on her shoulder. No, not her shoulder. The top part of her arm. That give me a surprise. She wasn't soft at all. She was hard like a man, and she was so small. Was what I remember more than anything, and I think about it all the way back, thinking, 'What kind of hard life they put that poor girl through? What kind of hard work they make this little child do?' When I get home the mother ask me, 'What you think of the child? The child all right?' She mean the little girl. I say yes. She say, 'What type?' I say, ' *'Pagnol* type.' I didn't want to tell her anything else.

"And then the usual thing happen. I say usual, but it not usual when it happen to you. Antonio was on a murder case one day. He had to go out to a ranch far out of town. Cattle ranch. Foreign people. Antonio hate that place. They build those big concrete sheds, and with all that land, and in all that heat, they keep the cattle pen up tight, and they feeding them chicken-shit and molasses. It had to end in murder. Antonio should have been out the whole day, but something happen and he come back early in the afternoon.

"Let me tell you now that there was a Syrian store in this town. The Syrian man live upstairs, but he also have a little quinta, a house with a little land, just outside the town. As he was coming back to the town Antonio see the little girl leaving the quinta with the Syrian man. He get *'basourdi* when he see that. As though somebody drop a sack of flour on his head.

"He couldn't bear going home. He went to the station and spend a couple of hours there. Then he went home. The girl was there now. She was in the yard. She was in a little open shed, with a concrete floor, with ferns in hanging baskets and plants in pots. A nice, cool place where she do her washing, and where they also sit out sometimes. She was doing something with the plants. He didn't say anything to her. He just stop in the yard, in the sun, and look at her, only at her face, and not at what she was doing. And as soon as she look at him she know she was in trouble.

"She left the plants and went to the house, to the kitchen. He went there too, and he sit down in the kitchen and now he look at the table. She leave the kitchen. He get up and draw his revolver and follow her. He follow her from room to room, from kitchen to drawing room to bedroom to gallery, waiting for when his finger would pull the trigger. She didn't try to run out of the house. Thank God. Otherwise the finger would have pulled the trigger. Then she stop walking. He come right up to her and she scream at him, 'You don't know how these Syrians like to take advantage of little girls? Why you don't go and kill him?'

"The words cut him like a knife. 'Taking advantage,' 'little girls'—the words cut him up. He get sad and foolish. He know he can't bear to kill her. He go to the little bedroom and lie down on the bed, in his uniform. The window open, the half-curtain hardly blowing. It still hot. He feel very peaceful, and he start sleeping right away. It nearly dark when he wake up, and he feel he come from far away. He stay lying down, smelling a neighbour frying fish, and he feel very peaceful, smelling that smell, and hearing the little noises from the houses all around. The noises sound as though they come from very far away. As he wake up a little bit more he know he feeling peaceful because he don't have to spoil his life or anybody else life. He don't have to do anything.

"It very dark when he get up. The house dark. He just seeing the few lights from the neighbours. It dark in the yard, dark in the shed outside, with the ferns in the hanging baskets, and the plants, and the chairs on the concrete. Nothing cooking in the kitchen, nobody outside. He alone in the house. The girl not there. She gone. He start walking through the house, round and round. He don't put on the lights. He walk in the dark.

"He go to the toilet. Then he go out in the dark yard. He walk about a little. Then he straighten himself, straighten his uniform, and pat the revolver in his holster. He get into his car and drive to the centre of the town, to the big park on the riverside.

"The river run on one side of the park. The Syrian shop is in a road on the other side. The road have a covered sidewalk with concrete columns at the side and a lot of advertisements one on top of the other on the columns. Is a long shop, with two wide doorways, but this evening one of the doors close. When Antonio go in he see the Syrian man at the far end of the counter, standing like a policeman in front of the shelves with the bolts of cheap cloth. He standing below a very dim hanging bulb, chatting and laughing with the people he cheating.

"Antonio study the laughing man and say to himself, 'Go on and laugh now. You going to stop laughing soon.' He check that the revolver there at his waist. He don't take it out, because this time he not going to wait for it to go off. This time when he take it out he going to use it. He start moving down from the open door. The Syrian man turn, and when he see the Guardia uniform he look a little respectful.

"In his own mind Antonio start talking to the Syrian man: 'Good. You showing respect. But is not enough to

show respect. I want to see the fright in your eyes. I want to
see your eyes when you start begging. That is when I will
send you home.'

"The Syrian man recognize Antonio. He don't look
shocked. He don't look frightened. He look vexed. Then he
look at Antonio with hate. That throw Antonio. Is as though
the Syrian man don't understand how serious the moment
is. The people in the shop understand, though. They stop
talking, and they stand aside for Antonio to walk between
them. He walk up to the counter, and the Syrian man now
look at him with scorn. All this time the Syrian man don't
move.

"And now a funny thing happen. In his mind Antonio
stop talking to the Syrian man, and he start talking to himself.
'Why this man scorn me so? Somebody tell him something.
I can't send this man home when his heart so full of scorn for
me. The girl tell him something, to give him this strength
over me. What she tell him?' All kinds of private things pass
through his head. The power flow out of him, and he begin
to feel cold, standing there in the shop. He begin to feel he
want to cry. The Syrian man say, 'Yes, Pepe?' Calling him
Pepe to insult him, in front of the other people, even though
he wearing his uniform. And Antonio could only turn and
leave.

"Somehow he live through the next few days. He send
a message to me, asking me to come and see him. I find
him in a state, and the house in a state. Is only the second
time I see the house. The first time they had it so nice for
me. The girl was in her nice clothes, and she was respectful.
Now she not there, and everything that I see make me think
of her. The little shed in the yard, with the plants and the
ferns, make me think of her. It was there that we sit out and
take tea.

"So when Antonio tell me the story I feel in my own
self a little bit of what he feel. He say he think he will have

to leave the Guardia—he too mash up inside to do that kind of work now. He start crying. I don't know what to tell him. Though I miss the girl and feel a little bit of what he feel, I don't have the experience to tell him anything. I can't tell him what to do to get people to like him or to stay with him.

"I grow up in the old days, with different ways. The older people used to look after that side for you. When I was twenty-two—it was the war, and I was working on the American base at Cumuto—my father just say to me one Friday when I come home for the weekend, 'You getting too damn big. Is high time you get married. I have my eye on one or two girls for you. I will go and talk to the families.' And that was that. I was a big man on the base, working with the Americans and everything, but I wasn't man enough to tell my father no. Before I could turn around, I have a wife and I start having children. It was like something that just happen to me, like something somebody give me. I didn't go out looking for it.

"And you could say something like that happen again after I cut loose from over there and bust it to here. I was living a runaway kind of life in Maturín, and I used to take my meals with this Indian family. I never talk nice to the daughter. I hardly talk to her at all. Somehow I just move in with them, and then she move out with me, and everybody agree, and nobody talk too much. And I must tell you I never touch the lady until we start living together.

"The funny thing is, as the children start growing up, it wasn't the boys I worry about so much as the girls. We can't arrange anything for them here, and they don't want anything old-fashioned like that. They want the modern way, to choose their own, and you know how girl children foolish. One piece of sweet talk, and their head turn. And when a girl have a child, that isn't something she can take back. Good or bad, is what she have, and her life follow that direction. But

Dolores and the other girl was all right. They have the right kind of looks, and they get a lot of offers, and they could pick and choose, and they settle down. And I know the other girls going to be all right, because that good example set.

"Was different for the boys. The girls could just sit and wait. The boys have to go out and get. They have to be men in a new way, and they don't really know what to do. They don't have the example from me. They just copying people outside without really understanding. And is extra hard for them, because all the time they still have the old-fashioned bashfulness which they get from me.

"It was easier for Antonio to get into the Guardia than for him to get that girl, and then he was so bashful about it he didn't tell me for a long time. He wasn't being sly. He wasn't worried about the girl. He just bashful. He feel it wouldn't be showing me respect, it would look as though he running me competition.

"And when he tell me, and I go to see them, I too was so damn bashful I can't bring myself to look the girl in the face, and Antonio so bashful he pretending he hardly know the girl. The only person who not bashful is the girl. And I think afterwards that all I know of the girl is what I see, that the girl is really a stranger, and that Antonio don't know much more about her either. And I feel now, as he and I talk in the house, that this is part of the mess he is in.

"We talk all day, and we talk until late at night. We talk and talk. We say the same things ten, twelve times, and then we start all over again, he is in such a state.

"I tell him God was with him that day, when his finger didn't pull the trigger, and then when he walk out of the Syrian man shop. I tell him that he don't really know the girl, and he can't talk of shame and disgrace. He must only think he make a mistake with her. The next time he wouldn't make a mistake. The girl probably make her own mistakes already, and the Syrian man, too. Everybody going out to look for boy friend and girl friend among strangers must make a mistake. And my feeling is that in the end what is really for you you will get.

"I say, 'I never had the kind of excitement in my life that you and your generation looking for in yours. Yours is the modern way, and I must tell you I jealous you a little bit for it, for the freedom it give. But if you want this kind of excitement, you have to pay the price. Other people must have their excitement and freedom too. You can't tie them down. You can't start thinking of fair and unfair. Once you start looking for this excitement, you have to put away this idea of fair and unfair.'

"So we sit down in the dark, in the shed with the fern baskets and the plants, talking and talking, and I search my mind for things to say to him, some true, some half true.

"People passing in the road all the time. They are like shadows against the lights of the other houses. I suppose some of them pick up the drama by now, and they know that the Guardia Nacional man and his father sitting and talking about the little girl and the Syrian man. I feel I can tell when people know. They don't want to look, and they walk as though they don't want to make any noise. They treat the house as though it is a house of sickness. Nobody mock. It is a side of the people here I never know about or had cause to look for, and it make me appreciate and respect them.

"I feel that as we talk, and as he get more and more tired, Antonio start calming down. But every now and then he break down and say that he will have to leave the Guardia. I don't really believe him now, but at the same time I have the feeling that, just because I am taking his grief very seriously, and because he is calmer, and because of all the sympathy he must know he is getting from the neighbours, he might want to show off and do something dramatic. I feel this is the most dangerous time.

"I tell him, 'I will say some prayers for you.'

"The idea did just come to me. And as soon as I say it, I see it was the right thing to say. He know that I have special prayers in mind. He don't know much about these prayers, but he know they are very important to his mother, and I take them seriously too.

"I say to him, 'I want you to promise that you won't do anything until I say these prayers for you.'

"He don't say anything, but I feel he agree. And that take a weight off my mind."

The special prayers Manuel Sorzano meant were readings from the Hindu scriptures. They required a pundit chanting in Sanskrit (or what in this far-off part of the world passed for Sanskrit), sitting in front of a low, decorated earthen altar, stuck with a young banana tree, and with sugar and clarified butter burning on an aromatic pitch-pine fire: old emblems of fertility and sacrifice. These prayers couldn't be arranged in Venezuela: Manuel Sorzano had had to return to Trinidad, where in an earlier life he had had another, and now unspoken, name. It was from those prayers that he was now returning, freshly cleansed in his own mind, not eating meat and not drinking, with the souvenir raffia basket with the jars and bottles of lime pickle and mango pickle and pepper sauce; and with the devotional Hindi records.

He said, "I hope I not coming back to big news." He struck his heart heavily with his braceleted right hand. "I can't tell you how much I feel that I am going to pay now for all my luck here."

Closer and closer below us now the windy grey and white sea, the blocks of flats, the long runways of the airport in the narrow strip of flat land between the sea and the mountains, the scarred red earth, the scores of yellow earth-removing machines, the many small white aeroplanes of the internal Venezuelan airlines, Aeropostal, Avensa, the larger jets of half a dozen international airlines beside the long terminal building: Venezuela of the boom, where in Caracas (reached by long tunnels through those mountains) in the more luxurious commercial centres a shirt could cost a hundred dollars, at a time when in New York a fifty-dollar shirt was an extravagance.

We stood in different immigration queues. As a Venezuelan he was quickly through. He waited for me, noticeable with his pigtail and his souvenir raffia bag.

The immigration official, when I got to him, waved my disembarkation form at me. He was about to say something when a colleague called to him; he called back, absently wrote something on my form, stamped it, stamped my passport, waved me on, and left his desk.

Manuel Sorzano lifted his chin and asked, "What he write on your paper?"

I looked. I had not written what my occupation was—and this was only partly an oversight: at that time writers were suspect: some guerrillas had been misusing the word. In the blank for occupation, the distracted official had written "*Ejecutivo*," executive.

Manuel Sorzano said, "You see why this is a great country? They treat you according to what you show yourself to be. They respect you just as much as you respect yourself. Nowhere else."

A man of the Guardia was looking at us. Manuel Sorzano had noticed, and he had very slightly adjusted his demeanour to show that he was on both sides of authority: a friendly acknowledgement of the uniform, together with a slight rounding of the shoulder to show deference to it.

In the customs hall he said, "But you should be a little careful. We have a few guerrillas here. Two or three times Antonio get involved in a little gunplay with them. One fellow write on his ID card *Director Ejecutivo*, Chief Executive. Boasting, nuh. Word get around, and one bright morning the guerrillas drive up and snatch him just as he was getting in a bus to go to work. A *colectivo*, one of those little private buses where you have to stoop. Everybody so busy scrambling on and minding their head, nobody notice. When they find he have no big company behind him, to pay up, they shoot him. In this country you have to know how to handle yourself."

CHAPTER 8

In the Gulf of Desolation: An Unwritten Story

A T O N E time I thought I should try to do a play or a film—
a film would have been better—about the Gulf. I saw it as a
three-part work: Columbus in 1498, Raleigh in 1618, and
Francisco Miranda, the Venezuelan revolutionary, in 1806:
three obsessed men, well past their prime, each with his own
vision of the New World, each at what should have been a
moment of fulfilment, but really near the end of things, in
the Gulf of Desolation. Separate stories, different people,
changing style of clothes, but the episodes would have developed one out of the other, as in a serial.

Raleigh in 1618, an old, sick man, waiting in the Gulf for
news of the gold mines which he had never seen and which
he no longer believed in, was like Columbus in 1498, complaining in his journal about his bad eyesight and bad health
and bad luck, pleading in advance for the sympathy of his
sovereigns. As he picked his way along the indentations of
this strange Gulf, partly salt, partly fresh, he saw himself
sailing between the island he called The Trinity and another
island (really the South American continent) which he called
the Land of Grace. He was offering place-names as prayers,
and exaggerating the wonder of what he saw. He had already
almost lost his dream of the New World; he knew that things

had gone very wrong with the little Spanish colony he had left behind on the island of Haiti. And at the end of this third journey he was to go back in chains to Spain. Just as Raleigh in 1618, when there was no longer anything to wait for, went back to the Tower and execution.

There is this kind of madness and self-deception—followed by surrender—in the later career of Francisco Miranda, the Venezuelan revolutionary who came before Bolívar. Miranda is not as well known as Columbus or Raleigh. His career is just as fabulous and original, but (for a reason we will come to later) he has no historical myth, and it is necessary at this point to establish his story.

In 1806 Miranda is fifty-six. He has been out of Venezuela for thirty-five years. For more than twenty of those years, in the United States, England and France, he has been touting around an idea of Spanish-American liberation. Technically, he is a deserter from the Spanish army. This means he has been cut off from such family wealth as he has in Venezuela; and he has been living on his wits. The South American revolution—and his potential place at the head of it—is his only asset. In 1805 he panics; he feels that the French under Napoleon might invade the South American continent and that there might be no revolution for him to lead. He leaves England and goes to the United States. With money from a merchant (who is willing to speculate in the revolution) Miranda buys a small ship, recruits two hundred mercenaries, and decides to invade South America.

It is a long, slow journey south. He quarrels with the captain, he quarrels with his recruits, and the invasion is a disaster. In a simple forty-minute action a Spanish ship cuts off and detains the two unarmed schooners that are being used to land fifty-eight of the invaders. Miranda, who has last seen action twenty-five years before, turns and flees in his own ship.

He is succoured by the British authorities in Barbados

and Trinidad. His unpaid, mutinous American recruits are brought to heel; he recruits more men from among the French in Trinidad; and he starts on a fresh invasion. Like Columbus, like Raleigh, he has a sense of history. He issues a proclamation: "The Gulf that Columbus discovered and honoured with his presence will now witness the illustrious action of our gallant efforts."

His proclamations are of another sort when, with covert British naval help this time, he lands without opposition in Venezuela. Local officials who do not give up their allegiance to the Spanish authorities, he says, will be treated as enemies. His idea of revolution is as simple as that. No one comes over to him; people run away from him.

He makes no effort to ransom or to rescue or to bargain for the fifty-eight men he had lost earlier. Ten of them are hanged and quartered, their heads spiked, their remains ceremonially burnt. The others are all shut up in dreadful prisons. Miranda never talks about them or expresses sorrow for them. They were mercenaries, gamblers. If the invasion had come off, they would have had a lot of loot. As it is, they lost; nothing is owed them.

He isn't strong enough—or skilled enough or confident enough—to move inland. After ten days he re-embarks. For some weeks he waits indecisively off the Venezuelan coast. British naval support, never officially authorized, is finally withdrawn; and there is nothing for Miranda to do but return to Trinidad.

For a whole year after this Miranda stays in Trinidad, and he is like a man marooned.

Until nine years before Trinidad was part of Venezuela and the Spanish empire. Now it is a British territory. Most of the island is forest, but it is empty forest: the aboriginal population has almost ceased to exist. Twenty years before, on the site of the old Indian shore settlement of Cumucurapo, the Spaniards had laid out a small Spanish-style town of regularly intersecting straight streets. Most of the residential plots away from the main square are empty and overgrown. Right at the end of the unfinished town, and going back to the hills and the forest on three sides, are the new slave plantations— newer than the town—set up on land that had remained bush for two hundred years, after the disappearance of the aboriginal people.

The planters are refugees from Haiti and the other French-speaking islands to the north. The planters are not all white. There are many mulattoes and blacks among them, and they are known, in the caste language of the time, as "free people of colour"; they are not called Negroes. An unusually high proportion of the slaves in Trinidad are "new Negroes," freshly imported from Africa.

The island now lives by and for these plantations, and away from them there is almost no life. Travel is controlled. There are no wanderers, no floating, free population. There is no place here for a metropolitan man like Miranda. There must have been times during the year when—waiting on developments, and at the mercy of the British government— he would have felt like a prisoner, and wondered whether he would ever get out, leave what had once been part of his native land, and go back to London, to his house and family.

After a long, idle year he does go back. This is where his story should have ended, with this escape from what had once been part of his native land. That would have been irony enough. But he isn't allowed to go out on a dying fall. He is too famous, has been active for too long, has talked too much. Another fate has been prepared for him.

Three years later the real revolution in Venezuela is started by Bolívar and others. They call Miranda out from London. They think they need him. Miranda is the most famous South American or Spanish American of his time; he knows important people in England and the United States. The revolutionaries also believe they need Miranda's military skill: the word among South Americans is that in military matters he is second only to Napoleon. (For eleven years he had been a captain in the Spanish service in Spain, North Africa, and the West Indies. Fleetingly, before he deserted and went to the United States, he was a colonel. But when he got to France he encouraged the French to believe that he had been a general in the American War of Independence; and, in the early days of the French Revolution, he had served for seven months as a general in the revolutionary army, until he was arrested for incompetence.)

So, unexpectedly, after the rout and disgrace and idleness of three years before, there is this complete triumph for Miranda. He lands in Venezuela to a ready-made revolution (such as he has been predicting for twenty years), and is received ceremonially as its leader and hero. For a while everything goes well. The Venezuelan revolution is triumphant, and Miranda as general secures its victories—though his engagements are particularly bloody, and the revolutionary who talks about civil liberty turns out to have a brutal, too assertive side. This brutality is one of the things that make people question the revolution.

Miranda had left Venezuela when he was twenty-one, and in 1810–11 he had been away for nearly forty years. And just as in that time he had made himself over many times—becoming a lover of liberty among the Americans; a revolutionary among the French; a Mexican nobleman and a count among the grandees of the Russia of Catherine the Great; a ruler in exile among the British, a man who could open up a whole continent to British manufactures—so in his projections Venezuela and South America had been steadily adapted to the fantasies of late eighteenth-century European thinkers. The people of the continent deserved the best. Both whites and Indians were worthy of Plato's republic. And then, in a further version of this fantasy, both whites and Indians somehow became Incas, as pure and as noble as the philosophers had judged such people to be.

But the Venezuela in which Miranda now finds himself

isn't like that at all. Venezuela is more like the Trinidad Miranda was lucky to escape from three years before. Venezuela is a colony in the New World, with slave plantations, and it has all the divisions of that kind of place: Spaniards from Spain, who are the officials; a creole Spanish aristocracy; creole Spaniards who are not aristocracy; mulattoes; the Negroes of the plantations; the aboriginal Indians. This kind of place is held together only by a strong external authority. When that external authority goes, people can begin to feel they are sinking. Freedom for one group can mean slavery or oppression for another group.

So the Venezuelan revolution, as it progresses, deepens every racial and caste division in the country, encourages every kind of fear and jealousy; and the revolution begins to fail. The ordinary people of the country begin to go over to the other side, the side of old authority, and the reverences and law and religion they know.

Miranda appeals to the slaves to join him. They don't listen; in fact, as the area controlled by the revolutionaries shrinks, the slaves of Barlovento rebel, and there is a moment when it seems they might capture the capital, Caracas. And now, to buy peace, or at any rate to buy time, some of the very men who had called Miranda out from London, to lead their revolution, decide to hand him to the Spaniards. They wake him up one night and march him to the dungeon of a coastal fort.

That is where it ends for Miranda: the fate he has feared ever since he deserted nearly thirty years before. This fear has grown through all his life as a revolutionary. He fears Spanish prisons as only a former Spanish officer can fear them; he fears the legal-religious cruelty and vengefulness of Spanish punishments as only a man who has dealt in these things himself can fear them. In the recent Venezuelan wars he has had men hanged; he has had heads spiked.

He is sixty-two now. He has four more years to live. All

these years will be spent in jail; some of the time he will be chained. He will never see London and his family again. He will move from the jail in Venezuela to the jail in Puerto Rico, to the dungeons of Cadiz. The dungeons of Cadiz are infamous. But when the captain-general of Puerto Rico, who handles Miranda with honour throughout, comes to tell him that orders have come for him to be taken to Cadiz, Miranda embraces the captain-general and thanks him. As though he is content at the end to lay aside the fantasies of thirty years— fantasies of an immense Spanish-American republic of Colombia stretching from the source of the Mississippi (all the land west of the river) down the length of the continent to Cape Horn, fantasies of Incas worthy of Plato's republic, fantasies which (like Columbus's ideas about the New World, and Raleigh's) also contained a dream of a fabulous personal authority.

THROUGHOUT HIS adult life Miranda was particular about his papers. He kept everything he considered important, sometimes even printed invitations. He did so at first as a traveller, one of the earliest South Americans out in the greater world; later he kept things out of a sense of history and personal destiny. If he isn't well known now it isn't only because he achieved little, and because the South American revolution doesn't have the universal appeal of the three great revolutions—the American, the French, and the Haitian— that came earlier. It is also because on the day he was betrayed he was separated from his papers—the sixty-three leather-bound folio volumes he had brought out from England two years before—and the papers were lost for more than a century. When the papers were recovered the South American revolution had receded, its history had hardened, and, as with the corpses at Pompeii, where Miranda should have been there was a void.

For Venezuelans Miranda is the Precursor, the man before Bolívar. And when I first read about Miranda and began to look at his papers, I too, but in my own way, thought of him as a precursor. I saw him as a very early colonial, someone with a feeling of incompleteness, with very little at home to fall back on, with an idea of a great world out there, someone who, when he was out in this world, had to reinvent himself. I saw in him some of my own early promptings (and the promptings of other people I knew).

I feel now that I was carried away by a private idea of an ancestry, and overlooked too much of what was obvious. There is something in the idea of colonial incompleteness, and his political cause cannot be denied. But Miranda was also, right through, from the time he left home, something of a confidence man. It was too easy: he was the first South American of culture (and often the first South American) people outside had met, and he found he could tell them anything about who he was and the place he had come from. He could tell the president of Yale, for instance, during a discussion of Mexican writing, that he had studied law at Mexico University.

This is the man we will see arriving—in latish middle age, thirty-five years after he had left South America—in the Gulf in 1806. And it is necessary now to go back and understand a little more of Miranda the confidence man.

He was born in Caracas in 1750. His father was a Canary Islander and a linen merchant. That is, neither a proper Spaniard from Spain, nor someone accepted by the creole Spanish aristocracy. But a rich man, rich enough to pay eight thousand pesos—a large sum—for a captain's commission for his son in the Spanish army; and rich enough to get a notary in Spain to prepare a genealogical account of the Mirandas, proving their Castilian purity and nobility through seven generations.

It is to take up this commission that young Miranda leaves

for Spain in 1771. In Spain he is enthusiastic for the sights, the wine, the prostitutes; he notes down everything. To cover some of his expenses (and this might be his merchant father's idea) he has brought four hundred and fifty pounds of cocoa beans—no doubt grown on the slave estates in the valleys north of Caracas. The cocoa fetches a hundred and fifteen pesos. This—to give an idea of the extravagance of the metropolitan life Miranda is hoping to enter—is what he pays for a silk handkerchief and a silk umbrella. And these are only two items in a long list of expensive dress things which he acquires on arrival.

A year later he receives his commission. He quarrels with people all the time. It is his nature; he is at once too assertive and—no doubt as a Venezuelan and Canary Islander—too easily slighted. However, the years begin to pass; there is a period of service in North Africa. As he settles into regimental life—he is imprisoned at least twice for insubordination—his assertiveness begins to show in other ways. On the parade ground one day he uses his sword to hit a soldier about the head and he damages the man's hearing; then he has the man taken down to the dungeon, stripped naked and beaten. He also begins to steal the regiment's funds. The practice is not unusual among officers who have bought their commissions and have in various ways to make their money back. There are complaints, delayed enquiries, rambling written excuses—much of the rest of Miranda's military life will be like this.

There is now the American War of Independence. Miranda very much wants to go, and he does. He is with the Spanish force at the siege of Pensacola. After the outnumbered British forces surrender, Miranda does some shopping. He buys three Negro slaves and a large number of valuable books. He buys the slaves one at a time in the course of two weeks and keeps the three receipts among his papers; the receipts are proof of his title. He also says that a British prisoner made a gift to him of a Negro man called Brown. These four slaves will be taken as contraband (no doubt on a Spanish military transport) into Cuba or some other Spanish territory and sold at a profit. There are pickings of this sort for Spanish officers in this war.

More is to come. The governor of Cuba cooks up a scheme. Miranda will be gazetted a colonel and sent to the British island of Jamaica to arrange the exchange of British and Spanish prisoners. The mission is genuine enough; but Miranda will also (after squaring the British authorities) buy two ships in Jamaica, load them up with Negroes and British china and linen, and take them back to Cuba. There everything (including the ships: a master stroke) will be traded. Miranda will be set down at the port of Batanabó with his harmless personal luggage (including the many fine books he has bought in Jamaica); the contraband ships and their cargo will make their own roundabout way to Havana. Miranda will take all the risks. The governor of Cuba, the patron of the scheme, will keep his hands clean.

It is a stupendous fraud, hard to keep secret, and there are Spanish officials who are outraged by it. Almost as soon as Miranda leaves Batanabó, with his six trunks in three carts, he is arrested and quite deliberately roughed up by excise officers. No respect is shown to his uniform or to his official passport. His excuses are ingenious, as always, but they don't help. The officials are implacable; even the governor is bypassed. The case—developing over twelve months—goes to the king of Spain, and the news that gets back to Cuba is so bad that Miranda decides to run. With the help of the governor he gets a berth on an American sloop and slips away to the United States. And that is just as well. The king of Spain's decision, six months later, is that Miranda is to be stripped of his commission and sentenced to ten years of garrison duty in Oran in North Africa.

By this time Miranda, in the United States, is mingling

with the highest in the land. The governor of Cuba has played fair with him; he has given him a letter to the Spanish minister to the United States, and the Spanish minister diligently introduces Miranda to distinguished people. For the first time in his life Miranda finds himself of interest as a South American and a cultured man, as a man in his own right; no one in the United States in 1783 would know or care what a Canary Islander or a Venezuelan creole is. And delicate gifts of social manoeuvre come to Miranda; it is as though he has been educating himself for this moment. At one gathering he says that the military man he has modelled himself on is General Wolfe. It just happens—and no one is more surprised than Miranda—that the man he says that to knows highly-placed friends of the general. Miranda is passed on to those friends; they pass him on to others. And so it goes on for a year and a half.

At some stage the idea gets around that Miranda's interest, or long-term cause, is an American-style freedom for Spanish America. The idea adds to Miranda's dignity; and he doesn't reject it. So when word arrives that Miranda is really a deserter from the Spanish service, it does him no harm. When he leaves the United States to go to England he has a letter of introduction to the secretary to the Treasury in Whitehall. He has moved very fast. Just eighteen months before, in colonial Havana, he was a contrabandist and a deserter; now, already, in London, he has become a kind of negotiator in the South American cause. And twenty years or so later Venezuelans, with colonial pride and exaggeration, will add a further gloss to Miranda's time in the United States: they will make him a general in the American War of Independence, standing shoulder to shoulder with Lafayette and Washington.

Miranda's travels continue, year after year: this has almost become his career. There is always someone willing to provide the would-be liberator with money. As for passion, there are constant brutal passages with chambermaids, servant women, prostitutes. There are also constant quarrels with servants. They often seem to sniff out his fraudulence or dependence, and he, with his Venezuelan-colonial ideas of authority, often roughs them up. At the upper level there continue to be introductions, onwards and onwards. The farther away from home he goes the easier it gets.

In Russia he becomes a colonel again, a Mexican nobleman, and a count. Catherine the Great herself becomes worried about what the Inquisition might do to him if he falls into Spanish hands. When he tells her that the Spanish ambassador has been challenging his right to call himself a colonel, she makes him a colonel in the Russian service. She gives him money; she tells him that the Russian embassies in Europe will always be open to him.

His reputation now feeds on itself; his failures no longer matter. When he goes back to England he enters into serious negotiations with the British government. The negotiations drag on for years, and nothing happens. But when he goes to France they make him a general in their revolutionary army. That ends in a military disaster at the siege of Maastricht, his imprisonment and trial. That doesn't do him any harm in England; in fact, he goes back, quite legitimately, as a general. For years, then, until he is fifty-five, British plans for the invasion or liberation of South America expand and contract and expand again around General Miranda. Once there is even a plan for a conquest of the continent with ten thousand sepoys from India.

Through these years of waiting and disappointment Miranda doesn't dwindle. He grows; he becomes more and more educated. Experience, knowledge of the world, and the acquaintance of great men have taken him far from the contrabandist captain of twenty years before. He handles himself as the head of a government in waiting. At the beginning he might have talked moralistically of the broken promises of ministers who have kept him dangling. But now he knows that men are linked by interest and he knows what he has to offer. A British invasion without him would be resisted by the people of Spanish America. Someone like him is needed. And it is only when he fears that he will lose his role, when he sees himself useless in London in old age, that he commits himself to his absurd one-ship invasion.

THIS IS the man who comes to the Gulf in 1806, after the failure of his first invasion. He should be ridiculous, but he isn't. There will be a new invasion soon, this time with the help of the British fleet in the Caribbean. The generals and admirals are all for Miranda. They want the great estates in South America that Miranda's victory will bring.

A British warship brings him from Barbados to Port of Spain. This is partly to protect him from the mutinous American mercenaries on his own ship, the *Leander*. They haven't been paid for the whole of the year, and they have no faith in Miranda's leadership.

Miranda is welcomed on the pier by the Trinidad governor, General Hislop. Hislop is a man of jangled nerves. He is forty, and fading. His last military service was twenty years before, in Gibraltar. He has been ten years in the West Indies in semi-administrative posts and drinks too much. He has been governor of Trinidad for three years, and he hates the island and the people.

Hislop has just had to deal with what he thought was a slave rebellion. That gave him a fright, and now he is nervous about the legality of what was done then—the hangings and the mutilations—and what has been done in his name since he became governor. He feels that everything he has done or presided over can be challenged, because since the British conquest there has been no agreed system of law. No one knows whether Spanish law operates or English law, and there are no proper lawyers to give advice about either system.

Miranda is without power. He lives on subventions from

merchants in London and now New York, and on uncertain grants from the British government. He depends now on British support for his second invasion attempt. Hislop is the representative of the British power. But at their meeting now Hislop is the suppliant, Miranda the man with the thing he can grant. Miranda recognizes that Hislop is a suppliant, and he knows that the request, when it comes, will be something like this: "General, should you have room in South America at some time for a military man, please do not hesitate to call on me."

They drive up through the wretched little town. Away from the principal square, near the pier, many of the building plots are empty and overgrown. The streets of the Spanish-laid-out town have now been given British names, of royalty and military men: King, Queen, Prince, Duke, George, Charlotte, Frederick, St. Vincent, Abercromby. It is the rainy season, and the dirt roads are muddy and the air is warm and moist.

Government House, where Miranda is to stay as a guest of the governor, is to the north, at the foot of the hills.

The two men talk about the invasion force.

Hislop says, "We can't give you any of our own troops, of course. But the Americans on your ship will have to go with you. Some of them are saying they will stay here, but I will let them know that they are allowed to be here only as members of your force. I have identified the ringleader among the Americans."

"Biggs."

"That's it. We can deal with Biggs. The Spanish authorities are another matter. They have been spreading the word that the island will go back to Spain when the peace comes. This means that none of the Spaniards here will volunteer. They are also spreading the rumour that you will set all the slaves free. This is to discourage the French volunteers. Rouvray has got about a hundred and ninety French volunteers. They will want to hear from you that you will secure property rights in slaves. That's what it always comes down to in this part of the world, as you know. Land and slaves. As governor of this place there are times when I feel I am just a jailer for the planters."

Miranda says, "I asked for letters to be sent here."

"You have quite a few. Some have been sent on from Tortola, some from the Leeward Islands station. And Mr. Turnbull has sent me boxes of leaflets and samples for you. You are to distribute them when you land in Venezuela. With your recommendations. Some people have a very simple idea of military operations."

Government House is in need of repair. Hislop apologizes. He says the Treasury of the island is empty. The previous administrator had very grand ideas of the style in which he and his family and his secretaries should live. He stayed for only six months, but he left a hole. After that there was the expense of fortifications, some of them now abandoned. The few public works Negroes that are now employed about the Government House grounds—mud-stained, in ragged brown linen clothes: the standard slave wear: Miranda has seen it on Negroes during the drive through the town—have been bought from the dealers on credit.

"They are not carpenters or craftsmen," Hislop says. "A carpenter would have cost a hundred pounds. These cost sixty. And they're new Negroes. From Africa. No good for anything except in a field gang, and they don't speak English or French. The story is that the trade is going to be stopped next year, so the merchants are bringing in as many new Negroes as they can now. That's creating its own problems. If you stay here long enough, that's all you start thinking about. Negroes and land.

"It will be no surprise to you, General, that you are in demand here. Miss McLurie wants to meet you. She's one of our ladies. She came in 1802 and is suffering from the lack of society. She wears a transparency. That's what she calls it. It shows her bosom. Apparently it's the latest fashion. She wants to hear from your very own lips about Lady Hester Stanhope and Catherine the Great. These stories have preceded you. That's the way it is with famous people, and you are the most famous man to have come here. Before you came, I suppose Commodore Samuel Hood was the most famous man we had here. Nelson's second-in-command at the Battle of the Nile."

Miranda says, "I met Hood before he came out here."

"And Be'nard wants to see you. He has been very pressing in the last week." Hislop pronounced the French name in an English way, making it sound like "Bennard." "He is a planter, courtesy of de Gourville. He is married to de Gourville's daughter. This makes him a relation by marriage of Baron de Montalembert. Be'nard doesn't let you forget it. The baron is one of our biggest planters. He will be a good man to get on your side. He came here from Santo Domingo five or six years ago. His estate is just around the corner from here. Just after he came here he lost a hundred and twenty of his Negroes by poison. It is a famous story. I am sure Be'nard will tell it again. He is going to call very soon."

"Bernard. I knew a Bernard in Paris. He later came to London. I sent out a Bernard here from England seven years ago. To keep an eye on things for me. He came and I never heard a word. Not a word. Will this be the same man? Worried that I'm turning up? Or deciding that there is something I can do for him? What do you think, General?"

"General Miranda, you asked just now about your letters. They are in your room. But there is another. It was thrown into the sentry box yesterday morning. It is anonymous. It may be abusive of me. It is what I've had to live with here. I am not sure that honour applies here, but I pass that letter on to you as a matter of honour. My request is that you will handle it in the same way. You have been the object of calumny and persecution yourself, General. It is very easy to be vilified in a place like this."

The men separate. Dinner is to be at three. Miranda goes to his section of the house, henceforth his headquarters. He sees the satchels with the Tortola and Leeward Islands mail. And the folded dingy anonymous letter Hislop mentioned.

The room is at the back of the house. The grass and trees outside are wet from the recent rain. A hill rises up not far away. The air is damp, and the very smell of rain and earth and dead leaves brings back to Miranda the smell of the cocoa valleys to the north of Caracas, and reminds him of the sacks of cocoa beans his father had sent with him on the *Prins Frederik* in 1771, to be changed for money in Cadiz.

The room is full of small, yellowish lizards; their droppings are everywhere. There is a muslin canopy over the bed, to protect it from dust and termite wood-dust and things like lizard droppings. The canopy is discoloured and in its folds or wrinkles grey with old dust; it sags in the damp air.

Outside there is movement, talk. The slaves are not speaking Spanish or French or English, but an African language.

He begins to shape a letter in his head: "My dear Sally, this is a kind of homecoming for me, after thirty-five years. It is quite amazing: I know this rainy-season smell. Soon I suppose the rain and the wind will bring the smell of the vanilla vine. I feel I know this place very well. It is my own. It exists in my mind. But it is now full of strangers. I don't like the sensation. I feel a great gap. Without the thought of you I would be quite lost."

He opens the Tortola satchel and soon, among the official, secretary-written letters, sees the broad, irregular, awkward handwriting he has been looking for.

"27 Grafton Street, Fitzroy Square, London. April 15th. My ever dear General, I embrace this opportunity of writing to you my dear Sir for wile I am a night and the two babies

are asleep it seames as if I am talking to my dear Friend
Himself and can hear his own voice. Leander has set down
his drum and sword and gun, we have had a fair in the Road,
and he makes such a noise my dear Sir saying Mamy I am
going to the war to fight for the General—"

Miranda thinks, partly framing his reply, "*Querida*. My
dear Sally, I love every misspelt word you write and every
mistake you make. These words you wrote four months ago
come to me now with your own voice. I can see my house and
the library and the books again. I think without you, my dear
Sally, I would become quite dizzy here, in this place I don't
know any longer, and try not to see too clearly or find out too
much about, where the Negroes talk in an African language,
and I can still smell the cocoa estates all around . . ."

"Leander sleeping is the picture of my dear Sir. My uncle
from Yorkshire is with us to keep us company and to get
some London portrait work. He sets Leander down in the
G's library, I must tell you I light a fire there one day every
week winter and summer, and my uncle draws his picture
but he doesnt set still a moment. And I am very flatter that
everybody says he has the Wisdom of twice his years. My
dear Sir I have followed all your Instructions and I now
propose to give you the regular Budget of news Mr. Rutherfurd says I should give you to keep your Spirits up in all your
trying circumstances. I talk in my mind every night to my
dear G, but I don't have news every day.

"My dear Sir your second son and mine Francisco was
born on the 27th of February. All that day my thoughts were
of you and your danger on the High Seas. You wished this
son to have your own name, and Francisco and Leander were
both of them Baptised as agreed on the 23rd of March. Mr.
Rutherfurd came in the morning with Mr. Longchamp and
they took us to St. Patrick's Soho Square in a Coach. Mr.
Longchamp responded for both babis. Father Gaffey wrote
Mr. Longchamps name wrong in the Register and had to

scratch it out both times. I give here the copy of the Baptismal Certificate for Francisco that Father Gaffey gave me for my dear Sir it's all in Latting so the G. must forgive errors. *Die 23a Martii 1806 baptisatus fuit Franciscus filius Francisci Miranda et Sarae Andrews. Natus die 27a Februarii praecedentis. Patrinis fuit Joannes Michael Jean du Longchamp. Per Daniel Gaffey.*

"When we went back to Grafton street Mr. Rutherfurd told me that not a few Eyebrows had been raised by the Roman Catholic Baptism with certain people we well know saying that you said one thing but in your heart of hearts were another. But I kept my peace about my dear Gen's intentions, and I thought hard of him and his dangers that day and the next when as agreed I knew that after the Baptism of our sons my G would be making his Officers swear to serve the people of South America and their new Flag. I think about that Flag my dear Sir the hours I spent making it here in Grafton Street spreading it out sometimes on the floor of the library, with Leander tied to the table leg so he couldn't get too close—"

"Sarah, I will never find the courage to tell you. The flag that carried so much of you was lost five weeks after you wrote that, when the *Bee* and the *Bacchus* were lost, with all the landing party. I waited until the 12th of March before I took the flag out of my trunk and showed it to the men on the *Leander*. I thought that Francisco would have been born by then. I know now that he was two weeks old. The *Bee* and the *Bacchus* were both unarmed sloops. The other ships we were expecting all the way down never came. After that long voyage, with those unruly, mocking Americans, butcher boys, I had to try to land. I couldn't just go away without doing anything. The Spaniards will dishonour that flag. They will find special ways . . ."

"First of May 1806. I wait for news of my dear Sir and try to guess what other people know. Mr. Holland the print-seller sent to my uncle for a Picture of the Gen, and my uncle sat down all morning at the small library table and drew one of my dear Sir in Profile with his long white queue hanging down his back tied up at the end with a little ribbing and with his silk cravat below his chin, all in Profile, very serious and stern, and my uncle says that in the Print the Engraver will show clouds and a Crown above the Gen's head. I thought this was a good sign, because as my uncle says Mr. Holland wants to sell his prints and he knows when to expect good news. But then Mr. Turnbull came and walked through the house in a way he wouldn't have dared if my Gen was here. Standing up in the library and Ex-Claiming when are those Volumes going to be paid for, they cost Thousand's, the booksellers and binders are sending their bills to the firm of Turnbull and Forbes, I never authorized that. Walking through the house as though I wasnt there, no bowing and no my good lady now, Leander and Francisco and their mother not much thought of now that you are not here. My dear Sir they are all snake's in the Grass as long as I live I will encourage Leander and Francisco to look for their Deseat. I was mighty sick after he left and my heart allmost broke. Take yourself out of their power my dear Sir, I nightly pray in the silence of the house for you soon to claim your own, and for that Crown to be sett on your head."

THERE WAS a disturbance outside. A number of men talking at once, an irregular hollow stamping on the ground, the sounds of harness, more talk, shouts, and then a slow, heavy crash.

Miranda was roused from the sound of Sarah's voice, from the flow of his own unspoken reply, from thoughts and pictures of his library, his sleeping sons, the London night, the silence of his house.

It was darker in the room than he had thought, as though time had shifted with his thoughts and it was nearly night here too. It was only the rainy-season weather of the estuary and the Gulf: one brief, violent downpour recently over, a remnant of its drizzle still about, another downpour about to come.

He went to the window. It was in the local style, the shutter roughly jalousied, hinged at the top (the better to keep out the rain), and propped open with a stick. Water dripped from the sloping sides of the shutter. The paint had long ago peeled, the timber had weathered grey; the sill had begun to rot.

The grounds at the back of the house were a mess of mud and rubble and bush, like a clearing in the forest. To one side—near the separate little cook-house, whitewash fallen off grey, soaked boards, smoke coming out of blackened open windows: dinner for the governor and his guest being got ready—there were old compacted mounds of kitchen ash.

In the mud directly in front, a mule had been unharnessed from a cart. The badly distributed load of rubble had fallen forward, breaking the front flap of the cart and pressing the shafts into the mud.

The three or four mud-stained black men around the mule and cart were talking in a language Miranda had never heard before. He supposed it to be a language of Africa.

If the men had been talking English or French or Spanish Miranda would not have noticed them as he now did. He would have seen only Negroes and he would not have been able to recognize them later. But the strange private language, and the whole internal, unknowable world it implied, made him consider the faces of the men.

They noticed him, too, almost at the same time, the old man with the long white pigtail appearing below the sloping jalousied shutter against the darkness of the window. For a while, waiting for they knew not what, looking at him, they stood still, and for those moments it was as if in their bewilderment—men who seemed not to have any idea what they were doing or why, or even where they were—Miranda saw something of his own disturbance, called away from London and his house and Sarah and her panic, to focus all at once on that piece of bush and those men.

He noticed their frailty. It was strange in people expected to do physical labour, but (and this was plantation lore, in Venezuela as well) the sturdiness of the plantation worker was grafted on to this kind of stock over later generations. Many Africans when they arrived were as frail as these men. A certain number were expected to die in the first year, from the water, the food, the new insects. On the established plantations there were ways of "seasoning" new arrivals and seeing them through their dangerous first year. These Africans in the grounds of Government House looked neglected. In the hollow red eyes of one man could be seen signs of a rainy-season fever. He was doomed, and so perhaps was one of the men with him.

That idea of doom, of another kind of life, coming to Miranda even while he was looking at the eyes of the Africans, re-established distance between him and the men he saw, and returned him to himself and the setting: the downpour coming, the wet, rotting window sill with disagreeable drifts of black-and-white lizard droppings in the eaten-away parts of the wood: the lizards now seen to be active everywhere around him, pale yellow creatures, almost transparent, like little crocodiles but with enormous lidless eyes.

He saw in a corner of the room now the three new deal chests, like seamen's chests, with the Turnbull and Forbes samples General Hislop had mentioned. The chests were painted with a style of lettering—thin horizontals, very thick verticals—that brought back the signboards and street signs of London: *Brig.-Gen. Thos. Hislop, Headquarters, Trinidad. For General Miranda. From Turnbull and Forbes, London.*

He didn't go back to Sarah's letter. It was an hour or so to dinner, time enough to consider other correspondence. The heavy roaring rain that came soon, beating on the ground and trees and the roof, helped his concentration.

Not long after the rain stopped a servant came and told him he had a visitor.

He went out to the verandah. He recognized his visitor as Bernard, last seen seven years ago in London. There was a mud-spattered calash with a wet black coachman in the drive. Though the rain had stopped, the drive was running with yellow water that came off the surrounding hills and made a general gurgling noise all around.

The calash made a good first impression; but then Miranda saw that the hood, which was up, was cracked and worn in the folds, the bodywork was dented and scratched, and the emblem on the low door was crudely painted. The wet coachman was wearing alpargatas, peon's footwear, a cheap kind of slipper with a very thin leather sole with woven cotton straps for the toes and the heel. The heel-straps of the coachman's alpargatas had long ago been flattened below the man's heel.

The verandah was wet and every little breath of air felt chill. The rain had blown in on three sides.

Miranda didn't ask Bernard inside. Both men remained standing in the verandah.

Bernard said, "General."

Miranda didn't speak.

"I never wrote. I know."

"There are so many letters," Miranda said. "You never wrote at all? Are you sure?"

"I put it off and put it off. Year after year. And then it was too late. Governor Hislop would have told you that I'm married. My wife is the daughter of the Chevalier de Gourville. Dupont Duvivier de Gourville. He's a relation of the Baron de Montalembert. No finer connection is possible in these parts. It wasn't something I would have thought possible for myself. I had to set aside thoughts of the revolution. You're a man of the world, and I feel I can offer you this explanation. I won't call it an excuse."

Miranda said, "I've heard of the baron. He came here in

1801 with a hundred and fifty Negroes, and he lost a hundred at one blow."

"A hundred and twenty. In the first month. After losing everything in Santo Domingo and Martinique. And there's no bitterness in him. He simply started up again. General, I don't want to take up more of your time. I thought it was my duty to make this call on you, to see you as soon as possible, and to declare myself. Times change, General. And though at one time I had to set aside thoughts of the revolution, I have these past few months been serving you in ways you don't know. I think it is important for you to know that. Of course, French people of standing here know of our old connection, and I have been able to reassure them—especially those who have volunteered for your new expedition—that there was never any political quarrel between us. Friends and foes have spread all kinds of stories about you here, General. The stories haven't been all about the court of Catherine the Great. Some have been about the French Revolution. You were a general in the army of the Revolution. But I've always told people that you will honour property rights in land and Negroes, that there is nothing to fear. People worry about these things here, and you can't blame them, after recent history. I hope you think I've done well."

"You've done well."

"Now I must go."

"Your calash?"

"My wife's. What you see on it are the Gourville arms. Roughly done, but it was painted by a Negro born and bred in Martinique and—you wouldn't believe—trained as a pastrycook."

"Pastrycook! The things you can get people to do these days!"

Bernard began to go down the steps. Miranda (never forgetting, with a remnant of shame, how, thirty-five years ago, eight fanegas, four hundred and fifty pounds, of Venezuelan cocoa had been converted in Cadiz into nothing more than a silk handkerchief and a silk umbrella) noticed how carefully, even with all the rain, the chevalier's son-in-law had dressed for the occasion: the pale yellow pantaloons, the white ruffed shirt, the blue silk jacket. Before he got to the bottom of the broad, semi-rotting wooden steps (the driver of the calash getting ready, shaking the wet off the reins), he turned and looked at Miranda. It was the moment Miranda— wondering about the purpose of the call—had thought would never come.

Bernard said, "General. The clerk of the Council died last week. Did Governor Hislop tell you? It means there is a vacancy. The fees are small. Over a month they wouldn't purchase you a dinner in London. But it's a position of some local dignity. It matters to me, to be something in my own right. You'll understand. I hope you'll feel able to recommend me for it."

AT DINNER Hislop said, "I know what he wants. You don't have to tell me. So far, when the messages have come I've pretended not to hear. Let's leave it like that. Let's have some wine now, to celebrate your homecoming. Because that's what it is: a homecoming after thirty-five years. And that's what I hope it will turn out to be in a lasting way."

Miranda said, "No wine for me, General. Just sugar and water. It's all I've had for years. It's what we used to drink in Caracas as children."

"Almost the only commodities we're not short of here. But sugar-and-water isn't the kind of story we hear about you."

"It's strange about those stories. I started some of them, or at any rate encouraged them. Now they're like stories about someone else. When I went to Spain in 1771, wine was one of the things I was travelling to know. It was something the poets wrote about. The wine of Europe, not the brackish church stuff we had in Caracas. I thought a lot about wine on the *Prins Frederik*. I expected nectar. As soon as I got to Cadiz I started to make notes about every wine I had, as I made notes about the women, the churches, the pictures. I don't know now how much I was acting for the sake of my journal. Acting being a man of culture. I was twenty-one."

"So the chevalier's son-in-law came in his calash. A famous calash. With its shop-sign coat of arms. I hope he was friendly."

"I don't know. He threatened me. He said I had a revolutionary past. He said he knew more about that past than anyone here, and some people might easily be made to feel that property wasn't safe with me."

Hislop said, "Unfortunately, he's right. It could be very damaging. The Spaniards have also been spreading rumours. The local Spaniards are already keeping out, and unless these stories are checked, your French volunteers might also drop away. They're refugees from the islands, aristocrats without money, and they're going into this business for the sake of property. Land and Negroes. To re-establish their fortunes. We all know that. I wish it were otherwise, but in this part of the world it always comes down to land and Negroes, as I told you. We have to take Be'nard's threat seriously. I'll find ways of letting him know that you've spoken to me, and that I've agreed to let him have the clerkship, but that I won't be making the appointment for a month. That should keep him out of mischief and give you enough time. Ah, the calash! Be'nard will feel it did the trick again."

"I couldn't really afford the money I gave him when I sent him out here in 1799. And yet when I saw him this morning I had to pretend to be stiff with him. It was strange. I felt no animosity towards him. And right at the end, as he was going down the steps and he turned and I saw how carefully he had dressed, my heart went out to him. He looked so vulnerable, so easy to hurt. It would have been so easy to call his bluff, to laugh at the calash and the barefoot Negro driving it. And simply because it was so easy I didn't want to do it. There's always a touch of pathos in someone like that. He's so exposed. I felt I was looking at a younger version of myself.

"I too had a coat of arms at one time. You need one to get a commission in a Spanish regiment. There are people in Spain who do these things. The man my father employed was called Zazo y Ortega. Zazo's method was simple. He linked the Mirandas of Caracas and the Canary Islands to the twelfth-century Mirandas of Old Castile. And although I knew precisely who I was, and was proud of my father, and very proud of our money, I also passionately believed when I got on the *Prins Frederik* at La Guaira that I was another kind of person, and that I was travelling to Spain to claim my rightful inheritance, of which the coat of arms was a part. The *Prins Frederik* was a Swedish frigate. It was utterly foreign. It helped me to feel that I had undergone a transformation. For years I lived like this, knowing who I was and at the same time believing myself to be somebody else. Holding those two different ideas in my head at the same time, even drawing the Miranda arms on the expensive books I bought.

"I will tell you something even more absurd. When I was twenty-five—just two weeks after my twenty-fifth birthday—I wrote to the king of Spain asking to be invested with the red cross of the Order of Santiago. This is a very grand order. The king himself appoints a commission to look into the nobility of your descent. The painter Velázquez was admitted to the order when he was sixty, and at the height of his reputation. I knew who we were, what we had come from in Caracas and the Canary Islands. I knew exactly how Zazo had gone about creating that genealogy for me. But I also thought quite seriously with another part of my mind that Zazo had turned up the truth, and I was worthy of the

king's investigation. I thought there was something wonderful within me, and I felt that the king would discover this. I
was twenty-five, a captain in the Princess Regiment in Africa.
"Later I became ashamed of all of this. I was glad there
was no reply from the king. I even forgot about it, until the
other day. And now I can look back on that whole business
with calm. But I can still see the logic of the young man and
understand why he did what he did. Something of that came
back to me when I saw Bernard go down the steps, about to
splash his delicate shoes and to spot his very expensive silk
jacket with the drips from the old calash hood."

Hislop said, "It's easy to look back at the past. It's not so
easy to be clear-sighted about the present. We don't always
know what we are doing now. We can just get dragged
along."

"General, you're frightening me. Of course I know it's
strange to be going on a campaign of liberation with these
French aristocratic adventurers who only want land and Negroes. But that's looking at it from the outside. I know the
logic of what I'm doing. I know how I've got here. You
know. You and I know all the twists and turns of events that
have brought me here."

"I was thinking of myself. I intended no rebuke to you.
I am a military man. That has been my ambition since childhood. My last active service was in Gibraltar. That was
twenty years ago. I have been becalmed in these parts for ten
years. I still think of myself as a military man, still think I
have a future. But really I no longer know what I'm doing.
They put you in a place called Government House and they
call you the governor, but you're really only a jailer for these
planters. I would much rather be with you. There, General.
I've said what's been on my mind these many months. I have
longed for this meeting. For the last four months I have been
learning Spanish. Learning Spanish one hour a day, and for
the last year or two I've been dreaming of an elegant society,

with fine houses and polished floors and beautiful Spanish ladies, where I might one day practise this Spanish. I have not seen action recently. But I could be on your staff. I could smooth things for you with our admirals and generals. I know many of them. I know their characters. I would know the words to use. The correct words are important with military people. That could be of value to you."

It grew dark, and the rain came again beating on the ground outside and the roof and making conversation difficult while the first onrush lasted.

Hislop said, "This is the kind of weather that can carry you off. Make you a banquet for the blue crabs, as they say here. Put on a jacket and you start sweating. Take it off and you shiver. After ten years in these parts my health has broken down. I dream of a June day in England. But to get to England in June a lot of planning is necessary. You have to be in Tortola in the Virgin Islands by March, for the convoys. I don't want to land in England in November."

"Caracas will be better for you. The seasons don't matter there."

"General."

"The Caracas valley is known as the land of eternal spring. The flowers have a deeper hue and the fruit are sweeter and bigger."

Miranda showed the anonymous letter that Hislop said had been thrown into the sentry-box. The seal was still unbroken. He put the letter to one side and said, "I thought it would be better to read it in your presence. Not now. A little later."

Hislop was moved. He said, "General."

The servants began to bring in the dinner, stamping with bare feet on the solid planks, bringing with them a smell of rain and leaf-mould, woodsmoke and charcoal fumes, from the kitchen hut Miranda had seen.

Hislop said, "No banquet, General. It's like living on a

ship here. We've got twenty thousand Negroes working on the plantations from five in the morning to six in the evening, six days a week. But the scarcest thing here is food. All they do on the plantations is cocoa and cotton and sugar-cane and coffee. The Negroes in their free time grow some ground provisions, cassava, yams, sweet potatoes. But they're not allowed to sell anything. The peons—the *'pagnols,* as they call them here—bring in a little wild meat from the forest sometimes, and some of the free people of colour sell a little poultry when they have it. But we're nearly always close to a famine. Nearly everything we eat here is smoked or salted and comes in a box from Canada or the United States. Beef, mackerel, salmon, cod, herring. Even tobacco comes in a box. Butter is orange-red with salt and costs six shillings a pound. No one thinks of churning it locally."

"You don't have to apologize, General. I know this food. I'm at home, remember. What's happening in your grounds? Do those men know what they're doing?"

"I doubt it. As a military man you must know that if you can't gauge what a group of men are doing, it is because they themselves don't know. They're just doing as they're told. We're trying to make the land slope away from the hills, to take off the flood water. At the same time we're digging in drainage trenches, with rubble at the bottom. It should have been done years ago, when they made this house Government House. You dig a ditch, you put in the rubble, and then you cover it up. It's to prevent water stagnating. As soon as water stagnates here you get mosquitoes. If you get mosquitoes, you can't live here. I tell the *commandeur* of the gang what to do, and he pretends he knows, but he doesn't really know why I am asking him to bury stones. Plantation people would have some idea, but these new Negroes know nothing about anything. I don't think they even know that they're working, doing something called work. They probably just think they're being punished. These Negroes believe that during

the day they're in hell. Literally. Did you know that? A
strange kind of hell, where it doesn't matter what they do or
what is done to them. When the sun goes down the real world
begins for them. Everything changes then. As soon as night
falls, and you know that in these parts night comes in five
minutes, things balance out for them. We become ghosts.
They become kings and queens and dauphins and grand
judges. They wear the crowns and have the whips. That's
what their sorcerers tell them. And it's what they believe. It
doesn't matter what you do to them or how much you try
to break their spirit. They believe that in the night the power
is theirs. It was one of the things that came out at an enquiry
we had earlier this year. You live in a place for ten years, you
think you know it, and then you find out that all the time
you've been standing on quicksand."

"In Venezuela we always knew that the Negroes liked
dressing up and playing games. They were great mockers. I
don't remember anyone thinking of holding an inquiry into
it."

"We had to. I don't know whether they told you in
Barbados, but last December we had a scare here. We were
very close to a full-scale rebellion. They were all in it." He
jerked his chin towards the servants. "Everybody's Negroes
were in it, whether they belonged to white people or people
of colour. It had been building up over some years, under
our noses, and we didn't know. One day they were going to
kill all the white people.. And then, when there was only one
colour—that was the way they talked at the enquiry—they
were going to go to church to take communion and then
they were going to eat pork and dance. That was as far as
they had thought in three years. They were going to eat pork
and dance and live happily ever after. You might say it's a
game, but they were going to kill people and burn the houses
and fields. Before, I never looked at a Negro. You know
what I mean. I don't want to look now, but I find I do all the

time. And I am not sure what I am seeing. Anyway, in a month or two all this is going to change. These people in the grounds will go to the galleys and proper public works, and other people will be working on the grounds here. No one here knows as yet. We have to keep it secret. We are getting some Chinese."

"From China?"

"Not strictly. From India, from Calcutta. But they're going to be the first Chinese ever in this part of the world. It was such a desolation around Government House when I came here three years ago. I thought we should have a botanical garden. They have them in the other islands. It isn't something the Negroes know about, and the planters wouldn't like it anyway. They don't want Negroes to do any agricultural work away from the estates. I wrote to London about the Chinese, and the wheels slowly began to turn. It's all taken nearly two years. The East India Company recruited the Chinese in Calcutta. You won't be here when they arrive, and I must say that I have lost interest. *Mi cama aquí . . .*"

"General!"

"Let me practise my Spanish, General. *Mi cama aquí . . .*"

"My bed here . . . Your accent is very good."

". . . *no ha sido . . .*"

". . . has not been . . ."

". . . *una de rosas.*"

". . . one of roses. 'My bed here has not been one of roses.' It has not been a bed of roses for you."

"Absolutely. I was hoping the Chinese would also grow vegetables. The Negroes don't really know, and the planters won't allow them to sell anything they grow. They say that after Haiti they don't want their Negroes to get any ideas. But I think they just want to grind the Negroes down, and they don't know where to stop. In my three years here I have seen more of human turpitude than in the rest of my life."

Miranda said, "Turpitude. I know the word. But I've never heard anyone use it in conversation."

"I suppose it's because I've spent three years framing that sentence. I constantly speak it in my mind. It comforts me. The French aristocrats we've assembled here have tainted everybody. You've been to France, you've been a general in their army. I am not telling you anything you don't know. The French aristocracy don't come out well, General. I can't understand them. They feel rich only if everybody else around them is in rags. They feel secure and well-bred only if everybody else is degraded. I understand now why they had the revolution in France. Then they had the same revolution all over again in Haiti, but a much nastier one. And now they've almost had one here. And they've involved me in it." Hislop struck his breast, and then struck it regularly as he spoke. "I had to get the troops out at midnight and go around picking up the ringleaders. If there is an investigation I will have to bear the responsibility. I and I alone. That's what Gourville and Montalembert and Luzette and the others think. They think they will simply stand aside, as they did with Picton. But I don't intend that to happen. I'm a military man. I'm responsible for the defence of this territory and for public order. I know nothing about the management and care of Negroes. I am not required to know anything about that. Garrow, the London lawyer, made it pretty clear at the Picton trial. I have the full transcript. I have studied it. An official who exceeds the law, Garrow said, is responsible for his action. So the planters of the Council and the jailer and everybody else have to take their share. They don't like what I am saying, but I have made my position clear. If you stay here long enough, General, you will find that I am not the most popular man on the island."

Miranda said, "Is there going to be an investigation?"

"Who can tell? There may well be. The news from London has been very strange."

"Is there a lot to be investigated? Was it very bad?"

"Three hanged. The heads spiked, the bodies hung in chains in the square."

"The bodies of pirates hang from gibbets on both banks of the Thames, half-way up to London."

"A lot of people mutilated. It's what they do in the islands."

"How do you mutilate them?"

"You cut off the ears. I've seen it in other places. In some of the very small islands they slit the nose, but here they just do the ears."

"I never saw that in Venezuela. But I can't trust my memory now. But if a punishment is customary, it's customary. You're too nervous, General. A rebellion is a rebellion."

"It's what I tell myself in my better moments. And Lord Castlereagh, the colonial secretary, sent his approval. He said he knew that that class of the community had to be watched. But if there's an investigation, what's that approval worth? If I am asked to state what law I was following when those men were given a hundred lashes and had their ears cut off, I wouldn't be able to say. All I would be able to say is that I followed the Council and the planters, and the jail staff seemed to know what to do. I never looked for the laws. I don't even know what laws we are operating here. The territory was Spanish until nine years ago. It might go back to Spain at the end of the war, or it might be given to the French in exchange for something somewhere else. No one knows. If you say that the laws should be Spanish, there is no one here to tell me what those laws are. The lawbooks and the lawyers are all on the other side of the Gulf. A military governor can only follow the advice of responsible citizens. That's what Tom Picton did, and that's what I did after him. And you know the full bill against Picton. Thirty-seven charges. Execution without trial, false imprisonment, torture, burning alive. Bail set at forty thousand pounds. The man ruined, his life darkened these last three years."

"You've been here too long, General. You're too jumpy. You can't compare yourself to Picton. He was notorious.

And most of those charges related to the regiment. The others were thrown out. There was a charge of using torture against a young mulatto girl in a case of petty theft. But that's going to be thrown out too."

"General, didn't they tell you in Barbados? The trial came up at the end of February, before Lord Ellenborough. General Picton was found guilty."

"At one time I would have liked to hear that. I thought that Picton had done me much harm and I thought I had a score to settle with him. But I don't think like that now. You can waste too much time settling scores. You can forget what you really have to do. He'll appeal, of course."

"He'll appeal. But he's ruined. And the planters who sat in the jail and had the people tortured, and devised ways of burning people alive—they're free men. Picton didn't build the jail. It was there when he came, with the jailer and the torture chambers, the special hot rooms. The planters had set it up. They paid the jailer fees for torturing or flogging Negroes. For the torture of the mulatto girl the planter who was the chief magistrate at the time paid the jailer sixty reales, about six dollars and sixty cents. Nobody's been investigating that planter, or the others. They've not been on forty thousand pounds bail. They're loyal to no one except themselves, those French aristocrats. If you stay here long enough your mind begins to go. You lose faith. You lose your way.

"I'll tell you. We had an invasion scare here last year. First it was the French. Then it was the Spaniards. The Spanish admiral Gravina appeared in these waters with quite an armament. I don't have to tell you how small our military establishment is, and how vulnerable we are to any sustained assault. We clearly can't defend the whole island—two or three hundred miles of coastline, some of it very difficult, and so much of the island is uninhabited anyway—so I thought we should decide in the Council what we were going to try to defend. I thought it made more strategic sense to defend the naval harbour at Chaguaramas. It's a small area and it's very defensible. If you defend the ships, they live again to fight another day. The planters said no, the duty of our military establishment was to defend property.

"Now, General, you have been following the debates about slavery and the slave trade in England. And I don't have to tell you that when planters talk about 'property' and 'the free transfer of property' and 'a free supply,' they are simply finding a way of not saying 'Negroes' or 'slaves.' They are not even talking about land. Most of them got the land free when they came. The Spaniards, to develop the island, offered a settler sixteen acres for every Negro he brought in. A white settler got thirty-two acres for himself, a free man of colour sixteen acres. Many of the people who came in, to put themselves under Spanish law, were running away from debts they had in other places under other flags. Many of the Negroes they brought in were mortgaged up to the eyes.

"So these refugee aristocrats were saying, in fact, while a big war was going on, that it was my duty as governor to prevent them from losing their Negroes. And they had powerful friends in London. So, after spending seventy-five thousand pounds on fortifying the harbour at Chaguaramas, I had to stop and think about fortifying the city and the plantations around it. That is why the Treasury is empty, and my servants and soldiers are in rags. I thought of enrolling a company of Negro Rangers, faithful and well-disposed ones, it goes without saying. The planters said they didn't want to lose their Negroes. I said, 'We'll have them fairly valued. You will be recompensed if they are lost or damaged.' They said that after Haiti they didn't want their Negroes to handle guns. I said, 'Very well. At least lend me some of your Negroes to work on that hill fort we are building west of the city.' They said they couldn't spare them. So where were we? What was the point of doing anything?"

"But you built your fort?"

"I had to. That was my duty as governor. I used Negroes owned by people of colour. The people of colour didn't like that at all, and the whites crowed over them. And now, of course, since the news about Picton's conviction, some of those people of colour are after me. One man of colour is already suing Picton for forty thousand pounds for wrongful arrest. I wait for something like that to be done to me. Night and day I cast my mind back over things that have been done in my time. I accuse myself, I defend myself. It's like a sickness. Those Negroes whose ears were cut off last December and January—they were also given a hundred lashes. In the Spanish time the limit was twenty-five. Picton raised that to thirty-nine—and that was under the influence of the French. Why did I let those planters tell me that those men should be given a hundred? After fifty lashes a man is half dead."

"General, General. A domestic misdemeanour is quite distinct from rebellion against the state. You are tormenting yourself needlessly."

"You think so? One man whose ears they cut off was a free man of colour. They were very down on that man. They said that a free man of colour associating with the Negroes was the most dangerous kind of man. They decided he was to be returned to slavery. They cut his ears off and sold him out of the island. It's what they do in the islands. As a punishment it is one step down from hanging, because that man's life isn't worth living afterwards. How could they do that to a free man? I should have asked them to show me the laws. Now the investigator will ask me that question. The laws of England wouldn't like that, making a free man a slave and cutting off his ears and selling him cheap to somebody outside who is going to work him to death. That is all you can do with a Negro whose ears have been cut off. You can't sell him.

"And I had actually forgotten about that until the Picton news came. Now I think about it five, six, ten, twelve times a day. When my time comes and I am asked about that man all I would be able to say is that the planters at that enquiry last December got me thoroughly alarmed and told me this was what had to be done. Of course I also tell myself that the poor man is now in no position to get in touch with London lawyers. He is not going to live long. You see, General. Having done that injustice to that man, or allowed that illegality to be done to him, I now wish for his death. I want to be free of this place, General. I feel I am sinking here. I feel I can no longer see my way. I told you a while ago that it is easy to see the past. My life up to ten years ago is absolutely clear to me. But now I am clouded. I no longer know why I do things. Ideas of obedience to my lawful superiors no longer answer. Those were the ideas that as a military man I was bred up in."

"It isn't the Picton case that's worrying you. I think it's the weather. I think it's your inactivity. As you say, you've been a jailer for too long. You are fighting phantoms."

"General. I haven't told you. There is a case that stands absolutely foursquare with the Picton torture case. It happened three and a half years ago, almost in the week I arrived. The chief magistrate, a planter, came right here late in the afternoon. My boxes were still being unloaded from the carts. He was in a little frenzy, the magistrate. He said they had discovered that a free mulatto had had dealings with a Negro sorcerer. The mulatto had been pestering a Negro woman, somebody's house servant, to sleep with him. She had turned him down. He had then offered his hand in simple friendship. She had taken his hand, and he had scratched her palm with his fingernail. She had right away started to have spasms, and her hand and arm had begun to swell. She screamed, and the other Negroes in the street became very frightened. Negroes here are always frightened of poison. Some of the Negroes ran for an alguazil and an alguazil came and took the mulatto off to the jail. The old jail, the one of Picton's time, with the hot-house torture rooms—we pulled it down two years ago.

"The magistrate went as soon as he could to the jail, to investigate. The mulatto said he hadn't poisoned the woman at all. He had only scratched a love potion into her palm. He had got the potion from an old plantation Negro. The potion, mixed with grease and quicksilver and nail-clippings, had already made two women love him madly. This time, he said, he had probably made the dose too strong. The Negro who had made up the potion for him had told him that there was this danger. The magistrate didn't find the story funny. He ordered the jailer to take the mulatto up to the attic, for torture. It was the place where, oddly enough, they kept white people. There was an Italian sailor there. He saw everything. The torture there was the piquet, the old cavalry-regiment torture. You tie a man's leg back, right leg to left arm, say, to convert him into a dead weight, and you suspend him by the left wrist until he can just rest his toe on the tip of a sharp piquet.

"Under torture the mulatto gave the antidote. Rum and asafoetida, I think it was. Of course it didn't work—it's amazing the magistrate thought that there could be an antidote. The woman remained swollen, and she kept on screaming, getting everyone thoroughly frightened. Old Vallot, the French jailer, strung the mulatto up again, and this time the mulatto fainted and lay for a while in a pool of cold sweat. When he recovered he changed the story about the plantation Negro. He said he had got the potion from a Negro sorcerer who had been banished from the island. I know today that as soon as a planter hears about sorcery he panics. I didn't know that then. It was my first week. The magistrate insisted we should get the mulatto off the island right away. He wanted the man banished there and then.

"And it was done just like that, right here. No papers,

nothing. I didn't actually forget about the case. But what I remembered more was the love potion and the asafoetida and the rum, not the sorcerer. And now I have had to dig it up from my memory, all the details of the conversation that day with the magistrate. Because since Picton's conviction they've all reappeared—the mulatto, and even the Italian sailor. Somehow they've all made their way to London, somehow they've found people to get them lodgings and pay their expenses, and somehow they've all been put in touch with lawyers. And all the people who supported the Picton prosecution are now behind them.

"The free people of colour are passionate about it. There are six thousand of them here. They can raise money. What is upsetting to me is that I've always been a friend to the people of colour, like Tom Picton before me. He was always against the legal humiliation of the people of colour, in spite of what you hear. He wrote many letters to London about that. Because that legal humiliation is what people intend when they speak, as you will hear them speaking, about the need for British laws and a British constitution and representative government here. We use words in a special way here, and what they mean is that they want to be their own legislative council and executive council and to set up their own laws.

"I'll tell you what some of those laws are going to be. They want to prevent people of colour from owning Negroes. That's pure malice. You make it illegal for a man of colour to have Negroes and you impoverish him at a stroke. There is no way he can run a plantation or make a living on his own in this kind of place. People do everything for themselves with their own Negroes. We have no free journeymen. The only respectable thing a free man of colour can do, if he has no Negroes, is to become an alguazil for the Council, a kind of general watchman. As in the Spanish time. He keeps an eye on the docks and the Negro yards in the town and he looks out for Negroes breaking the curfew. Sometimes he lends a hand in the jail. He isn't allowed to own Negroes, and for good reason. There would be all kinds of abuses—kidnappings and disappearances of new arrivals, and so on. There are only six alguazils here, anyway. It's all the Treasury can afford. And there are six thousand free people of colour. If it becomes illegal for a man of colour to own Negroes, he will have to sell those he has for what he can get, or they will be confiscated. Either way there are some people here who are going to make a great profit. At least half the Negroes here are owned by people of colour. So we are talking about a lot of money. And we are talking about a great deal more if, as is almost certain, the African trade is stopped next year, and 'supply,' as our friends say, becomes purely local.

"There is something else the Du Castellets and the Montignacs and the Montalemberts are planning. They want to prevent people of colour from buying houses. It's a piece of antique French legislation from the islands. Where do they expect the people of colour to live? And what is their definition of a house? Do they mean an estate house, or a house in the town? I will tell you: it will mean what they want it to mean. It will become a simple means of persecution. You take away people's livelihood. You plunder them of their little capital, and then you degrade them.

"There is something else. It's so terrible you won't hear about it while you are here. The French are not going to tell you, and the people of colour are too frightened and ashamed to talk about it. The white planters are letting them know, very quietly, that when British laws come in, they, the people of colour, will be liable to be whipped for misdemeanours. Only Negroes are whipped now. So the people of colour, who are now free men and proprietors, will be indistinguishable from Negroes. They will have no money, no resources, and many of them will certainly be enslaved again. And all this will be done in the name of law and the rights of man and the clemency of a British constitution.

"They know I'm against it. So they've blackened my character in London and up and down the islands. I'm a tippler, a sot, too fond of the pleasures of the table at Government House, dead to the world after dinner. Too little dignity for a governor. The pleasures of the table—red, salty butter, no vegetables, and this ship's food.

"You will see now that the worst thing I could have done was to have allowed that man's ears to be cut off. A free man reduced to slavery, and treated as the worst kind of Negro. It's really what the French want to do to all the free people of colour. They infected me at the time of the enquiry. They talked to me about Martinique and Haiti. They talked to me about having to burn Negroes when they became too steeped in sorcery and magic. One man told me that a friend of his in Martinique had had to burn four of his Negroes. They told me that a free man of colour who habitually mixed with Negroes was very dangerous. They made me want to hurt the man very badly. After all the evidence at the inquiry, after hearing those simple-looking people talking very calmly about murdering people as though it was a continuation of their king-and-queen play at night, I saw the island and the town going up in flames. I never asked to see the laws. I never saw the man or what they did to him in the jail or asked how they sold him out of the island. I wonder now whether I would have even thought more about it if the Picton conviction hadn't occurred. The turpitude, General. The turpitude I've lived with these past three years."

Miranda said, "These people are my volunteers. I have no other now."

"Your volunteers. Not your masters. As a military man I have been bred up in the virtues of obedience to my lawful superiors. I've never knowingly—as a military man—done an illegal or wrong or insubordinate thing. Most military men can say the same. It is particularly galling to me now to live with the prospect of being dragged before the public as an oppressor. Especially as the oppressor of people whom I've considered it my duty to protect. If there is an investigation or enquiry or trial, I wouldn't know how to defend myself. To defend myself, I will have to put myself on the side of people whom I consider infamous. The people of colour have said, after the Picton conviction, that they intend to make an example of me. They are not nice words to hear. And I have reason to believe that they are being encouraged by the French, of all people, just to do me down. Nothing is clear to me now, General. I have become clouded."

"Your bed has certainly not been one of roses. *Claro que su cama no ha sido una de rosas, como ha dicho.*"

"I feel I need to make a fresh start."

"You certainly can do that in Caracas."

"General."

"But you'll be on the same side as the French volunteers."

"That will be accidental. I will have the clarity of your own purpose and vision."

Miranda said, "Let me read this letter from your sentry-box. It might be from one of your mulatto friends, you think? Please, General. Allow me that joke. The letter's not in French. It's in Spanish. A scrivener's hand. So at least it's formal. I'll skim. It may be nothing. It may just be standard abuse. It begins politely. Too politely—a bad sign. Sure enough, it soon becomes very passionate. I recognize the manifesto style of certain Spanish official pronouncements. It's a letter from the Spanish authorities. It's very serious. It warns me of the fate of Tupac Amaru. Tupac Amaru was the Inca name taken by the leader of a very big Indian rebellion in Peru in 1780. He was horribly tortured when he was caught. His tongue was cut off while he was still alive, and then, while he was still alive, he was quartered by four horses pulling in different directions. The four quarters of the man-

gled body were placed in four specially prepared leather cases
and sent to different places in Peru. Every officer in the Spanish service knew about the fate of Tupac Amaru. I was in
Jamaica at the time, a newly brevetted colonel, negotiating
an exchange of prisoners with the British. The idea of people
preparing the four leather cases for a man who was still living
was particularly upsetting to me. I think it was one of the
things at the back of my mind when I decided to desert two
years later. When I was in the United States there was another
rebellion. Another man took the name of Tupac Amaru, and
was killed in the same dreadful way. But let me read the letter
more carefully.

"*Esteemed sir: Liberty is the watchword of our times, in all
continents. As Spaniards, in a land which has been ours immemori-
ally, we have aspirations like your own. Our purpose is to tell you,
always with the respect due to a distinguished compatriot, how we
have fared under your British patrons since the British conquest of
our island. Picton, the first British military governor, who is now
in London expiating his crimes, sought simply to cut off the Spanish
head. He expelled nearly all Spaniards of culture and breeding and
professional attainment. You will not hear from your convivial host,
Hislop, how he has dealt with the peon remnant of your compatriots,
the keepers of grog-shops, the boatmen and huntsmen, the charcoal-
burners, the hawkers of tallow and dried horse-meat, simple people
like those you surely would remember from your childhood, people
who do not know fine words and in their current humiliations are
protected only by their faith and pride. Hislop—who in his craven
way has not dared to touch the French of family, holding their very
Negroes inviolate, exempt even from the corvée—has made militia
service compulsory for all Spaniards. This entails a charge of one
hundred dollars for uniform and equipment. Hislop himself has fixed
this charge. Very few of our peons can pay this sum, so most will
have to leave the island or take to the high woods, abandoning in
either case what little property they have to Hislop's Treasury. So,
in less than ten years of British rule, we have become runaways and*

outlaws in our own land, and our language is judged to be a servant's language.

"And now you come among us. On both sides of the Gulf we have got to know the prospectuses of your London sponsors, Turnbull and Forbes. They offer many desirable modern manufactures at a fair price, but it cannot be a surprise to you if in the eyes of some of us you appear less a liberator and a lover of freedom than a Caracas man who has remained true to his origins, and has returned as the factor of a British commercial enterprise that seeks to reduce the people of the continent to peonage, as has happened to people in large parts of Asia, and as has happened here.

"Since the British conquest you and Picton between you have used the language of liberty and revolution to seduce many good people away from the fear of God, the sentiments of humanity, and the no less sacred duties of religion and society. You have lured these people to this island, your base for subversion, and you have kept them here like caged wild animals, to be released at your whim on an innocent populace. These misguided people have been ready to give everything to you and your cause. You have given them nothing. Your revolution, because it is baseless and finds no echo in the souls of good men, because it has degenerated into a personal enterprise and is without nobility, has never come. And when these proud Spanish spirits, recognizing their error, have rebelled against their betrayal by you and Picton, ways have been found of silencing them. Think of Juan Mansanares, for some time so loud and boastful in the grog-shops of this town, and flush with English money, then mysteriously dead at the age of thirty-six; old Manuel Gual, at first hidden away by Picton, then cruelly poisoned with pills of opium mixed with crushed glass; his friend José España, driven by his despair back across the Gulf, betrayed in his own hearth, beheaded, his fair body quartered, his head displayed in an iron cage at the Caracas Gate of the port of La Guaira; Andrés de España, languishing for years in the infamous jail here; Juan Caro and Antonio Vallecilla, both dead, their graves unknown. Think of these men, and all the others whose life and passion you and Picton ate away

month by month and year by year, and wonder that you felt so little
trepidation at setting foot on this bloodstained soil. Wonder that you
never thought that your fate might be like theirs, and that this
usurped island might also become your prison and grave.

"Whatever encouragement Hislop gives, his word is worthless.
He is a soldier; his honour lies in obedience. He will feast you today;
he is famous as a good host. He will turn his back on you tomorrow,
if he is required to do that. You may discover, as we have done, that
he has claws. Justice approaches for the fifty-eight men you aban-
doned off the coast. Justice approaches for you too. You are more
alone and unprotected here, in what used to be your homeland, than
you ever were in London. Six copies have been made of this letter.
At least one will get to you, and you will think of TUPAC
AMARU."

Hislop said, "General, General. I shouldn't have shown
you the letter on your first day. It has unsettled you."

"It has. I know Spanish hate, but it's always a shock
whenever I am reintroduced to it. This is a letter of hate. You
were talking earlier of the hatred the people here got you to
feel for the free man of colour whose ears they wanted to cut
off. They made you look at him. They told you he believed
in his own powers. They showed you hell in his eyes. They
made you feel you didn't have just to punish the man, you
had to destroy what was inside him. Spanish hatred is like
that. It's never far away, and it's mixed up with ideas of faith
and truth and retribution. As a punisher you're in the right.
You're in the place of God.

"I know about this hate because it's in me too, after all
these years. I have dealt in it myself, and I know that what
I've done is partly responsible for this letter. Hate against
hate. I've said things about Spain and the Spaniards I
shouldn't have said. I said foolish things, wounding things.
I know how to wound them. When I left Caracas in 1771
Spain was the centre of the world for me. History, culture,
elegance. The United States didn't exist—the American colo-

nies were poorer than we were—and the French Revolution was twenty years away. I'm ashamed to tell you how much money I spent on clothes in my first month in Cadiz. It was some years before I saw that the ideas I had had about Spain and its position in the world were exaggerated. When I deserted from the Spanish service and went to the United States in 1783, at the end of the war, I found for the first time I could say things about Spain that I had grown to feel. And it actually did me no harm. I saw that. And then there was the execution of the second Tupac Amaru. That affected me more than the Americans I was with. I began to say things I shouldn't have said. The president of Yale rebuked me one evening. He said the Spaniards had a higher regard for law than I allowed. I said I knew about Spanish legalism: I had graduated in law from the University of Mexico. I made that up on the spur of the moment. It came out very easily, and it silenced him.

"It was much worse when I went to Russia. I felt I was so far away that it didn't matter what I said about Spain or myself. I made full use of the freedom, I should tell you. And the empress and her nobles were so interested, so protective. I was dazzled. I felt it was what I was born for. I had never felt so safe. I said things about Spain to please them, dreadful things about the Inquisition and superstition and Spanish ignorance and degeneracy, dreadful things about the Spanish king and his son, the Prince of Asturias.

"I was in demand. One night at a gathering in St. Petersburg a fine gentleman I hadn't met, as soon as he caught sight of me, came right across the room towards me. I smiled and bowed, getting ready for his Russian French, expecting him to be hampered by the language but friendly and interested and as anxious to invite me to his house as so many of the other Russian noblemen I had met. It wasn't French that came out of this fine gentleman's mouth, but Spanish, the Spanish of Spain, spoken in a tone and with the forms you would use

with a servant. He was the Spanish chargé d'affaires, Maca-
naz. He wanted me to produce—there and then, almost—
the Spanish patents which made me a colonel and a count.
That was my style in Russia. It did no one any harm, and it
gave the Russians pleasure. I was staggered by his contempt.
It was the contempt of the well-born Spaniard from Spain
for the South American. I felt shabby, caught out. It was like
being pushed back to the Caracas of twenty years before. I
was about to say that I had served for some time in the
Princess Regiment and had retired from the service as a colonel. But at the last moment I changed my mind, and the
crudest street-corner obscenities of Caracas came out of my
mouth. In any other setting he would have had to draw his
sword. But in that room he had to digest the insult. He
didn't forget, of course. He wrote to the ambassador, and the
ambassador wrote around to other people about me. I
thought about that incident quite recently, when the *Bee* and
the *Bacchus* were cut off. It was very strange. I was leading
an invasion, something I had talked about for years, and then
with the memory of that far-away St. Petersburg room I
thought, 'And now you've put yourself within their reach.' "

Hislop said, "What will happen to those men?"

"No question. The Spaniards will treat it very seriously.
The officers, Donohue and Powell and the others, will be
executed. The men will all be imprisoned. I always told them.
Tell me—this is about something in the letter—why do you
think all the agents I sent out here failed me, or went bad?
You know about Bernard. I know about the others."

"They got tired of waiting. They lost faith. Like Picton.
In spite of what people say about him, he didn't come here
to buy estates. He never wanted to be a planter. He is a
military man, and he came here hoping for action. They
promised big things in South America, but the alliances kept
changing in Europe, and the politics kept changing in London. The invasion was postponed and postponed. You can't

ask a man to wait and wait. Not everyone has your steadfastness, General."

"Steadfastness. I don't know. Perhaps there has never
been an alternative. No second possibility ever came up. No
one has ever offered me a second idea."

"No one would ever think of doing that, General."

"There was a time when I used to talk against Picton in
London. I thought he was destroying my agents and destroying the revolutionaries from across the Gulf. I was wrong.
Old Manuel Gual and the others who were killed here were
killed by a Venezuelan I now know about; Caracas recruited
him and gave him the famous glass pills. The one man of
mine Picton expelled and sent back to Europe turned out to
be a fraud. My bad judgement again. The man could write
me a witty letter about the unreliable revolutionaries of
France, and then, almost on the same day, write a tearful
letter to the king of Spain, begging to be forgiven. Picton
expelled him almost as soon as he saw him. I was enraged
when I heard, but he did me a service there.

"Actually there was another reason why I talked against
Picton. But I couldn't admit it to anyone. In 1798, without
knowing anything about me or my past or all the work I had
done for the revolution, he wrote to London about me. He
said they might find me useful, but I shouldn't be told too
much. The actual words were much worse. I can't forget
them. They were reported back to me by my friend Rutherfurd. Those words did me much harm with the ministers. I
know them by heart. 'There is a native of Caracas now in
London who might be useful on this occasion, not that he
possesses a great local knowledge, or has any considerable
connection, being the son of a shopkeeper of Caracas . . .'
This was nearly thirty years after I had left home. I had done
so much, established my cause and my character, taken so
many risks. He had ignored all that. And he himself had done
nothing."

Hislop said, "He was only repeating what the Caracas people had put in his way, to damage you."

"I know that. I knew it then. And things like that don't worry me at all now. But I couldn't forgive him then. I always talked against him. So much so that when the ministers in London decided to replace him by commissioners and to have him investigated, the news was brought to me as good news, and I was asked to send out one of my own people with the new commissioners. I thought I should send the most reliable man I knew, to re-establish my credit generally. I couldn't have chosen anyone worse. Bernard, you know, came out and never wrote me a word. This man wrote all the time. His name was Pedro Vargas. Every two or three weeks, when the mail ships arrived from Barbados or the Leeward Islands station, the people in Whitehall would send me bundles of letters from the first commissioner's office, from my man Pedro Vargas. Every word was false. I should have spotted it. The language was rhetorical, in the Spanish manifesto style. Vargas was a master of that. I was a messiah, a redeemer. Everyone in Venezuela and New Granada was waiting for me, ready to give their lives and property to the cause.

"One letter made me lose my head. He said that he was writing in great excitement. For various reasons the moment for action had absolutely come. We shouldn't wait. If necessary the two of us alone should start the revolution. Once we landed, at any spot on the coast, people would flock to our banner. I took the letter to ministers. I showed them what Commissioner Vargas—giving him this false title—had written. I nearly caught myself out, with that exaggeration of the dignity of Pedro Vargas. I told the ministers I would be willing to forego the allowance I had from the British government if they would give me a ship and equipment and allow me to go to Trinidad and raise a force from among the black troops there. Fortunately they refused. I don't know whether they knew more about Vargas than I did. Can you imagine what would have happened if I had turned up here and asked for black troops to invade the continent? You hardly have enough men to defend this little town. And the planters wouldn't have given me their Negroes. I would have had to go back to London and ask them to give me my allowance again.

"I later discovered that Vargas hadn't even embroidered some little incident or some piece of local gossip. He had written that letter just to give a little variety to his reports. He had attached himself to the suite of the first commissioner as a kind of secretary and assessor in Spanish law. He would sit in the first commissioner's house—this very house—and every few days write me a fairy story. He was getting an allowance from me, ten shillings a day. He was getting a good deal more from the first commissioner. He had been a revolutionary at one time. He had been part of a conspiracy in New Granada and had exposed himself to real danger and had suffered. But what mattered to him now was getting that regular money from the first commissioner."

Hislop said, "It was Vargas's evidence that condemned Picton at the trial in February. I've read the transcript. Vargas was called as the Spanish legal expert. He was the only man in England—if you would believe it—who had the relevant Spanish lawbooks. He said that there were very old Spanish laws that permitted torture, but no modern ones. And that was it. Strange that all the bigger charges of hanging and burning should have been thrown out, and this case of petty theft should have brought Picton down. Signing the order that the very respectable magistrate brought him for the torture of the young mulatto girl. And Picton is tried, and the magistrate is untouched. And very strange that Picton should have been ruined by this man you sent here who let you down. He has opened up the possibility of all those charges against me now. The mulatto and the love potion, the very first week I came here. Every night in my head I work out my defence in the Court of King's Bench. I wonder who I'm going to call as a witness, and how I'm going to prove that the Spaniards do torture. And then I think it's a waste of my life, all this worrying about something I had almost nothing to do with."

Miranda said, "Even when I was enraged by Picton, I didn't want him brought down like this. He would despise the lie and he would despise us for it. I certainly didn't want him brought down all these years later by someone like Pedro Vargas."

''MY DEAR Sally, all goes well. You see, you are too nervous. With Hislop's help we have brought the *Leander* Americans round. There are still days when they get drunk and make a racket, but discipline gets better and better. We drill them and the French every day at the local barracks. Count Loppinot de Lafresillière refused absolutely to serve under an American, and we have decided it is better to keep the two groups apart. This time we will make a little armada of ten ships. The British are helping unofficially with the ships, and I can gauge the strength of my support in London from the attitude of people like Admiral Cochrane and General Maitland and Hislop here. These men court me. I can see regard in their faces. They still think I am the man who can do things for them, and I thank God for that. Hislop thinks I can give him a good job, and Maitland and Cochrane (his immense greed makes him easy to manage) expect me in due course to grant them vast estates on the continent.

"It is wrong, *querida,* for you to think of these men as snakes in the grass. When I was young I used to complain in that way. I was wrong. You must not encourage Leander and Francisco to expect more from men than they should expect. You must not talk to them about snakes in the grass. These men, Cochrane, Maitland, Hislop, owe me no loyalty. A mutual interest draws us together. When there is no interest, we will pull apart. There will be no immorality or disloyalty in pulling apart. If you don't start thinking like that, *querida*, you will eat yourself up. You will be in a perpetual moral frenzy in which you will condemn everybody except yourself, and people would start wondering what it is about you they don't like. It is something I've talked to you about. I think it is most noticeable in your attitude to certain members of your family.

"As for Turnbull, he is my oldest friend. We met more than thirty years ago in Gibraltar, when he was a young factor and I was a captain, and we have been friends ever since. Whatever happens now, he will have regard for me afterwards, and I for him. I will not find people like Turnbull and Rutherfurd again. The time for that kind of friendship is past. If Turnbull gets impatient with me, I get impatient with myself. A friend doesn't have to watch his words always. Don't be suspicious of him. Don't be unhappy about him. I write this only because, as you know, I am worried about your nerves.

"My serial letter, or my letter-journal, never stops. I speak to you constantly in my mind. I report everything to you, sometimes very small things, because I love your love. You have almost become my waking mind. But not everything I speak I will write.

"We are about to go now. The ships are ready. I will not be on the *Leander*. I will be on H.M.S. *Lily*. This is Cochrane's idea: he thinks that if there is a battle the Spaniards will go for the *Leander*, which flies American colours and is known to be my ship. The men are as prepared as they will ever be. But—this is something I wouldn't write, and want no one to know—my spirits are low.

"A second Spanish letter was thrown yesterday in the sentry box here (and Bernard later sent a copy of the same letter that had been left at the Council room). This one is about the big thanksgiving service they held in the Metropolitan Church of Caracas for the capture of the *Bee* and the *Bacchus,* and about the sentences at Puerto Cabello on the fifty-eight men. Sixteen days ago they were all taken out in ankle fetters to the prison yard and made to kneel down while their sentences were read to them. The ten officers were to be hanged. All the others were sentenced to eight or ten years in prison with hard labour. They are to sleep on beds of stone, with pillows of brick, and they are to wear twenty-five-pound chains. The ten executions took place seven days ago. I know that the Spaniards would have hurried through the legal process so that all this news could get to me before this second attempt.

"It would be nice if the details were exaggerated. But I know they are not. The scaffold was outside the prison gate. The ten men, in white gowns and white caps and in leg-irons, were led out to it. After each man was dropped the hangman, a Negro, slid down the rope and sat on the shoulders of the hanged man. The bodies were then decapitated and cut into quarters. The quarters were heaped together with the uniforms and arms of the dead men, covered with the torn-up scraps of my Colombian flag, and set alight. I knew that they were going to do some special dishonour to the flag you made in Grafton Street, Sally. But I won't tell you.

"The atmosphere of the Inquisition, my revolution treated as heresy—it is more undermining than I would have thought. If I, at one time, knew how to wound them, they still know how to trouble me. One of my first thoughts, when I read this letter, was that I had done the right thing to have the boys baptized. When I was thirty-five or so, and after just fifteen years abroad, when I was in the United States and then when I was in Russia, the whole world of my early years in Venezuela seemed very far away, seemed to be part of another life. I felt I had forgotten so much. Now it's as though I've never left, as though 1771 was last year."

. . .

"MY DEAR Sir, We are in such a State here. My uncle has just brought back six copies of your Picture from Mr. Holland the Printseller. My uncle says the engraver should have done better but these people have to do too much and they cut corners and they don't try to understand the work they are copying, before they finish one job theyre looking for the next one. The picture shows the Crown in the Clouds above your head and my uncle says it is poor work that crown, badly drawn but people don't care. He says the picture is in Mr. Holland's window and people stop and look at the crown and wonder so perhaps Mr. Holland knows his business. But the deseat of these London tradesmen my dear Sir they give no Credit to my uncle for the picture which he did at the small table in the Front Library. They say it is done from the life by their artist with the Navy in the Barbadoes my Uncle says it's the kind of thing they always say. Below your picture they have engraved the names of the ships of your little fleet My dear Sir. What a fleet my dear Gen I never had the least idea. We daily wait to hear good news. What pretty names your ships have Lily Attentive Bulldog Trimmer Mastiff. I cannot tell you how Excited Leander is that one ship has his name, he pulls his toy ship on its wooden block all over the house and he says Mamy I will take my ship and go to the Genl. When I tell him that the ocean is very big and his ship wouldnt sail very far he says Mamy I will buy a bigger ship and go and fight for the G. He reads his book well and he promises not to trouble little brother who is now sleeping and is as pretty as your picture My own dear General. These are their happiest days my dear Sir."

"OH, SARAH. We are separated by more than the ocean. We are separated by time, by three to four months. You write about things here as they were four months ago, and what I

write now you will read in two months. I don't know what
will have happened by then. It's failed, Sarah. The whole
thing failed. You were right. The people in London let me
down at the last moment. They withdrew their support. And
I'm back in Trinidad.

"I am not at Government House. Officially I have no
position here. I have no headquarters. I am a private person,
and while I am here I must give up all attempts to revolution-
ize the continent. On the morning I arrived I went to call
on Hislop. He couldn't pretend he didn't know me, but he
behaved as though he knew nothing about what I had been
doing. When I asked for permission to stay, he said it was
out of his hands. He said the merchants didn't want me to
land. They had made a petition to him. They said that for six
months they had been cut off from trade with the Main
because of me, and they were being ruined for nothing at all.
The petition was going to be debated that very morning in
the Council. Hislop thought I should attend the meeting. I
suppose that was friendly advice. If I hadn't gone, perhaps
Bernard wouldn't have spoken up for me as he did, and if
Bernard hadn't spoken up, the vote would have gone against
me. Hislop would have been full of regrets, of course, but I
would have had to leave. Heaven knows where I would have
been now.

"And things seemed to be going so well in the beginning,
Sally. Ah, those good beginnings! I've had so many of them.
How they encourage, and at the same time how they unsettle!
We sailed without interference to the town of Coro. We fired
at the fort. There was some return fire and then the Spanish
soldiers withdrew. We landed and entered the town with no
trouble. Just three men wounded. Then we found there was
nothing to celebrate. We had entered an empty town. Not a
soul. The Venezuelan agents in Trinidad had done their work
well. They knew our strength, and exactly where we were
going to land, and they knew that the British were only going
to support us from the sea.

"For years I had believed—and people like Gual and Caro and Vargas had encouraged me to believe—that when I landed the people would flock to my colours. No one came now. I thought they had been threatened by the authorities, and I thought I should deal with the situation in a Spanish or Venezuelan way. That side of my character took over. I felt that, having appeared with such a naval force, I should speak very loudly. I issued a proclamation. I said that Spanish rule had ceased, that all officials should come forward and declare their loyalty to me or suffer the consequences, and that all able-bodied men should enrol under my colours. It was a wrong thing to do. No one came forward, and my authority with my own men was further undermined. I sent out small parties to the villages round about to reassure the people. I found the Spaniards had forestalled me. They knew how to fight this war. For weeks the priests had been preaching against me. Everyone who helped me was to be excommunicated. The bishop of Mérida had declared me a heretic.

"For the next ten days the Spaniards who had withdrawn from Coro shadowed us, fifteen hundred of them to four hundred of us. No question of engaging them, no question of making a march over the hills to Caracas. The strain began to tell on our volunteers. Their discipline began to break. One day there was an incident between the two groups, the French and the Americans. Three more men wounded, a cook killed. This greatly alarmed me. I thought we should make our way back to the coast. We had no carts, of course, for the wounded and the sick, or horses or mules. We had to use litters, changing the carriers every half hour or so. It slowed us up. I felt I had walked into a Spanish trap. I felt that at any moment the Spaniards might fall on us. I drove the litter-bearers hard. At one stage I threatened to shoot some of them with my own hand. They haven't forgiven me. I am not staying in Government House, and now they shout abuse at me in the streets.

"Late one night we re-embarked. I didn't know what to

do. I had waited so many years for this moment. I wrote to
the British governor of Jamaica for help. It was foolish. Of
course he couldn't send troops to me. I waited six weeks to
hear that, our supplies running out, food very scarce, people
getting sick and mutinous. And then a message came from
Admiral Cochrane, telling me he couldn't help any more.
London had forbidden it. His help to me was to be limited to
protection from a naval force of the enemy, to prevent enemy
succours being landed, and to secure my re-embarkation. In
short, it was finished. I had thought of Cochrane as an avari-
cious man, easy therefore to handle. Now the style of his
letter, so precise and pointed, like instructions on the battlefield, spoke to me of the capacity that had made him an
admiral, and of a power that I had never possessed.

"This was the mood in which, after beating eastwards
against the wind for five weeks, that wind like the wind of
my misfortune, I returned with my ragged force to Trinidad,
and on the very day of my return had to show Hislop a good
face, and then, like a man still only a step from power, had
to sit in the Council while the contraband traders debated my
future.

"Cochrane shows me honour still, in a way. He has arranged for me to stay in the house of Lieutenant Briarly, RN.
Briarly is so far correct. He lives in greater style than Hislop,
but as the leading Navy man here he does run something like
a parallel government. He enforces the Navigation Acts here.
His command is only a dismasted hulk in the harbour, but
when he is aboard that he is outside Hislop's jurisdiction.
Such is the power of this Navy. The Navigation Acts have
to do with trade. This means that Briarly is a kind of customs
officer. This means that he splits with the contraband traders
and the ship's captains and offers protection to others. He is
making a fortune. He knows to the last shilling how much
he is worth, and I have already been made to know it too. I
know that this Port of Spain house where I am staying is

worth ten thousand dollars (and he keeps on saying he can sell it any day), and I know that in addition he has a large country estate worth fifteen thousand pounds, with eleven mules and thirty-three Negroes. He is forever writing down the names of these thirty-three on little scraps of paper, and putting numbers next to them, as though he wants to count his Negroes and add up their value all the time.

"The Spaniards and Venezuelans here, the traders and the peons, still hiss me in the street. They did it the morning I arrived. I thought they would have stopped by now. They do it in a way that always takes me by surprise. They don't look at me, so when the sharp hissing sound starts I can't tell where it's coming from. It is a terrible sound. It would cut through a military band.

"A defeated man has to put up with criticism, and I thought at first that they were mocking me because I had failed. Then I thought it might have been because of the American malcontents from the *Leander,* who make endless scenes in the streets and are dunning me for money I don't have. Terrible stories have been spread, too, about our retreat to the coast and my threatening of the litter-bearers. Then I thought they were hissing me simply for being alive, after so many men had died. I know now that almost on the day we left for Coro the Venezuelan agents here began to spread the story of the executions at Puerto Cabello, the hanging and the burning of the men in white gowns and white caps, the twenty-five-pound chains for the living, with the beds of stone and pillows of brick. And then I thought it was quite simple. I felt that I had let them down because I had failed. I thought that because I had failed I had exposed them as South Americans to ridicule.

"This was so wrong. It is vanity on my part to think like that. I am assuming that these people look on me as their liberator, look to me to restore their dignity. I am assuming they look on me as I look on myself and have been looking on myself these past twenty years. The opposite is true. The peons here look on me as a heretic and traitor. They are happy that I have been defeated and the men from the *Leander* are in rags. The Venezuelan agents have taken good care to circulate the bishop of Mérida's proclamation against me. I am an atheist, a monster, an enemy of religion, leading a gang of scoundrels from the United States and the islands against my country.

"I have never these past twenty years, in the United States and England and Europe, had to defend myself against that charge, and I don't know how to do so here. I don't know how my life has been so twisted that this distorted picture of my character can be thrown at me. This has caused me much distress, Sally, as much distress as the defeat and the humiliation and the idleness I have to endure here. I begin to feel, not only very far away, but also that I am losing touch with things.

"I don't know how to say to the peons here, what the world knows, that since I left the Spanish service I have held no job and had no idea other than that of South American independence. That is how I define myself in the will I made just before I left London. You will remember I say there that I have known no people anywhere else so worthy of a wise and just liberty. What means do I have of making them understand that here? The six thousand books you look after in Grafton Street have been left, in that same will, to the University of Caracas when freedom comes, and I leave the books in memory of the literary and Christian values the university taught me. My sons were both baptized before I set foot on my native land, and when we were coming south in the *Leander* I never stayed on deck when on Sundays Captain Lewis read prayers. The Spaniards have taken all the accidental things in my life, the wild things I said in the United States and Russia when I first felt myself a free man, and the fact that I now need all the volunteers I can get, the Spaniards have taken these accidental things and created a picture of me that I do not recognize. I know that I have followed a straight path, and I am very clear in my own mind about what I want. But I have no means of making myself clear to these people. And, worse, everything I do now confirms their picture. I have written to London for four thousand men. Rouvray has gone with the request. That, too, will add to this picture of the traitor and atheist.

"Briarly, regularly counting his Negroes and adding up his fortune, has begun to sense my solitude and friendlessness, my loss of direction, my floating state here. He has so far been correct with me, treating me as the colleague and friend of his admiral. But now I get some feeling of a change, and this might mean that the ministers in London have given Cochrane more urgent things to attend to. I am nervous of the ruffianly gang of midshipmen who serve Briarly. They have been corrupted by their licence as young officers, tormentors of ordinary seamen, and enforcers of the Navigation Acts, and they take pleasure in chasing and beating up unsuspecting people. They don't touch Negroes, who would have the protection of their owners. But they can give poor white people and free people of colour a rough time. The other day, in daylight, they chased an Englishman through several city yards. They said he was an informer. He ran into somebody's yard and they ran in after him. They pulled the poor man from under a bed in a Negro hut at the back of the yard—it was an enormous joke to them that he was hiding there—and to complete the joke they tarred and feathered him, and Hislop's alguazils could do nothing.

"I've been reporting my doubts about Briarly. His attitude to me has changed. I know it now.

"At dinner yesterday he said, 'I've had a run-in with Biggs the American, the man from the *Leander*. He's not exactly friendly towards you. You haven't paid him or anybody else for six months. He's told me a lot of other things.

He says he's going to write a book about this whole business of yours.'

" 'I know. I'll have to take what comes.'

" 'Let me be blunt. Why is it that whenever you've been put to the test as a military man, you've let people down?'

" 'I did well in North Africa. At Melilla. But that was thirty years ago.'

" 'Exactly. I was thinking of the siege of Maastricht when you had bluffed your way into command of the French.'

" 'There was a trial in Paris. I was cleared of all charges. Biggs should have told you.'

" 'And Puerto Cabello in April, and now.'

" 'I suppose you can say I had bad luck.'

" 'I have good luck.'

"As sometimes happens when I am in an unequal relationship with a man in authority for whom I have no regard, I began to exaggerate the side of my character that was opposite to his. It can look like irony to some, but it really is a form of unhappiness. I became soft, over-cultured. I said, 'Cicero says good luck is one of the four qualities of a successful military man.'

" 'What are the other three?'

" 'Talent, military knowledge, and prestige. The words have very wide meanings.'

" 'Don't you think it would have been different at Coro if you had had a man of luck at your side? A man who believed in his luck wouldn't have been so much on the defensive. He might have shown you some way of cutting off the Spanish force that was shadowing you, squeezing them between you and the ships, and then marching on Caracas.'

" 'I had no faith in the men. They had begun to fight among themselves.'

" 'How are you going to pay them off? And settle the master of the *Trimmer*? He's going to sue you. He says you hired his ship in Barbados. Why don't you sell the *Leander*?

It will fetch a good price. You will pay off everybody if you sell it well.'

"'Who will buy it?'

"'I will buy it. That's not charity. It's a business deal. I will refit the ship in Antigua or Barbados, get it up to Admiralty standards, and sell it to the Navy. The Navy needs ships. I know exactly what they need.'

"He said no more, and now to some extent I wait on his decision. He knows that, and for some days he has not mentioned the *Leander*. I feel uneasy, because it seems too easy, and because I'm not sure now what's coming from Lieutenant Briarly.

"I got to know today.

"He said abruptly at dinner, 'I think before you sell, the *Leander* should make one last run under American colours. Up the river to Angostura. That's where you should have gone in the first place. The river is narrow, the town is not well-protected. I know the place. As a good Navy man, my first thought when I look at a town from a river or the sea is, "What's the best way of attacking this place?" It's a mental exercise for me. And the Venezuelan ship captains bring me information all the time. I know exactly what to do at Angostura. An hour's hot work by good Navy gunners would deal with the military barracks and such fortifications as they have. We could then move up and down at will, covering you. We could hold the town for quite a while. You could land and proclaim your republic. If it works you stay. If not, in five days you are back here.'

"I know it's an act of piracy he's proposing. That's the idea he has of me and my cause. It's the idea the Venezuelans have spread, and it's exactly the way some of the *Leander* men used to talk at the beginning. And, of course, I would be completely in his power. He could withdraw his force, he could hand me over to the Spaniards, he could do anything. But the insult! The insult!

"Two days later. Nothing said in the interim. Now: 'Have you thought it over?'

" 'Angostura is better fortified than you imagine. An attacking force coming upriver would be very vulnerable.'

" 'So your answer is no?'

" 'I fear so.'

"He was enraged, icy. He said, 'The *commandeur* of my property here has been complaining to me. You have been making far too free with the mules and the Negroes. To the general prejudice of the place. The *commandeur* says he is not able to get on with his proper duties.'

"I said, 'You offered the facility. I have been transferring supplies from the *Leander* to a warehouse. You know that.'

" 'I gave permission for one day. I didn't give permission for a week. I think you should leave. I have in fact drafted a letter to Admiral Cochrane telling him that I feel compromised in my dealings with Spaniards and others by your continued residence here. In the circumstances you will understand that I have to decline your offer of the *Leander*. I think you should leave as soon as possible.'

"I left the next morning. I was relieved to get away from the house. But I was sorry about the *Leander*. He had encouraged me to think that the deal was all but struck.

"I went to McKay's Hotel. It is next door to the military barracks, where for four weeks or so I drilled my men. Downstairs, McKay's is a tavern with a billiard table for merchants' clerks. Upstairs there are four or five rooms overlooking the parade ground.

"McKay came here just after the British conquest. He had heard from someone that the island was empty and they were giving away land. He found when he came that they were indeed giving away land, but only in large acreages and only to people who could bring in a large enough Negro *atelier*. He said as a joke to the chief magistrate one day, 'Suppose I start clearing five acres of forest for myself, what will happen?' The chief magistrate said in the same spirit,

'Vallot's jail and Negro's punishment, thirty-nine lashes.' Vallot was the jailer at the time, a Frenchman from Martinique, a figure of terror to the Negroes. It is a tavern-keeper's story, the way McKay tells it now, and of course he has done well with the billiard table and the dubious rooms upstairs, and has a few Negroes of his own. About the billiards: McKay says every table pays a tax, and the money goes straight to Hislop as part of his official fees as governor.

"I have written down that story about McKay for you, Sally. What I will not write about is my mood. The fact is I don't know what to do now about anything—not even about the *Leander* people—and I don't see there is anything I can do. I have simply to wait until I hear from Rouvray in London. That will be three months at least. I know how to wait. It's the one thing I have learned in the last twenty years. What I don't know is how well I will get on here. I am among people who don't really know who I am. They have their own ideas. They are ready enough to go by the regard of people like Hislop and Cochrane, but when that regard isn't there they don't know what value to put on me. I am not like anyone they know.

"It's strange, but I have never been in a situation like this before. In Caracas I was the son of a rich and prominent man. Even as a child I was known. I grew up feeling famous. Later in Spain I was an extravagant colonial, and then I was a captain in the Princess Regiment. I suppose I floundered for a while when I left the Spanish service and went to the United States. I had to pick my way, and I had to improvise all the time. But at the end of my time in the United States I had given myself a character that well-placed people could recognize. In England, France, Russia, I became known for my political cause. It is a very special cause. I have always been somebody. Here now, so close to home, I see no kind of recognition in people's eyes, and I feel as though I am losing pieces of myself.

"And then, Sally, after all that worry, I didn't have to stay at the hotel. I was rescued. McKay's people were bringing my boxes up when Bernard came, running up the rough plank steps in his heavy boots. He was in his planter's working clothes, and looked quite different from when I had last seen him, on the verandah at Government House. He was in his London clothes then.

"Bernard said he had just heard about Briarly, and he had come to take me to his estate house. My boxes were to be taken down again—he gave the orders. He spoke generally with great authority. We were to leave at once. I would be comfortable in his estate house. I would be looked after. I was not to worry about Briarly. I had lost nothing by the quarrel. No one cared much for Briarly and his ruffianly gang of midshipmen. The wonder was that I had stuck it out at Briarly's for so long.

"He had come in his calash, with the Gourville arms. I didn't want to notice its condition now, didn't want to look at the coachman's alpargatas. I appreciated the style. I had been so cast down—for so many of those days at Briarly's, as I now realized—that the regard I saw in the eyes of McKay and even the sickly young billiard-playing clerks downstairs was like balm.

"Bernard's estate was in one of the valleys to the north. So we had to drive right through the town, from south to north. It was like a public display of my worth, in streets where the *Leander* Americans still made trouble and the Spaniards and Venezuelans still sometimes remembered to hiss. And I knew that other people as well (in spite of what Bernard said) had begun to be uncertain about me.

"It was an act of pure friendship on Bernard's part. There is now nothing I can do for him. Friendship like this wasn't something I had ever looked for from him, and I felt it was a correct instinct that had prevented me from treating him roughly when he came to see me at Government House. I had seen something like pathos in him: he had dressed with such care. My heart had gone out to him. Such emotions are often reciprocal, and it occurred to me as we drove that perhaps at that same moment six months ago, when my position here was unquestioned, when my headquarters were at Government House (not far away now) and my authority exceeded Hislop's, Bernard had seen a similar pathos in me.

"We left the town. We entered the narrow winding valley road. After a mile or so, we began to pass a new estate. It was Bernard's, or perhaps the Gourvilles'. Cocoa and coffee grew together, and young shade trees, *samaan* and *immortelle,* perhaps no more than fifteen years old, both now in flower, rose above the low cocoa woods. The red-and-yellow *immortelle* flowers on the ground looked like bright paint. Heavy cocoa pods, all the colours from green to yellow to red to purple, grew directly out of the young black trunks and boughs and hung by short thick stems.

"I got the very smell of damp earth and dead leaves of the cocoa valleys to the north of Caracas. But no vanilla. Instead, an acrid smell of fermenting fruit, which became more pronounced near the house: like the smell of maturing casks or vats of wine.

"Bernard said he was so used to the smell he hardly noticed. He thought I was smelling the tonka bean, an acid, pulpy fruit used to give flavour and body to cocoa. Then he said no, he knew what it was: they were 'sweating' the cocoa beans in the cocoa house. We went out to the cocoa house and he showed me. Cocoa beans grow in a pulp inside a cocoa pod. When the pods are cut open, beans and pulp have to be sweated or fermented for a week or so until the pulp rots. Fermentation gives the cocoa bean its flavour; and that is why some people say chocolate has a slight narcotic effect. I used to hear as a child that certain people in the bush drank their cocoa cold and bitter.

"I said, 'I always thought I knew about cocoa beans. And I'm sure I did at one time. I knew there were many processes, as with so many ancient foods. But I'd forgotten about the sweating. When I left from La Guaira in 1771, my father made me take eight fanegas of cocoa beans.'

"Bernard said, 'That's a lot of cocoa beans. Most of a cocoa pod is pulp.'

" 'The beans were an extra form of currency, if all else failed. It was no trouble to me. The carts brought the cocoa from my father's warehouse to La Guaira. The sailors stowed it in the hold of the *Prins Frederik,* and Aniño, our agent, took charge of it in Cadiz and some time later sent me the money. I don't think I actually saw or smelled the beans.'

"A little way from the sweating shed I saw a strange sight. About twelve women or girls moving very slowly, and in silence, hardly bending their knees, on four raised platforms. There were three girls on each platform. At the side of each platform was a pitched roof of wooden shingles that looked as though it had slipped away from its platform. The fully sweated cocoa beans were drying on those platforms. They took some days to dry. At the slightest sign of rain the seemingly slipped roofs were to be lifted over the platforms; the beans would rot if they got wet. From time to time the drying beans had to be turned over. That was what the twelve girls were doing. They were 'dancing' the cocoa, moving slowly, toes pressing down, through the beans. 'Dancing'—that was the word used here, Bernard said. At the end of the dancing, after some days, the dried beans would have a slight shine. The girls were not all moving in the same direction, and the slowness, and the different positions of the girls on the raised platforms, the seeming self-absorption of each girl, did suggest a strange, subdued dance.

"One girl was lame. I asked Bernard about her.

"He said, 'Marie Bonavita. She was one of the queens when they were planning the rebellion last year. At night she was a queen. She would take one of the estate mules and ride off to their meeting place. When she was there she was not allowed to walk. She was carried everywhere. Her courtiers wore wooden swords painted blue and yellow. Her king was Samson, a carter on Luzette's estate. He had his own uniform, with blue facings. Once she had a big loaf baked here in our oven, and she gave a piece to all her followers. They paid two bits each for that. People were very upset when they heard about that mock communion.'

"'Marie Bonavita. Mary of the Good Life, Mary the Pure.'

"'My wife gave her the name, and always cherished her. After they had killed everybody, she was going to be one of the Negro queens. It came out at the enquiry. Quite a few of these girls were in it. Most of them got away with a whipping. Twenty-five lashes. Marie Bonavita got a little more than that, and she has to wear that ten-pound iron ring on her right ankle. The blacksmith made it for her. She is all right now. She's not dangerous. She's calmed down. She always asks after my wife.'

"'How long will she have to wear the ring for?'

"'Forever.'"

"'MY EVER dear Genl, Your rebuke gratefully accepted, your good words about friendship striking straight into my Heart. Mr. Turnbull heartbroken by your news, after all the High Hopes, and he came here to sit in the Little Library for a quiet half hour he said and to think of his old dear Friend far away. He exprest Sorrow and Regret for the unkind Words he had passed in my Presence. He said he had since gone into the matter and only three booksellers Accounts not paid up Dulau, White, Evans, and he had told them that if they pressed Gen M too hard their Goods wld be returned to them without any Thanks. He said there was still Hope, all the Manufacturing Towns of England were ready to send supplies to my dear G for a new attempt. But this time with an adequate force of reliable men. So my Gen must be patient.

"Both Mr. Turnbull and Colonel Rutherfurd are keeping

an eye on the politics here with the new ministers. My Gen can imagine the to-ing and fro-ing, and Mr. Rutherfurd says that being on the spot as my dear Sir is and ready to move is more than half the battle. Mr. Turnbull sends a messenger with fifty pounds the first of every month from the money you left with him I never have to ask. It was Mellancolic my dear Sir the old greyhaired man angry with the Gen when things were going well and now grieving for my dear Sir's misfortune. Colonel Rutherfurd came with Colonel Williamson in a post chaise, such a commotion in Grafton Street, Leander thought it was his Father coming home as he continuly dreams and he was Overjoyed. He stared all the time at Colonel Williamson and the colonel said he was affected seeing the face and actions of my Gen in the boys every movement. I find much Conciliation in my boys in the absence of my dear Sir who must learn to find Patience as we do here."

''AFTER ALL these weeks Bernard is still friendly and protective. His estate is like a private domain, and the *Leander* people and others have to keep their distance. No one hisses me here. I haven't heard from Rouvray in London. I don't know what the new politics are like there now. I am ready to wait. It is something I have learned, but I have less to do here than I have ever had, and it is hard to be idle in the middle of this very busy estate routine. Bernard is on his feet from morning till night.

"Bernard's wife sometimes has dinner with us. There is something wrong with her bones—Bernard doesn't say what, and perhaps no one knows. She doesn't move easily, and it is a strain for her to sit with a stranger and make conversation. She has a pretty young-woman's face on an old, heavy body. Bernard is devoted to her. They have no children. He loves serving her and looking after her. He loves everything about her—her name, her estate, her fragility, her old-fashioned French. When I first met Bernard in Paris he was a firebrand. That was why I thought him good for my purpose. I never thought of him as a tender person. The tenderness I have seen in him here has probably been brought out by this lady.

"I have not seen any member of the lady's family in the house. Nor have I seen anyone like the Baron de Montalembert. The story here is that Bernard's head was turned by these people of title and he didn't press at the time of the marriage for all that he might have got. They say that among the Gourvilles he is a kind of subordinate, hardly more than the manager of his wife's estate. There is more to his position than that, but there is nonetheless something in the story.

"The people who tell me these things are people to whom Bernard introduced me. Bernard would think of such people as his friends. I don't think they can see the effect they are having on me when they tell me these stories. I cannot conceal from myself—and I wish the idea hadn't occurred to me— that through my association with Bernard I have fallen among the second rank of people in this place. That's not my judgement alone. That's the way they judge themselves. They instinctively put themselves in the second rank. So far as they are concerned, Hislop and Cochrane and even Briarly are people of authority, way above, out of reach. They tell blood-curdling stories about Briarly and Cochrane and absurd sto-ries about Hislop's gluttony, and they think they are being very frank and critical. But, really, they never question the authority of these people.

"The people they try to damage are people like them-selves. As soon as they get you alone—and you have just met them—they tell stories against their friends. So I am nervous of their welcome now. They are so very warm when they meet you; and then you see the other side so soon. I feel that when they offer friendship it is a way not only of claiming me, but also of pulling me down, and when they appear to be sympathizing with my misfortunes they are speaking as good and proper people who have never got above themselves.

"I feel they will soon start telling stories about me. Sometimes when I am with them I find it hard to remember that when I first came here, and was staying at Government House, I looked upon Hislop as a minor local official.

"I have been out of touch, on a tour in the countryside, but have now come back and still find no news from London. It was a month-long tour of English-owned estates with Colonel Downie and Miss McLurie and some others. It was good to get out for a little. It was Downie's idea—he has hopes of serving in my army when the time comes, and his interest makes me feel that things may not be as hopeless in London as I sometimes think. The English are very recent immigrants here, and some of the newer places we went to were very rough. In one place on a Sunday afternoon the whole *atelier* were mustered in clean brown-linen clothes in front of the house and they sang English hymns. I couldn't of course show any interest and this caused a certain amount of bad feeling.

"When I was on the *Leander* coming south from the United States I made a point of not showing myself too often to the men, for the sake of discipline. On this small island you see the same people all the time. It is like being on a ship, and I began to feel half-way through the tour that I had shown myself too often here and was getting a little too well known. I felt that my reputation was dwindling, and that people were already criticizing me, as they criticized their friends.

"At the end of the tour, at a dinner at Miss McLurie's, Colonel Downie presented me with the journal he had made of the tour. I was touched by the gesture—I had grown so melancholy towards the end of the tour, yet never able to show anything—but as soon as I opened the roughly bound book I saw that the journal was the work of an uneducated man. I saw that I had been taken in by Downie's manner and accent, having very few British people of quality here to set him against.

"I looked up. Miss McLurie (who was in her famous transparency, showing her bosom perfectly) was waiting to catch my eye. She said, 'You know, of course, that he's not a colonel.' I didn't know—I had been cherishing him because of the shine he gave to my own hopes. And I had always thought that he and Miss McLurie were special friends. And he was right there still, one of the guests, at the other end of the table.

"I asked him later. He said Miss McLurie was right: he wasn't a colonel. He had called himself that after he had come to the island; he had military ambitions and was looking for an opening somewhere. I said he had misled me, and this could have been damaging. I had suffered enough from the *Leander* people, who had thought that service with me was only a matter of rations and plunder. My venture was likely to have its desperate passages. After my recent reverses I needed men not only with military experience but also with a record of proven luck: he should have known that.

"He hung his head and said he was sorry. But he didn't think he had done worse than other people I knew, and no one criticized them. It was well known, for instance, that Archibald Gloster, the local attorney-general—another person I keep meeting all the time in various houses—wasn't a lawyer. He had simply bought a lawyer's licence from the Council secretary in the time of the first British governor, Picton.

"Bernard later told me it was true about Gloster. It was no secret that the attorney-general wasn't a lawyer at all. And there was a further story about that, Bernard said. It came out during the enquiry into the slave rebellion that had nearly happened.

"Gloster had a personal servant called Scipio. People here often give their Negroes the better-known classical names— Hercules, Hector, Cupid, Caesar, Pompey, Agrippa, Cato, Scipio. At night—this was in the months during the preparing of the rebellion—Gloster's Scipio would leave his quarters at the back of Gloster's yard in the town, and go the five or six miles to the seaside village of Carenage. The Negro known as King Edward had his court at Carenage, and Scipio's loyalty at night was to the *convoi* or regiment of King Edward. Edward's courtiers had wooden swords painted white and green.

"When Scipio first joined the regiment, King Edward offered him a sword and a title: 'My Lord St. John.' Everybody who joined a regiment got a title which he had to use at night. Scipio said no, he didn't want to be My Lord St. John. It didn't mean anything. He wanted to be attorney-general, like his master. Edward said that wasn't a proper title for a courtier in his regiment. In the end they decided that Scipio was to be clerk and secretary—the job Bernard now has in real life—and at night, at Carenage, while King Edward's dauphins and dauphines and princes and princesses drank white rum and sang and danced and ate things that had been cooked for the party in the various estate kitchens during the day, Scipio sat in the light of a flambeau and turned over the pages of one of Gloster's lawbooks and then for ten or fifteen minutes at a time made a pretence of writing. As secretary, though, he had a serious enough job: he became one of the organizers of the rebellion. He was one of those who got a hundred lashes and lost their ears.

"After he told me this story Bernard said, 'Somebody out there is studying me. And somebody is studying you as well, I'm sure. At one time I used to think it was harmless. After what nearly happened to all of us, the mockery seems horrible.'

"So the world shrinks around me while I wait, Sally. I no longer want to go out. There is very little to go out for.

I have heard everything they all have to say. I feel that, as the world around me gets smaller, I dwindle with it. I hope I don't have to wait here much longer, and I hope the waiting has been worthwhile. I cannot hold on to large ideas in this setting. My instinct now, my passion, is to get away, just as it was in Caracas in 1770, thirty-seven years ago. It's as if after half a lifetime I have made a circular journey back to what I was—though I do not remember Caracas being as small as this. The people cannot be blamed. The merchants mix only with their fellows in the very small town, and people like Bernard are tied to their estates. And it is Bernard now who, after his Council meetings, comes back in his calash with news of the bigger world both for his wife and for me.

"At one end of the front verandah of the estate house there is a projecting room, jalousied on three sides. On hot days Bernard's wife moves there for the air, from her inner room, and she gets a girl to sit with her. As I read and write in the verandah—decorated down the length of its inner wall with a simple, bright pattern of flowers and curling ribbons, the work no doubt of the pastrycook who did the coat of arms on the calash—I sometimes hear Bernard's wife talking to the girl with her.

"I hear intonations rather than words, the intonations of someone lying on her back. She is really trying to talk herself asleep, and the girl with her regularly says a few words to show that she is still there. The girl's words are clearer, because she is sitting, and the girls—there are different ones—are amazingly affectionate. It isn't always *madame*. It can be *mamselle, mama, dou-dou, ma 'mie, mon enfant, ma petite*. It is very strange and lulling, and on a hot day, in the wine-cask smell of sweating cocoa beans, I can listen to the rhythms of the talk and watch the long-tailed cornbirds weaving the long, sock-like pouches of their nests on the *samaan* or *immortelle* trees. Often the girl falls asleep before the mistress.

"One day I thought, 'This is practically all the society Bernard's wife has.'

"Every day before nightfall, at about six or just before, Bernard goes and locks the mule sheds. He doesn't want the Negroes to go wandering about on the mules at night, as they did before. And often, even after this, he gets a feeling that things are not right outside. It's just a feeling, but it eventually makes him go and check the mule sheds and the Negro houses. He has said more than once to me, 'There are so many of them, and there are only two of us.'

"In the morning he is up very early, to check the yard and the houses and the stores and the kitchen, and to unlock the mule sheds. After morning tea—there are three estate meals: tea, breakfast, dinner—he has to give out the work in the cocoa sheds and cocoa woods, and after breakfast he has to go and check the work, and he often has to show how everything is to be done, because some of the people who did a job quite well the day before will now say they have forgotten how to do it. The recently arrived Africans, or new Negroes, as they are known here, are especially difficult that way. They believe that if they do their tasks badly often enough they won't have to do them at all, and might somehow even be sent back home.

"So Bernard is as tied as any Negro to his estate. If he didn't have the secretaryship of the Council he would be quite immured here.

"After the recent trouble he can take nothing for granted. Every morning when he makes his round he is hoping he isn't going to find a corpse—a poisoning or a suicide. Even while I have been here Negroes have been poisoned or have committed suicide on estates quite close by. There have been a number of suicides on the La Chancellerie estate, which is another estate owned by a woman, Rose de Gannes de la Chancellerie, Marquise de Chaurras. They commit suicide by eating dirt over many days. The eating of dirt is something the new Negroes rather than the creoles do, and those suicides come in batches. They give encouragement to one another.

"When something like that happens, or when news of it comes to Bernard, I can see it on his face. He doesn't like talking about it. He would prefer to keep it from his wife, but he knows that it's something she will hear about from the girls when they go to sit with her in the room with the jalousies on three sides. Perhaps something has even happened here in the last few months. If it has, Bernard wouldn't want me to know. When I hear the women talk, I hear only *maman* or *madame* or whatever, and the rhythm of their patois. Perhaps without knowing it I have been hearing the women talk about a death in one of the little houses.

"I don't remember that it was like this in Venezuela. Was it because I lived in the town? When I visited the plantations or estates of friends, they seemed easygoing places. I took it for granted that they would have their own rules and customs; everywhere had its own rules. Of course, it was a long time ago, before the great revolutions, and perhaps there were things I would think differently about now.

"Twenty years ago, when I was in Russia, I went and spent an hour in a public bath. This was in Moscow, in 1787, in the early summer. A Russian I had got to know told me it was something I should do. It was one of the sights for visitors. I found when I went that you could see the women from the men's area. They were completely naked and you could see the lacerations and whip-marks on their bodies. The bath attendant allowed me to walk among the women. No one paid me any attention. It wasn't arousing. The indifference and the damaged bodies were things I couldn't ignore. I don't think my Russian friend saw it like that. I kept my thoughts to myself, and very soon allowed myself to forget what I had seen.

"No one can ever read the eyes, Bernard says. There is no way of knowing who has begun to eat dirt or who has laid by a store of poison. A few years ago the poisoner on Dominique Dert's estate, on the western boundary of the town, was the *commandeur* himself. He had formed a strong attachment to his master. Bernard says this often happens with trusted estate servants. The *commandeur* poisoned his fellows whenever he thought they were getting too close to Dert. When the *commandeur* was found out, he had the *atelier* assembled—as though he was still *commandeur*—and the story is that he made quite a speech to them. He became quite exalted. They didn't know, he said, but for months he had had it in his power to poison them all. Then he spoke directly to Dert. 'I could have poisoned all these Negroes of yours at any time. In one night I could have ruined you.' That speech was the big moment of his life. It was like something he had been living for. The master, the *atelier,* the estate—this was his complete world. Nothing existed outside. A few days later he took some of his own poison.

"The poisoner on St. Hilaire Begorrat's estate in one of the valleys to the west was the nurse in the estate hospital. This was a famous case, Bernard says. Begorrat was an early immigrant from Martinique, and he is very much like one of the old Venezuelan marquises of cocoa and tobacco, as we used to call them. Though Begorrat is a good deal more educated than they were.

"At the time of the hundred and twenty poisonings at Montalembert's some of Begorrat's people were also poisoned. The old marquis of cocoa didn't like this at all. He thought it showed disrespect. Montalembert was a newcomer. He, Begorrat, was the senior planter in the place. He had established the style of the place, and even some of the institutions. Everyone deferred to him on estate matters.

"He pretended to be very angry. He lined up everybody on his estate, had one of the corpses brought out, and said he intended to find out who the poisoner was. The estate doctor cut the corpse open and he and Begorrat began to look at it very closely.

"It was too much for the poisoner, who was the hospital nurse. Her name was Thisbe. She broke from the watchers and ran through the cocoa woods to the neighbouring estate and asked there for sanctuary. Bernard tells me that this is what they do in certain parts of Africa: people from one village can claim sanctuary in another village nearby. She was handed back. Begorrat had pack thread tied around her thumbs and she was suspended by the thumbs until she gave the names of about twenty poisoners and sorcerers on other estates.

"It frightened people that there were so many. That very day they were all picked up and taken to Vallot's jail in the town. They were kept apart from one another. They were chained or put in irons and some were shut up in the special hot chambers below the roof. Some of them were chained so that they couldn't move. Some of those in the hot chambers quickly became demented. They were fed on plantains and water and over three weeks they were examined and examined in the jail by Begorrat and a poisoning commission of planters. Thisbe was repeatedly tortured. When it came to the judgements the planters followed Spanish forms. The people judged to be poisoners and sorcerers were heavily chained and made to kneel to hear their sentences. Some of them were hanged and decapitated. The new Negroes among them were first baptized; Africans are considered infants by the Church, and can be baptized without instruction. One man was burned alive. Thisbe was hanged and decapitated. Her body was burned and her head was staked on a pole in Begorrat's estate.

"Begorrat tells Thisbe's story like a story he has told many times. The pole on which Thisbe's head was staked is still there, facing the Negro houses, almost on the spot where the corpse was cut open.

"He said with a smile, 'There's nothing there now. But they see the pole all the time and they know what they're seeing. It's magic against magic. I've told Bernard many times. It's the only way. Here it's my magic against theirs.'

"He told this story in the little grotto he has created in the hillside, and his current favourite—Bernard says he has had several—threw himself about with laughter whenever Begorrat smiled. He smiled often. He smiled especially when he talked about opening the corpse and pretending to look carefully at it, like a Roman reading the entrails, and when he said it was his magic against theirs.

"His lips are soft, but his speech is precise, biting and witty. The elderly cocoa marquis is much better educated than most people here, and he knows it. The people who defer to him tell you behind his back that when he came here from Martinique all those years ago he was bankrupt. All the Negroes he brought with him were mortgaged in Martinique; so the big tract of valley land he got free from the Spanish administration, sixteen acres for each Negro—the land that is today his little kingdom—was fraudulently obtained. I am sure he knows the stories. I don't think he minds in the slightest. He has calculating, merry eyes. He is like a man who knows he can afford to laugh.

"It isn't only Thisbe's head-pole that's still there at Begorrat's. The old jailer Vallot is also there. He is the man who tortured Thisbe and many others. He would like to go to the United States, to Louisiana. He says he has relations there, and he might get a job. There is nothing for a free man to do here. But Hislop is not giving him a passport. It was Vallot who tortured the free man of colour in Hislop's first week as governor here—the man of colour who used a love potion to get the black woman to sleep with him, and got people frightened all over again with thoughts of poison and sorcery. This is the case that has been tormenting Hislop ever since the Picton conviction last year. The free people of colour have raised a fund and retained a lawyer in Red Lion Square in London and are pressing the matter hard. Hislop is determined that if the case comes up, Vallot will bear responsibility as an official who exceeded his duty.

"Vallot is an elderly, pasty-faced Frenchman from Martinique. He came here in the Spanish time and acted as jailer for thirteen years. He has had no job for some years now. The local people decided to get rid of him at the time of Picton's arrest. He has used up his savings and is dependent on Begorrat's charity. He lives on slave rations in a Negro hut among people like those he used to flog and mutilate. Apparently they accept him. And he, curiously, has no feeling of humiliation or danger. Bernard says that no one at Begorrat's will poison Vallot. Poison is a weapon only against the master. The man who is almost certain to be poisoned is Begorrat's current favourite, and everyone knows it.

"Vallot doesn't know anything about me—he doesn't know much about anything outside the island. They had told him I was a general, and he had put on quite good clothes (possibly pawned in the old days by a prisoner, or offered instead of the jail fees) to come and tell me his story, and to ask for my sympathy and help. He talked a lot about the illness of his wife. She has a lovely name: Rose-Banier. He says that she used to serve all the paying prisoners with her own hand and used even to make coffee for them in the mornings. She was up and down the three floors all day, he said. Now she is old and ill and can hardly look after herself and their one-room hut.

"And all the time old Begorrat, in his pantaloons and buckle shoes, in this cool cocoa valley that is his kingdom, smiled with his soft lips at Vallot's tale of hardship, and his favourite laughed and rolled about the floor of the grotto.

"There have been great revolutions on both sides of the Atlantic. There is a war in Europe that will further change the world. Great admirals and generals and new inventions are constantly altering the nature and scale of war. Even Mr. Shrapnel's recent invention will in time be part of the general change; when it is taken up there will have to be new battlefield tactics. But here we might be on another planet, or in

another age. Here they have their own heroes and histories
and mythical events and sites: the hot chambers of Vallot's
jail, the dismissal of Picton, the *commandeur's* last address to
the *atelier,* the poisonings at Montalembert's, the opening of
the corpse at Begorrat's, Thisbe's running through the cocoa
woods to ask for sanctuary, the spiking of her head. Here
they attach different events to years as they pass; it is almost
as though, like the Indian nations of the continent, they have
another kind of calendar.

"I dwindle, Sally. I sit in Bernard's verandah and look at
the cornbirds' long straw nests hanging from the *samaan* and
immortelle branches, and hear the women talk in the jalousied
room, and I write essays about the liberation of South
America for future publication, and compose this journal-
letter to you.

"I mentioned Shrapnel in this letter yesterday. His name
simply came to me as I was writing, one of the hundred
London names I carry in my head. You will remember that
four years or so ago he wrote to me at Grafton Street about
his invention and asked me to a demonstration in some fields
somewhere. It is strange to be where I am and to think about
reading Shrapnel's letter in the library at Grafton Street and
arranging with others to go to his demonstration. It is as
though it hardly happened, or happened to another man. I
feel—with Vallot—that there is no room for me here. I have
no function. I lose touch with myself, even with my ambitions.

"It was just a week ago that I met Vallot. Today—would
you believe?—when Bernard came back from the Council
meeting he brought me a letter from a Swedish sailor in the
new jail in the town. Not the old jail—that was pulled down
four years ago by the Council, to prevent anyone seeing what
Vallot's old arrangements really were like. You have to ask
and ask before they even show you where it was. The Swede
is in jail for disorderly behaviour—that means drunkenness.

They feel here that drunken—or 'disguised'—sailors are bad for local discipline. 'Disguised' is the word they use. The alguazils get a small payment for every disguised sailor they pick up, and they are very eager.

"The Swede says he can't pay the jail fees, and he is being kept on bread and water. He appeals to me as a friend of liberty to rescue him. That is easy enough to do. But his letter also makes me think of the day thirty-six years ago when I went aboard the Swedish frigate, the *Prins Frederik,* at La Guaira, and for the first time felt myself a free man. I had to get so many permits and certificates, from the Church and others, before I was allowed to leave Venezuela. There had been months of little worries and setbacks, even with my father's influence, and I didn't feel I was leaving until I was actually aboard the *Prins Frederik.* I can go back easily to that moment now: the hills behind the little town of La Guaira were like the hills I see here, and I can give this ever present wine-vat smell of Bernard's estate house to the eight fanegas of cocoa beans in the frigate's hold.

"And now, and now, Sally, after all these months, letters come from you and others that tell me plainly what I have always felt in my bones: that I have been wasting my time here. I used to be told that it was half the battle to be here, on the spot, and that I had to be patient. Now you write, and Rutherfurd writes, and Turnbull writes, and a few other people write as well, that I should get back to London as soon as possible. Things have changed, ideas have grown. An immense military action with a great commander is being planned, to seize the South American continent before the French do. This is the very idea I have been putting to British ministers these past few years. It has been taken up now, and I am so far away. All the letters agree—and they are already two months old—that if I am not in London at this stage of the discussions there may be no room for me in what is finally decided.

"So I stand to lose the fruit of a life's dedication. Oh, Sally. I have been dwindling here; I have shown myself too often to these people. I have been dwindling in London as well; I haven't shown myself to people there. You might think that a man carries his personality, his soul, within him. But here—like a man in prison, I suppose—I have grown to feel removed from both the world and myself. I have to discover myself again. It may take me time to be what I was, and I may discover that I have changed.

"Today Bernard, as secretary of the Council, brought back news from Hislop for *Mister* Miranda. Hislop says he is unwilling to give Mr. Miranda a passport. He thinks that to do so might expose him to criticism and perhaps to legal action because of Mr. Miranda's dispute with the *Leander* men, who claim their wages, and the master of the *Trimmer,* who claims his fee for the hire of his sloop. He says also that there is a directive from Lord Castlereagh, the foreign secretary, that nothing that can be construed as official British support is to be offered Mr. Miranda.

"Bernard said, 'That's what he has to say. That's what will go on the record. But he really wants to talk to you. He has an idea that something is afoot in London and he wants to know what you can do for him. I think you should go and see him. He can't actually detain you here, but he can delay you for many months. A letter to London for advice—six weeks. Another six weeks for a reply. A further six weeks for a letter seeking certain clarifications, and so on. Time is valuable to you. He can help there, and perhaps you can think of something to offer him.'

"This was Bernard's last service to me, making it easy for me to deal with Hislop. I began to feel I was leaving, and I began to feel I was escaping, and lucky, as I had felt thirty-six years before when I had got all my permits and certificates and could go aboard the *Prins Frederik* at La Guaira.

"Bernard, whom I had sent here some years before, when he was the dependant and I the patron, was staying. He would never leave. He had nowhere else to go. I felt for him then all that I had felt when I had seen him in his London silk at Government House. I felt afresh all his pathos and anxiety, and the fragility of the life he had made for himself with his wife.

"We were standing after dinner in the verandah, looking across the narrow valley. This was what Bernard would always see or, if his circumstances changed, grieve for.

"His hand was resting on the banister of the verandah. I put my hand on his and told him, 'I don't know what would have happened to me here if you hadn't come to see me that day a year ago at Government House.'

"He looked at me, considered me. Tears came to his eyes. He said, 'I hope it goes well for you, General. I am sure it will.'

"Hislop will not refuse what I offer, Sally. I have something quite important to offer him. The ways of the world are returning to me already, and Leander might see his father even before you read this letter."

WHERE THERE had been Africans in the grounds, speaking an African language, there were now Chinese. They were small, shrunken men with bony faces. They wore conical straw hats and long black pigtails. Their sun-browned arms were stringy and looked very thin in the very wide short sleeves of their cream-coloured tunics. Their wide, slack pants, in material of the same colour, came down to just below the knees. They looked very old; their eyes looked pulpy and vulnerable.

Some minutes after the servant had taken in Miranda's name, Hislop came out to the verandah. And it was there, standing, that they talked. The rain and sun of a year had further darkened the pine floorboards, eaten away a little more of the soft wood between the ridges of the hard wood.

Hislop said, "I've got your letter, Mr. Miranda, but you

will understand that my position is not easy. Be'nard will have told you about Lord Castlereagh's directive."

Miranda said, "The directives of ministers are variable, because they do not always remain pertinent. Lord Castlereagh sent his congratulations about the way you dealt with the slave conspiracy. But that has not prevented the free people of colour agitating this past year about one of their number whose ears were cut off. That is potentially a serious matter, and I think you will find that if it goes much further, Lord Castlereagh will distance himself from the action. In fact, I want to talk to you about legal matters. What I have to say will interest you."

"That was what you said in your letter."

"I campaigned against Picton when he was governor here, and to some extent I am responsible for his dismissal. Afterwards I sent out an agent here, Pedro Vargas. He didn't attend to his obligations to me. The reports he sent me were dangerous lies and nonsense. He attached himself to the commissioner who was investigating Picton's rule. He was described as an assessor in Spanish law and as such he became one of Picton's accusers. His evidence at the trial condemned Picton. He said that Spanish law didn't permit the torture of free men. This is nonsense, as we all know. But Vargas was the only man in London with a copy of the relevant Spanish lawbooks, and in a time of a great war it wasn't easy to get another expert in Spanish law."

Hislop said, "I've spent many nights wondering how I could prove in a London court that the Spanish practise torture."

"Vargas was a brave man at one time. He took part in a dangerous conspiracy in New Granada. He was imprisoned and tortured. Somehow afterwards he made his way to England. This was in 1799. He turned to me for help when he arrived. He wrote me a long letter full of circumstantial details of his torture. This letter, if produced in a court of law, will destroy the evidence he gave at the Picton trial. The case against Picton will disappear. And so will the case the free people of colour are preparing against you about the man of colour who used a love potion and was tortured by Vallot."

"You never told me this. We sat in this house a year ago and talked about this matter."

"I had forgotten. I was reminded of it only a few weeks ago when a sailor wrote me from the jail here. I began to think in my idleness of all the appeals and the begging letters that had been sent me. I don't think I remember the names of those people. I've already forgotten the name of the Swede. And I don't think that, apart from the details of the torture, the Vargas letter could have been much good. It would have been full of rhetoric, like the nonsense he wrote me from here. There is another reason. All of us who are political exiles and have dealings with the government have secret names that are used in correspondence. Vargas's secret name was 'Oribe.' That was how he wrote me, and that was how I remembered it. My secret name, as you know, is Mr. George Martin."

"This letter is among your papers in London?"

"The papers of thirty-five years. They are in thirty cardboard boxes and two leather portfolios. I have a rough idea where to look. It would be impossible for anyone else to find. The Picton appeal is coming up soon."

"It might be useful for you to be there beforehand."

"Important things are preparing, General. A big force, and General Wellesley. I think you have an idea. If I don't get to London in time, there may be no room for me in the plans now being made. And there may be no need for me to have a staff. If I were to have a staff, I would need someone who has a knowledge of Spanish and would know how to deal with British military people at the highest level. I know very well it's not been a bed of roses for you here."

"General."

"As far as the Spanish government is concerned, they need only know that I am leaving this place, abandoning my enterprise, leaving my ship behind, my supplies, and going back to London. Lord Castlereagh will not be embarrassed in any way. And success, you know, General, wipes out certain things. Of course, since I am going back to London I have no further need of my ship. The ship can be sold or in some way disposed of. There is solid value there. I will leave you as my agent. You will do me that service. I am sure that, between you and Briarly and the master of the *Trimmer* and the disgruntled Americans of the *Leander,* certain matters can be adjusted."

"Something can be done. About Briarly, I think I should tell you that I sent him to the jail for a while."

"Did you, did you?"

"He complained from the jail about the stench and the filth. I handled his complaint with perfect correctness. I passed it to the provost-marshal. The jail is his responsibility. He collects a portion of the jail fees. The provost-marshal said the jail was as clean as a jail could be kept. It was washed down every day. I passed that message back to Briarly in the jail. I don't think it did him any harm. He had really become quite impossible. He seized the ship that brought the Chinese from Calcutta. It's an East India Company ship, but he claimed there had been some irregularity. We are still wrangling about that. Nobody's sure who's paying for the ship and the Chinese. Our Treasury here is quite empty. We don't know whether we are supposed to be paying the Company, or the London government is paying. Until that is cleared up we don't have a ship to send the Chinese back. They didn't work out. I feel that when the East India Company people in Calcutta were told by London to send Chinese to us, they just went out and emptied the first opium houses they found. I don't believe these people ever planted a tree in Calcutta or grew a vegetable or hoed a weed. They are city people. And nobody in London or Calcutta thought about women. These Chinese wouldn't look at Negro women. And no free mulatto woman would look at the Chinese. So they have just gone mad over the year they've been here. They've been here for as long as you, General. They hate being stared at, and there are still people who want to come and look at them. They've been keeping going only on the opium. Many of them have died. I want to send the rest back as soon as possible."

"A six or seven months' journey back. The same time to come over. A year or more here. I wonder what memories the survivors will take back to Calcutta of this part of their lives. Will they know where they've been? How they stare!"

"They've gathered to look at you. I think it's because of the long white pigtail you have. It's unusual here. It's longer than the Navy pigtail, and you are older than most Navy people. They probably think you are one of theirs, come to take them back home. A passport will be made out for you, General. The *British Queen* will be leaving for Tortola in the third week of October. That gives you enough time to order your affairs here. In Tortola you will join the convoy for England. That will leave in mid-November. The flagship will be the *Alexandra*. I think they will find a cabin for you. You will be in London before the end of the year."

The Chinese looked silently at the two men as they talked, and when Miranda began to go down the verandah steps they came a little nearer to consider him.

Miranda said, "Will anyone in Calcutta believe them when they tell this story? Will they believe it themselves, after a while?"

"General. The active years that remain to me are few. This makes them all the more important to me. My principal aim is, of course, to be creditably employed, but naturally without prejudice to my private interests. General, I think we should understand one another. Service with you will be a privilege, but I should find it hard to accept any rank lower than major-general. It is not from vainglory, I assure you. It is more for the sake of others. I have certain obligations, and I will not be able with a full heart, at this stage of a life with more than its share of hardships and cheated hopes, to accept anything less than I have said."

"General, you need say nothing more."

WE JUMP six years. Venezuela is in turmoil, a land of blood and revenge after three years of revolution, and Miranda is a prisoner of the Spaniards, in Morro Castle in Puerto Rico. He is waiting to make his last journey across the Atlantic, to Spain, to the dungeons of La Carraca in Cadiz. Cadiz was where the *Prins Frederik* took him in 1771. It was the first city he saw in Europe. It was where he bought his silk handkerchief and silk umbrella, and it will be where he will spend the last three years of his life, sometimes chained.

THERE HAD in the end been no major British invasion of Spanish South America. Such an invasion, though, was being seriously planned when Miranda went back to London from Trinidad. General Wellesley (who two years later became the Duke of Wellington) was assembling a large invasion force in Ireland. Miranda—as a South American who would have given legitimacy to the British action—would have had an important place in his army. But then, as so often with Miranda, plans had to be changed. Almost at the last minute the French occupied Spain; Spain all at once became an ally of Britain's in the war against Napoleon; and the British army that should have gone to occupy Spanish South America went instead to the Iberian peninsula to fight a war of liberation.

Miranda was fifty-eight, white-haired. It might have seemed now that after all the years of waiting there was nothing left for him to do. But then, two years later, Venezu ela declared its separation from Spain. The twenty-seven-year-old Simón Bolívar came to London to get help for his country, and Miranda went back to Venezuela with him.

He must have thought he was going back to a revolution that had been accomplished. He found a country split into all its racial and caste groups, a civil war beyond any one man's managing, and far beyond his military skill. After twenty months the first phase of that war was over. The revolution had for the moment been defeated; in the jails revenge was being taken on republican prisoners; and Miranda—like a man who had run to meet the fate from which he had more than once escaped—was a prisoner himself, betrayed to the Spaniards, his old enemies, by the man who had called him out from London, and had gone to tea one day at Grafton Street.

He was kept for five months in the jail at La Guaira, from where the *Prins Frederik* had left in 1771. Then he was moved to the fortress of San Felipe in Puerto Cabello, where in 1806 ten of the officers of the *Bacchus* and the *Bee,* dressed in white gowns and caps, had been hanged and quartered and burnt with their uniforms and arms and Miranda's own South American flag. Five months later he was taken to Puerto Rico, to Morro Castle, where thirteen men from the *Bacchus* and the *Bee* had for some time been imprisoned, loaded with twenty-five-pound chains, and given beds of stone and pillows of brick.

IT IS there now, while he is waiting to be transported to Spain, that Miranda is allowed visits by a Venezuelan, Andrés Level de Goda. Level is thirty-six, and a lawyer by profession. Thirty-eight years later, when most of these passions have turned to dust, and the reputation of Miranda has been all but erased, Level in his memoirs will provide the only witness (apart from official jail-book entries) of Miranda in captivity.

Level is of a creole landowning family, with (at least until the revolution) cocoa and sugar estates on the Venezuelan side of the Gulf. He is a royalist. He wants Venezuela to hold on to the Spanish connection. He thinks the revolution Miranda was called out to serve was started by local aristocrats—second-rate people, in his estimation—to settle personal grudges and to secure their own position, and had no popular support. A Venezuela set adrift from Spain will live through an unending civil war, Level thinks: the country is too full of factions and castes and hatreds.

Politically, Level and Miranda have been on opposing sides. But in Puerto Rico they are meeting in a kind of understanding. Miranda has been betrayed by the revolution and is now beyond politics. Level has been turned by the troubles in Venezuela and Spain into a wanderer with little money. He cannot for the time being go back to Venezuela: the revolution has caught alight again and he has been declared a proscribed person. In Puerto Rico he is dependent on the generosity of the captain-general, Meléndez, who is a friend. So both men, Miranda and Level, are also meeting in a kind of shared destitution.

On many afternoons Level goes to Morro Castle to sit with Miranda in his cell, and they talk while Miranda drinks his daily cup of tea. The head of Miranda's special guard leaves the cell door open when the two men are together.

Level's admiration for Miranda grows: the fluent speech, the authority, the voice, the physical presence of the old man, the knowledge of men and books and great events.

Meléndez, the captain-general, shows Miranda every regard. He has Miranda's meals sent from a tavern outside. He even arranges for Miranda to get money (against funds in

London) from an official on the British island of St. Martin, which is only a few hours' sailing away.

Miranda is interested in the news from Spain, and Meléndez passes on the Cadiz newspapers as soon as he gets them. In them Miranda reads of the war against the French in Spain. He reads of the battles and growing reputation of the Duke of Wellington and General Picton, the former governor of Trinidad. The old man must suffer, thinking of his own fall, but he shows no emotion to Level or Meléndez.

He drinks his tea in a special way. He squeezes half a lemon into a cup of tea, and while he drinks this mixture he nibbles at the hull of the lemon, taking care (almost as if he is racing against himself) to finish both drink and lemon hull at the same time.

He says one afternoon to Level, "Why are you staring? You remind me of the Chinese in Trinidad. They thought I had come to take them home. Did Hislop tell you about that?"

Level knows the reference. He worked for some time in Trinidad as an adviser in Spanish law to Governor Hislop.

He says, "I'm not staring, General. I'm looking, to remember. I was thinking that one day I would be telling people that General Miranda turned his tea into a lemonade."

"It's what my father used to do on hot afternoons in Caracas. I began to do it when I came back."

"When I'm with you I think of all the places you've been to, and all the people you've seen, and I can begin to feel that I myself have entered history a little. It is a feeling so precious I can hardly hold on to it. General, I've been trying for some time to put this to you. It is something I know I shouldn't put to you. But, equally, I will not forgive myself later for not doing so. I want to know about Catherine the Great. If you think the question is wrong, please forgive me. If you think it is too intrusive, please consider it as never having been spoken."

"It was one of the stories I encouraged, almost something I spread myself in the beginning, in my thirties, after I had left the Spanish service. Like so many of the thoughtless things I did then, it came back later and did me much harm. It exposed me to a lot of jealousy. Not in the way you might think. Venezuelans loved the story. They didn't see it as a tribute to me. They saw it as a tribute to themselves. Some of them behaved as though I had taken away something from them. They felt that I had misused something that belonged to them. I had come between them and the arms of the empress. And then they extended this to my whole career. Whatever I had done in the world I had done, according to this way of thinking, only because I was like them, my critics. Whether in Russia or England or France or the United States, there was nothing personal about my achievement. If they had been where I had been they would have done what I had done. I had gambled nothing of myself, taken no risks, exercised no personal will. And this was extended even further. They had done it for me. I had done nothing. I was nothing.

"I told Hislop in Trinidad—I don't know whether he told you—how Picton had damaged me in 1798, nearly thirty years after I had left home. He had written to the ministers in London that though I was important, I was nothing, the son of a Caracas shopkeeper. Of course he had got that from Caracas—and even at all the removes I could detect the voice of the Venezuelan who felt I had sullied the empress's arms and spoilt what was his due.

"Something like that happened again when I came back. I had been called back by Bolívar, as you know, and I was going to stay in his house in Caracas, because after forty years I had none of my own. I didn't go there directly. I thought I should behave formally and show respect to the revolution. When I landed at La Guaira I wrote to Roscio, the junta's secretary for foreign affairs, asking for permission to go to

Caracas. His reply was insulting and extraordinary. He said that I should never forget that I owed more than most to the country, because I had been unusually privileged and had spent many years abroad in the courts of Europe. What he was saying was that during my forty years abroad I had actually been exploiting the country, living off the national patrimony, and now should pay back a little of what I owed. And I knew at once that, though we were talking about the revolution, it was the old Catherine-the-Great jealousy at work on Roscio. That story did me much harm. I should never have come to Caracas after receiving that letter of Roscio's. I should have known that the situation had been misrepresented to me. I should have stayed at La Guaira and gone back to Curaçao on H.M.S. *Avon*. I should have made them wait, for a year, if necessary. That's how I should have handled it."

Level says, "Our hate, General, our hate. It isn't like the hate of other places."

"The Spanish empire damaged us in that way. It kept us backward, gave us very little to do. It gave us as men no way of proving ourselves. It never made us believe in human achievement. It made us believe only in luck and birth and influence and theft and getting patents from the king. It made us cringe before authority and mock it at the same time. It made us believe that all men at bottom were worthless. Many of the stupid things I did in the early days were because of that. It was ten years before I understood that things were different in other countries."

Level says, "At one time I used to think the jealousy you talk about was harmless, like the jealousy of a grocer for a man who comes and sets up a shop next door. After the revolution this jealousy turned to hate. We've all surrendered to this hatred. People won't stop now until they see the white bones of the enemy. I never thought it would happen. I thought people would be too frightened. I remember the early revolutionaries, Gual, España, in the late 1790s. They sent people to our estates and to others and tried to get us interested. They said they were going to have a republic and the flag was going to have four colours, for the different races. White, blue for the Negro, yellow for the mixed, red for the Indian. The four colours would also stand for the four aims of the republic. Liberty, equality, security, property. Property for the white, liberty for the Negro, equality for the mulatto, security for everybody. They were going to give everything to everybody. How were they going to do it? When you asked them they couldn't answer. They hadn't worked it out. They had thought only about the flag and the colours. Sometimes they got angry. 'You're an *americano*. You should be a proud man. How can you talk in this low way? Don't you care about your country?' I would say, 'It's wrong of you to put it like that. You can't tell me that my country is your flag. The question to ask when you talk about independence is: "Who is going to rule over us?" That's the question everyone will ask, and that is where the war will begin.' And, actually, that's how it happened. Now that we are launched on that four-colour war I don't see how it can stop. There will always be someone looking for a final victory, and someone wanting revenge."

Miranda says, "I don't think anyone can work out a constitution for a place like Venezuela. It's the Spanish legacy to us. Those people you mention, Gual, España, and the others—they suffered too much to think more clearly. I can also tell you now that the constitution I worked out for Venezuela was absurd. And yet I spent so much time on it. It was half Roman and half British. I didn't have consuls. I had officials I called Incas. A local touch, you see. I persuaded myself that I believed in my constitution, but I also know I had devised it to impress people abroad. Perhaps there is a genius somewhere who can work out a constitution for us. But he certainly isn't Venezuelan, because no Venezuelan will be calm enough to manage things wisely, and he can't be an outsider because he wouldn't begin to understand the divisions and the passions."

"In all your years of writing about Venezuela and South America, you simplified it, General. You talked about Incas and white people. You talked about people worthy of Plato's republic. You always left out two of the colours. You left out the black and you left out the mulatto. Was that because you were far away?"

"No. I did it because it was easier for me intellectually. Most of my ideas about liberty came to me from conversation and reading when I was abroad. So the country I created in my mind became more and more like the countries I read about. There were no Negroes in Tom Paine or Rousseau. And when I tried to be like them I found it hard to fit in the Negroes. Of course, I knew they existed. But I thought of them as accidental to the truth I was getting at. I felt when I came to write that I had to leave them out. Because of the way I have lived, always in other people's countries, I have always been able to hold two or more different ideas in my head about the same thing. Two ideas about my country, two or three or four ideas about myself. I have paid a heavy price for this. You mustn't rebuke me now.

"I got to know William Wilberforce when I went back to England from Trinidad. I admired him greatly. I thought of him as a philanthropist, a protector of the oppressed. I knew he wanted to talk to me about Negro slavery, but the first time I dined with him at Kensington we quickly got on to the subject of the Inquisition, and that led to a wide discussion about South American liberty. I felt I had to get him to understand the humiliations someone like my father had had to live with. And someone like poor Manuel Gual whom we've been talking about—after thirty-three years of service, only a captain in the Veteran Battalion, poor Gual, because higher ranks were reserved for Spaniards from

Spain. About the constant, humiliating obedience in all matters required from us. Obedience to the Church, obedience
to the king and his officials, the humiliation in which we felt
we walked. I had to get Wilberforce to understand those
things—they are not easy things to explain—and I felt that
to go into the Negro question with him would have been to
waste his interest in us. It would also have added an element
of confusion to what I was telling him about South America.
I knew how important Negro emancipation was to Wilberforce, and I made it clear that I accepted his views without
question. But I felt he was talking about other places. I felt I
was dealing with another matter altogether. I wasn't the only
one to think like that. You will know how badly Hislop
wanted to leave Trinidad and serve the South American
cause.

"And then many months later, when I remembered, I
wondered what that very fine man Wilberforce would have
thought if he had known that after the siege of Pensacola
I had in a matter-of-fact way bought three Negroes as a
speculation, and that just a few years later I had had to leave
the Spanish service because I had tried to smuggle two boat-
loads of Negroes from Jamaica to Cuba."

"There was that story," Level says.

"It was true. But it isn't a fraction of the truth about me.
It occurred at the very beginning, thirty years ago. I was
starting out. That was the world I found. There was a whole
life after that. That later life was what I was responsible for.
I didn't feel I had defrauded Wilberforce. Though again,
when I took Bolívar and the others to meet him, and he was
so gracious, saying how fortunate he was to be in London
just then, I wonder what he would have thought if he had
known that my fear of Spanish jails and the Inquisition—and
a lot of the politics I talked to him about—had begun with
that smuggling incident. I would have had to do ten years in
Oran in North Africa, if I hadn't deserted.

"For many years after I deserted I visited jails wherever I went. It's one of the things travellers in Europe do. But I was also testing myself. The jail at Copenhagen was the worst. Some of the prisoners were chained. Some of them were only debtors. The excrement wasn't removed from the latrine for months. I was so frightened by that I wrote to the authorities about it. And now I'm here. So I suppose that score's been settled all round."

Level says, "Hislop and I talked a lot about your time in Trinidad. I myself felt when I was there that I was in Venezuela. Didn't you feel at all when you were there that you had been given a glimpse of what lay on the other side of the Gulf?"

"Again, I knew it and didn't know it. There were two moments when I knew, very clearly. The first was on the day I arrived, after Puerto Cabello and the *Bacchus* and the *Bee.* My homecoming, you might say. I heard some Negroes talking in the grounds outside in an African language, and I went to the window. We were all surprised, all momentarily lost. It was in the middle of the day, but it was raining and dark. The Negroes looked at me as though they had seen a ghost—my white hair and long pigtail. I saw it clearly in their eyes. I felt very far away from the world. The second moment came about two or three months after I had come back from the Coro venture. A man called Downie and a lady called Miss McLurie and some others took me on a little tour of the island. One of the places we went to was an Indian reserve. There were a few places like that where the Spaniards had settled the remnants of the Indian people. Little missions, clearings in the forest, with the Indians in carat-palm huts and the priest in a little wooden house, and the church sometimes of adobe. All very rough and depressing. The Indians had become alcoholic. Miss McLurie and Downie and the other English people in the party became very angry on my behalf when we were in this mission. They thought the Spanish priest was a scoundrel, using the Indians as very cheap labour, getting them to cut down cedar trees and saw up the timber, and making an extra profit out of them by selling them rum. They wanted me to make a scene. They wanted me to abuse the priest. I thought it was strange, their concern, and then I realized that they were treating the Indians as my own people. I had a glimpse of the place as from a distance and I felt I had trapped myself there and would never leave. But then I put it out of my head."

"You had a bad time in Trinidad. I know. I talked to people. It could have ended for you there. People in that little place were so full of their own hatreds they hardly had time for you. If you had stayed for another year or so you might have lost the few protectors you did have. The amazing thing is that, having had the luck to get away, you so quickly decided to risk it all again and come back. I don't know what Bolívar told you about the state of the country. I don't think he could have told you that the royalists held both the east and the west."

"He seemed to be using my own words. He made me feel that what I had been prophesying had come true. The trouble I had, to get permission to leave England! It was almost as hard as leaving Venezuela the first time. It was much harder than leaving Trinidad. The ministers didn't want it. They didn't want their Spanish allies in Cadiz to think that they were encouraging the break-up of the Spanish empire. In the end we compromised. I would leave England on a warship and they somehow wouldn't notice. But they in-sisted that for appearances' sake Bolívar and I should travel on different ships. So Bolívar went ahead with my papers. I tell you this so you would understand I had complete faith in him and his family. I had had my papers beautifully bound the previous year by Dulau. Sixty-three volumes in three new boxes, with a brass plate with my initials on each box."

"If you had known that at the end the whole country was going to be against you, would you have come out?"

"After thirty years I couldn't have stayed away. I had to see it through to the end. Even to that moment you talk about. I had to see all my ideas turned inside out, as it were. That became a kind of release, in fact, right at the end. For years I used to tell people that if I could be set down on the Venezuelan coast with two hundred men, or fewer, the whole country would come over to my flag of liberty. It didn't happen like that to me. It happened to the other man, the rough naval officer the royalist authorities sent against me. He was blessed with luck. He landed with a hundred and twenty sailors and everybody began to go over to him. In twelve weeks he overwhelmed us. He could do nothing wrong. The Indians went over to him. The mulattoes, the *pardos,* the dark people, were with him. The mulattoes fought like demons at Valencia. Even when the white people surrendered they fought on. I had five thousand men. The mulattoes fought on even when there were only five hundred of them. For them, as you say, the question of the revolution was: 'Who is going to rule over us?' And they simply didn't want to be ruled by the people on my side. I had to make two assaults on Valencia. Eight hundred people were killed in that little siege, and fifteen hundred people were wounded. I remembered, too late, what Hislop had told me about the free people of colour on the other side of the Gulf—and I had never begun to think that that might have anything to do with me.

"I thought later, when things became hard, that I should enrol Negroes in my army. I offered them freedom if they served for ten years. I don't know what Wilberforce would have thought of that—this was just a year after our meetings in London. But at this stage everything I did was going to be wrong. The offer to enrol Negroes didn't get me suitable soldiers, and it turned everybody else against me. The royalists at Curiepe in revenge turned the Negroes from their plantations on me. They sent them marching to Caracas to loot and burn the place down.

"This was the end. I was quite encircled. After Bolívar lost Puerto Cabello we were absolutely without resources. People were leaving me every day. I could depend on no one. I couldn't carry on the war. At the beginning people like Roscio wanted me to keep out of their revolution. Now they left me alone with it. Everybody focussed his resentment or fear or hate on me—republican, royalist, all the four colours. I saw then what you have said, that the war was unwinnable, that if somehow the revolution could be reconstituted and we could go back to the beginning, it would all unravel again, and in almost the same way. I realized in those last days that for all those years abroad I had been speaking only for myself, that the revolution I had been working for would have come about only if all Venezuelans were like me, coming from a family like mine, and having a career like mine. It was what the Spaniards had always said, that my revolution was a personal enterprise.

"The knowledge was a kind of release. I wouldn't have arrived at it if I had stayed in London or if I had left the war half-way through. I would have been nagged by the feeling that there might have been something I could have done, that in spite of the four colours and the marquises of cocoa and tobacco and everything else I had always known about Venezuela, the ideas I had worked out might have proved right. Perhaps the philosophers were right. Perhaps below all the accidental things about people—birth, character, geography, history—there was something truer. That was what I had always felt about myself. Perhaps all men, if they were given a wise or rational liberty, became worthy of Plato's republic.

"I had no half-feelings or misgivings now. I knew I had seen things through as far as they could go. The unimaginable moment came when I realized that I no longer had a side, and that apart from personal dependants there was no one with me. My thoughts then were all of Grafton Street. The territory I controlled or was safe in was shrinking day by day. Soon it was reduced to the city of Caracas and the mountain road to the coast, to La Guaira. A few square miles. Think of that! Two or three years after I deserted I used to present myself to foreign governments as the potential controller of a territory stretching from the source of the Mississippi, all the land to the west of the river, down to Cape Horn.

"A British warship was waiting at La Guaira for me, to take me to the British island of Curaçao. I sent my three boxes of papers ahead with a loyal follower. I took the precaution to address those boxes not to me, in case they were captured, but to a British firm on the island. I did the same with the twenty-two thousand silver pesos and twelve hundred ounces of gold I took from the Caracas Treasury. It was with a perverse pleasure that right at the end I assumed the character my enemies gave me. My feeling was that this was owed me, for all that I had done for the country, and for the forty years I had been cut off from my family fortune. But I didn't manage to board H.M.S. *Sapphire,* as you know. It sailed with my possessions to Curaçao. My information is that the firm to which they were addressed claimed the money as their own, and were very happy to recover this fraction of what they had advanced through me to the revolutionary government in Caracas. So that account, too, has been settled all round."

Miranda makes a signal to someone outside. Captain Lara, the head of the special guard, comes and stands outside the open door, and Level de Goda knows it is time to leave.

· · ·

LATER THAT night, when the town was quite asleep, Level was awakened by Meléndez, the captain-general, in whose quarters he was staying. The captain-general was formally dressed, with his officer's jacket, and he carried the polished baton of his rank.

He said, "It's very hot, Andrés. Put on some clothes and come and walk with me by the sea."

They walked a short way along the sea wall and stopped by a pier. Ships' lights were reflected in the water of the harbour and masts were dark against the sky. A night breeze blew off the sea. The sails of one ship were bent for sailing. A small boat rocked near the pier steps. It wasn't empty: there were two oarsmen and two soldiers in it. The soldiers got out now and stood to attention on the steps. Along the sea wall then appeared Captain Lara and Miranda arm in arm. Behind them walked a Negro carrying a small wooden trunk on his head. Level recognized the Negro: he came from the inn that for five months had been preparing Miranda's meals.

Meléndez said, "The ship is waiting, General. It only remains to say goodbye. Lieutenant Ibáñez has given his word that no restraint will be placed on you during your voyage to Cadiz."

Miranda said, "No chains?"

"You will be treated with honour."

Miranda said, "I give thanks to God that I am going to Europe. Captain-General, I will never forget this kindness you have done me."

He embraced Meléndez and then, before being handed down into the boat by the soldiers, he embraced Level. Level remembered the embrace as the embrace of a friend.

LEVEL WROTE his memoirs—and gave that little formal farewell speech to Miranda—thirty-eight years later, when he was seventy-four. This was in 1851, when, as Level said, the Venezuelan revolution or civil war was still going on after forty-one years, and seemed set to go on for another forty-one. The memoirs might have been one of the casualties of the war. They were never absolutely finished, and (perhaps also because of Level's politics) were not published until 1933, and then only in a Venezuelan learned journal.

Level would have known that Miranda had died in jail in Cadiz just about thirty months after he left Puerto Rico. He wouldn't have known that Miranda had died painfully, over four months, racked by one affliction after the other, violent fits, typhus, and towards the end by an illness that made him haemorrhage from the mouth. He was buried unceremoniously, lifted away from the hospital of the jail in the mattress and sheets of his deathbed, and in the clothes in which he had died, and set down with it all in his grave. The men who took him away then came back and gathered up his other clothes and possessions and burnt them. Knowledge of the spot where he was buried was soon lost.

Miranda's second son, Francisco, was seven when Miranda was in Puerto Rico. Level might not have known that this Francisco, his father's namesake, left London when he was grown up and went to fight in the South American civil wars. He was executed in Colombia in 1831 (the year after Bolívar's death), when he was twenty-five, in one of the many purges of the war.

Level remembered, very delicately, Miranda's concern about a lady in London, to whom he would have liked to send money, and to whom, through Meléndez, he sent a letter about household matters. Level would not have known that in 1847, four years before he began to write his memoirs, Sarah had died in the house in Grafton Street. She was seventy-three. She had lived in the same house for forty-eight years, and for the last thirty-seven of those years she had been years, and for the last thirty-seven of those years she had been without Miranda. The census of 1841 records two women servants in the house, and it is possible that Miranda's library—valued at nine thousand pounds in 1807, with debts to booksellers of five thousand pounds—provided her in the end with a fair income.

It would have been a slow fading away for her. At the time of her death Miranda, once so important and busy in London, was hardly a name. His three boxes of papers had apparently been lost; and, as with the corpses at Pompeii, where Miranda should have been in historical accounts there was a void. Sarah vanished with him. The date of her death, and even the fact that she had kept on living at Grafton Street, was uncovered by a researcher from the Venezuelan embassy in London only in 1980.

Miranda's papers were found more than a hundred years after his death. In the second decade of this century an American scholar, William Robertson, had the idea that (though the money and the gold had been seized) Miranda's papers might have been sent on from Curaçao to London, to the appropriate British minister; and that they might subsequently have become part of the minister's own archive. The appropriate minister in 1812 was Lord Bathurst, secretary of state for war and the colonies. In 1922 the sixty-three volumes of Miranda's papers were identified by Robertson in the Bathurst library in Cirencester in Gloucestershire. Perhaps a speck or two of Venezuelan dust still adhered to them from the two three-hour journeys they had made more than a hundred years before on the cart road between Caracas and La Guaira. The papers were acquired by the Venezuelan government, and then made their last journey to Caracas.

The first volumes, heavily edited, with many things suppressed or omitted, were published in Caracas in 1924. The final volumes were published in Havana in 1950 for the bicentenary of Miranda's birth. These Havana volumes, in which the papers appear just as Miranda preserved them, the ephemeral mixed up with more formal things, without editorial gloss or interference, seem still warm with the life of the man.

CHAPTER 9

Home Again

THE FIRST black African country I went to was in East Africa. I was in my early thirties. I was loosely connected with the local university, and I lived in a little low bungalow in the landscaped grounds of a government compound on the edge of the town. Most of the people in the compound were expatriates—mostly British, with a few Americans—serving the government in various ways. Some were directly employed by the government; others had been sent out (like me) by foreign foundations or aid agencies.

The country was newly independent and was thought of as revolutionary, but the compound still had a colonial feel. It made me think of the expatriate compounds of the Trinidad oilfields, and it probably had been laid out at about the same time, between the wars.

The bungalows and flats in both places were quite modest. It was the setting—the many acres of landscaped grounds—that made them special, suggesting separateness and privilege. The land seemed to have been scraped clean of haphazard local bush. There were no internal fences, no middens that showed, no junk, no obvious patches of waste ground. The open spaces between houses were grassed. Every local tree and shrub, however common outside, cassia,

coconut, flamboyant, hibiscus, seemed in this stripped enclo-
sure to have an extra, exotic beauty.

The idea of privilege—or protection: almost the same
thing—was not wrong. The East African compound was like
a little welfare state within the country. There was a whole
side of life we didn't have to worry about. A special department looked after the flats and bungalows. It did repairs
and replacements and attended to complaints. And though it
wasn't part of the official deal or issue, nearly everyone who
came soon got a servant or houseboy who was used to the
ways of the compound.

I was self-conscious with these servants in the beginning.
I was embarrassed by the idea itself: African servants in East
Africa—settler country in parts, still, and safari country as
well—came with too many associations from books and
films. But then I saw that most people on the compound,
even the servants, were living unnatural lives. Everyone had
been presented with a style—in some ways as formal as that
of an Oxford college—that couldn't exist outside. After a
time the idea came to me that it might have always been like
that on the compound, even in colonial days.

Because the compound was on the edge of the town and
there were no buses or taxis, I had to have a car. And because
I couldn't drive, or didn't trust myself with a car, I had to
have a driver. It would have been convenient if one man
could have done the driving for me and the cooking and the
looking after the bungalow, but in the compound it didn't
work like that. I had to have a professional driver.

Just after breakfast the man would come, respectable and
neat in creased trousers and clean shirt and shining shoes, and
ask about the day's programme. Most of the time I didn't
have a going-out programme. I was working in my bungalow. So he would sit in the kitchen and wait, at first looking
up whenever I passed the open doorway, then conscientiously
looking down. He took later to bringing comic books, maga-

zines, and then proper books to the kitchen; he wrote letters. Sometimes in the morning I sent him home for the day, and then a few hours afterwards I wanted to get out. Compound life, with all its privileges, had its complications.

The servant and the driver had been found for me by Moses Lubero, who worked as a houseboy for a young English couple some houses away. Lubero was a heavy, slow man with bright, rolling eyes. I sometimes saw him with clothes-pegs in his mouth hanging out baby clothes. Baby clothes! Lubero was more important than that. He was said to control the houseboys on the compound. When he was out and about and he heard or saw my car coming he did a slow swivel of the neck and a very slow roll of his eyes to consider the car and me and the driver. It was as though there was something wrong with the muscles of his neck; but it might just have been his way of letting us know that he was keeping an eye on things.

He wore the standard houseboy whites: a short-sleeved shirt and shorts. From a distance they made him look like a fat boy. As you got nearer, his appearance changed: the fat boy wasn't a boy at all. He was a middle-aged man who had seen much; there were deep lines from his cheekbones to the corners of his mouth, and frown lines on his forehead. The paunch—creasing the waistband of his white shorts—didn't suggest softness. It suggested strength, authority, self-regard. Close to, he didn't look friendly; he had an air of tribal authority. His surname indicated that he came from the centre of the continent; a grandfather or someone further back might have followed an Arab or Indian trader down to the coast and become beached there.

To control the houseboys on the compound was to have power. The jobs were better paid than comparable jobs in the town, and every bungalow or flat had well-maintained "quarters," a servant room; many people in the town would have liked those quarters. There was also, with expatriates coming and going, a whole system of trade in the cast-off goods. The houseboys were controlled in other ways. It was Lubero who arranged everything when my own servant bought a broken-down old bicycle (borrowing through Lubero to do so, and also buying ill-fitting white-rimmed plastic shades to go with his new bicycle style).

THE COUNTRY was a tyranny. But in those days not many people minded. Africa had just begun to be independent, and the reputation of the president was that of a good man using his authority only to build socialism.

There was a section of the expatriates who saw themselves as serving this cause. It was one of the things that had attracted them to the country. They liked their closeness to power, and their simple but protected lives on the compound; though it worried them that they had to have the houseboys—they talked about that. Some of them even liked the idea of the shortages and austerity outside, and the disciplining of the people. They thought it was what had to come before things became better. They thought it right that people in the villages should be prevented from migrating to the capital. In this way the town didn't grow, people were protected from the corruptions of town life, and it was easier for villages to be collectivized and returned to the socialism of traditional African ways. I think now that for these expatriates compound life would have provided something of what ashram life or the life of the religious commune provided for others elsewhere: liberation, new rigidities, a new self-awareness and self-cherishing.

Moses Lubero controlled the houseboys, and Richard kept an eye on the expatriates. Richard was English, a slender man in his thirties who used an ivory cigarette-holder. He invited people to dinner in his apartment when he felt they were straying. He worked for the planning department, but he was better known on the compound for the letters he wrote to foreign newspapers and magazines when they published critical things about the country and the president. He wrote not as an official but as a private person. He wrote of socialism as of an austere faith that was its own reward. He might say, "Why shouldn't a poor African country be allowed to develop its own brand of socialism?" And he might say of the president: "He may not leave his country richer than he found it. But there isn't only one way of measuring success, and this new man of Africa will have the satisfaction of having ruled according to his own high principles."

Richard had an easy, self-mocking manner which made you feel that he was half on your side and that you could joke with him about what he had written. You couldn't. He was humourless; he simply couldn't take in a point of view that was different from his own.

One afternoon—I had sent the driver away for the day—I took the car out, to practise. I went on the airport road. It was the least busy of the roads around the capital. It went through no villages and it had a nice long straight stretch. On this stretch after some miles I saw a black-uniformed man on a motorcycle coming down towards me. And then I saw another uniformed man on a motorcycle. The men on the motorcycles were gesticulating. They appeared even to be half standing up on their bikes. When they came nearer I saw they were gesticulating at me. It became clear that they were furious with me, and it also became clear that they intended to drive me off the road. I pulled over on to the verge, without accident. Behind the motorcyclists was a big black car, and in the back seat were two men in off-the-shoulder African cloths. One of the men was the president. There was a smaller car behind, and behind that another motorcycle.

A few days later I saw Richard walking in his usual brisk way in the compound.

I said, "The other day the president drove me off the road."

The fixed, meaningless smile left his face. He became

severe. "You are making this up. You know you are making this up. The president doesn't do that sort of thing."

"That's what I thought. But then I had never met him on the road before."

"You can write what you want, of course. You have that freedom and you know it. The South African exiles here will certainly be grateful to you for your satire."

He spoke satirically himself. The country offered ready asylum to political exiles from South Africa, and in the compound we had a number of them. They made a distinct, depressive element. A few of them were black; many more were white. The whites were unhappy, damaged people. They might have been damaged by defeat, or it might have been that exile had brought out the melancholy or incompleteness that had always been there in their natures, below their political cause. I had never known revolutionaries before, and I suppose I had theatrical ideas of what they would be like. These people on the compound—whom I saw from a distance, and whom I found hard to get to know—were not defiant or fierce or full of faith. They were more like people who had been dealt a bad hand, had taken a wrong turning, and who would somehow always be out of reach, always dealing with their private demons.

THE COUNTRY was full of a special hate. It was for the small Asian or Indian community who, as elsewhere in East Africa, were mainly traders and shopkeepers and made a closed group.

There would have been ancient connections between the coast and India. It was an East African pilot who showed Vasco da Gama the way to India. The Victorian explorer Speke even published a map, said to be based on old Hindu texts, giving Sanskrit names for the rivers, lakes and mountains of Uganda. There would have been an Indian element in the mixed Swahili culture of the coast. But people didn't carry this kind of history in their heads; and the Asian community that was hated was the more recent one that had come over and settled in the half century or so of British rule.

The hate was in the newspapers, in the parliament, in the compound, in the university. It was open; it was licensed; it brought about no retaliation. Expatriates dealt in it to show their own commitment to the country. Some political people saw it as part of the business of building socialism, and gave it a doctrinal gloss.

The Asian shops in the capital would have been drab enough with all the regulations about imports and foreign exchange. It didn't take much to see that in the background there was a further constant plundering of the shopkeepers by officials, important men in the president's party, blackmailers, and finance houses in England and elsewhere who were being used to get money out of the country. The shopkeepers, Hindu or Muslim, were stoical; this was the gift of both religions. They didn't complain, and they wouldn't have wanted to do so to outsiders. But the griefs of those shops, dark wooden or concrete boxes that attracted such hate, seemed a world away spiritually from the landscaped grounds of the compound and the even more splendid campus of the new university, which had been built with foreign aid and seemed to speak of foreign approval of what the president did.

It was well known that in his early political days the president had been helped financially by some people in the Asian community. The president himself sometimes mentioned this when he attended certain ceremonial Asian occasions. I met one of those helpers one day. He was in his sixties, heavy, ill-looking, his active life in the past. He came of a merchant family who had migrated to East Africa at the turn of the century. Unusually, he had not gone into the family business. He was a lawyer. Perhaps because of this separation from family ways, and his isolation, he had been marked, more than most Indians I had met in India or East Africa, by the racial cruelty of pre-war East Africa. (It was the distorted echo of that cruelty that had in the beginning disturbed me even in the revolutionary compound, in the conventions about houseboys, their uniforms, their quarters.) It had been especially hard for him in the pre-war years, when he had felt himself caught between the humiliations of colonial East Africa and colonial India. After the independence of India he had devoted himself to the East African cause. He had got to know the president when the president was a schoolboy, and already famous, already spoken of as a leader. He had always admired the president; even now he admired him.

After he had talked of the excesses of the president's rule—the cruelties in the villages, the harassment of the Asian community, the censorship of the press, the regimentation of the students in the university—the lawyer went back to talking of the qualities he had admired in the president. It was as though, in spite of everything he had said, he had reached a personal point of rest and reconciliation, and had a bright vision of the future. There were three or four British people like that on the compound, not old, and one or two with some family connection with Africa. They loved Africa for the landscape, the peoples, the mysteries of the religion, the animals, the spaces. They could live nowhere else, and they intended to stay, regardless of politics, as long as they were allowed.

I thought it was to a point of rest like this that the Indian lawyer was taking me, that he was looking to a future beyond the current excesses of the president's rule.

I said to him, "But how are you going to spend the next few years?"

He said with deliberation, "I will be doing everything I can every day to getting every shilling I possess out of the country."

The lawyer was not without his family and caste sense for the accumulation of wealth. But he had become far more than a man of his caste. The charitable impulses of his faith—connected with the idea of merit and the good life—had been converted by him into a lifelong political idealism. He knew very well that to do what he had said would be to waste the little life that remained to him. But he was speaking seriously. The situation in the country was just as bad as it appeared, and he was talking out of despair and the knowledge, hard to bear at his age, of his own futility.

EDUCATION WAS free, and most of the students at the university were the first of their family or village to get higher education. They brought certain village habits to the campus. They could drink with a great, sullen seriousness for two or three days; and many of them did so when they got their monthly allowance from the government. They slept with their room lights on because they didn't like sleeping in the dark. The students' residential blocks blazed with electric light throughout the night, and a visitor might have thought that the students of this new African university were working night and day, to catch up.

In fact, some of the students brought fresh and sharp minds to the university. It was at the university they learned to be dull, through the political training they received: learning about the president's thought and the principles of his African socialism. It was as though they had been brought from their villages to the university to be re-initiated, re-tribalized, given new taboos and made narrowly obedient again. At the end the successful ones were fit and ready to serve the president and the state; and this was just as well, because there was for them no other way of earning a livelihood.

This was the future they had to show themselves worthy of. They learned to walk out in a body during lectures given by visitors. Few of them could say why; all they knew was that the leader of their group had given a signal. This walking out on foreign lecturers was a form of aggression that got talked about by expatriates, and it appeared to corroborate an idea the tyranny promoted about itself: the country was moving fast under the president, but not fast enough for the students, who were getting impatient and angry, and pushing the president, almost against his will, into more revolutionary postures.

The students constantly demonstrated. They demonstrated against South Africa and Rhodesia. They demonstrated against those African countries whose rulers were critical of the president. And more and more now they demonstrated against the local Asian community for sending money abroad and sucking the country dry. The government newspaper reported these demonstrations and at the same time ran editorials asking the students to show restraint; though I felt sometimes that the newspaper was reporting demonstrations that hadn't taken place.

Two or three years before, the president had invited a famous Hungarian economist down from London to advise on the socialist restructuring and unifying of the half colonial, half informal-African economy. Now the rumour began to go around that another foreign adviser was coming to look at ways of controlling the flow of money out of the country. Whenever he did radical or difficult things, or extended his own powers, the president didn't like to appear to be acting on his own. He liked it to appear that he was only following good socialist precedent, and taking the advice of reputable people from reputable countries.

Richard stopped me on a path in the compound one day. He said with his seeming smile, "Do you know a man called Blair? He's coming here, to keep us all in order."

I could tell from Richard's tone and the brightness in his eye that he was talking of the president's new adviser.

He bit on his empty ivory cigarette-holder, flipping it up

and down and then up again. "He's from your part of the world. The story is he went to school with you. Used to be a minister. Now is a kind of roving ambassador. Soon you'll have no secrets."

And of course now I knew the name. Blair and I hadn't gone to school together—that part of the story had been garbled. But his name was a name from the beginning of my adult life: for some months in 1949 we had both worked in a government department in the Red House in Port of Spain. I was playing at being a civil servant; he was entirely serious.

I was an acting second-class clerk, a copyist, filling in time and earning a little money before going to England and Oxford on the scholarship I had won. He was a new senior clerk in the department, a tall and grave black man who had made his way up. He sometimes came and sat beside me at my table at the end of a morning or afternoon, to check and initial the certificates I had written out.

He was more than ten years older than I, and in Trinidad that difference in age was important. It meant he had been born in a darker time. His education hadn't been as straight-forward as mine. He came from a poor family in a far-off country area and he had made a late start. That late start had put him at a disadvantage in the educational system. He had had to go to rough elementary schools and then to "private" high schools run by people with the barest qualifications. He would always have been too old for the better schools, and he would never have had the clear vision of a way ahead that had been given to me at an early stage: elementary school, exhibition to a secondary school, scholarship to a university abroad. He would have always had to feel his way. And when, after all of this, he had entered the government service, just before the war, his prospects were still limited; the senior posts were reserved for English people.

That had changed. He wasn't thirty, but he was already a senior clerk, higher in the service than he could have imagined when he entered it. He intended to rise further: it was known that he was studying for an external London degree. And yet in the office I was seen as the man with the real future: Oxford, and a career in the wider world. Blair himself seemed to think so. He might have felt that in other circumstances his chances might have been more like mine, but he showed me no grudge. In Trinidad in the 1940s—before the full postwar opening up of the world for people, and while the society was still colonial—scholarship-winners received a special admiration; they were admired almost as much as cricketers. Blair offered me this admiration.

And then over the years things had evened out for us. My life abroad, so brilliant to think about in the Red House in Port of Spain, had turned out to be hard and mean. My career had taken many years to get started. I had had to learn to write from scratch, almost in the way a man has to learn to walk and use his body again after a serious operation. And even then after ten years I couldn't feel secure, worrying always about finding matter for the next book, and then the one after that.

Whereas for Blair the world, so constricting when he had started, was soon to change dramatically. Even before I had published my first book, the new liberating politics of a Trinidad soon to be independent had come—with constant night meetings, like religious occasions, in the old British-Spanish colonial square next to the Red House—and Blair had been swept up to the heights, swept out of that government department where I had got to know him, swept out of that kind of government employment altogether, and into ministerial office: travel, ambassadorships, United Nations postings, and now this job for the president, reporting on the outflow of money. He had been born at the right time, after all.

''SOON YOU'LL have no secrets," Richard had said. He didn't mean anything by that; he was just using words, to appear to be saying more than he had said. It was like his fixed smile, which wasn't a smile at all. But this time he had drawn a little blood: he would have noticed that I was embarrassed by his news.

I hadn't met Blair since 1950, and I didn't want to meet him now. I didn't like the politics he had gone into. The almost religious exaltation of the early days of the black movement had given way very quickly to the simplest kind of racial politics. In Trinidad that meant anti-Indian politics and constant anti-Indian agitation; it was how the vote of the African majority was to be secured. Though I was no longer living in Trinidad, I was affected. I found when I met people I had known there, even people I had gone to school with, that the racial question couldn't be ignored. There was a self-consciousness on both sides, a new falsity. And I found, with every visit I made to Trinidad, that I was more and more cut off from the past.

The politics that supported Blair's career were more than politics to me, and I didn't like to think of him coming here, to this African country which thought of itself as revolutionary, to unsettle things further. I had got used to the unnaturalness of compound life, with its semi-colonial formalities. The local Asian community, with a sense of clan and caste far stronger than anything we knew in Trinidad, never saw me as one of themselves, and I had found ways, as a man on my own, of detaching myself from the racial undercurrents of the place. I felt that with Blair here all that was going to change.

I couldn't say that I had really got to know Blair in 1949. I was very young, seventeen. I never met him outside the office, and in the office he revealed little of himself. He was a big man but he moved quietly, without disturbance, as though he didn't want to draw attention to himself. His handwriting was very small and neat; it spoke of confidence, method, ambition. He was formal and always controlled. His thoughts often seemed far away, and I thought this was because of the studies he was doing at home for the London external degree. He didn't drink with the others on pay-day after the office doors had been closed. He didn't hang around after work. He wheeled his bicycle out of the bicycle-rack, lifted it down the Red House steps, and was off.

He was considered an exemplary man and everyone in the office respected him. His correctness seemed to be part of his character, and the correctness was something he got from his background, which was special. He came from an all-African village community in the north-east of the island. For various reasons—remoteness, bad roads, the "witch-broom" blight that had destroyed cocoa estates, the Depression—the community had kept its separateness for some generations, and in the wreckage of the old estates they had developed a kind of gentle pastoral life. They were self-possessed and calm, without the scratchiness of black people elsewhere. They were famous for their honesty, their un-locked front doors, and they had good manners. They said "Good morning" or "Good afternoon" to strangers and ex-pected to be greeted in the same way. They never spoke of a date to come without adding "please God": "Next month, please God," "Next Friday, please God." They were slow, but they were thought of as good people and were liked for that reason.

Blair would have been one of the first of the community to be educated, and the strange thing was that he seemed to come perfectly equipped for a civil service career. I used to think, being just out of school myself, and considering Blair's correctness in the office, that the manners and attitudes of Blair's slow, pastoral community had given him the de-meanour of a school prefect, a head boy: someone subordi-nate, but on the side of authority. He had joined the civil service in the colonial time; he would have been ready then (like some of the older clerks) for a life of subordination; and in those early years he would have been just as correct as he was when I knew him, a newly appointed senior clerk for whom the world was opening up. Buried or submerged below the man I knew in 1949, and the later politician whom I didn't know, was this calmer man from another age who wanted only to make his peace with the world and was willing to settle for what he could get.

I don't think Blair would have liked to be reminded of this earlier man. Though it would have been his instinctive feeling for authority, his acceptance of it and his sense of where it lay—together with his discovery of racial passion— that had pushed him into politics and kept him always close to power, while others came and went. His correctness didn't leave him in his new career; he was trusted by his superiors and looked up to by others. The stories that were spread of his corruption (and might have been exaggerated) were of a piece with his past: he was the man who arranged things for more important people who wished to keep their noses clean.

RICHARD HAD appeared to say that he was going to ask me to a dinner he was arranging for Blair. No invitation came, and it was through Moses Lubero, the compound fixer, and my own servant Andrew that I learned about Blair's arrival. The houseboy whom Lubero assigned to Blair came from Andrew's tribe and was possibly a close kinsman of Andrew's. He hadn't worked in the compound before, and Lubero had to get a permit for him to leave his village and come to work in the town. The place was full of regulations like this, which meant that at every stage there were people who had to get a little money.

The new houseboy looked like Andrew, I thought, but was younger and smaller. He didn't wear houseboy whites, like Lubero; he followed Andrew and wore flared blue jeans. The jeans he wore were a little too big for him (they might have been Andrew's) and he had to have big turn-ups. For a

week or so he spent much time with Andrew in the small
bungalow kitchen (getting crowded, with the driver there as
well) and I believe Andrew was teaching him how to cook
and generally do things. One morning I saw the new man go
to a hibiscus shrub outside the bungalow and very carefully
cut and strip a little twig. Andrew would have sent him out
to do that and was no doubt keeping an eye on him at that
moment: at lunchtime I saw two sections of the very twig
sharpened to a point and stuck on either side of a piece of
boiled corn. So I knew that one day soon Blair would come
back to his bungalow or apartment from his discussions in
the Ministry of Finance or wherever and start his lunch with
boiled corn with hibiscus handles.

At the end of the first month Andrew sold his bicycle to
the new man, and Andrew (through Lubero, of course)
bought another, better bicycle, which would have made him
borrow a little more. So now the new man would come
cycling up to my bungalow to be with Andrew. Sometimes
he did so in the middle of the morning, and sometimes then
Andrew would cycle away with him, no doubt to straighten
out some disaster in Blair's kitchen.

Houseboys were free in the afternoon, and for two or
three weeks Andrew and his kinsman spent some of this free
time cycling about together in the compound. It was a form
of celebration. They were showing off their new bicycles and
happiness and style. The new man began to wear Andrew's
white-rimmed plastic shades. They were small for him, too,
and the arms sloped high above his ears. Andrew two or
three days later began to wear new wrap-round shades; and
then, stealing a further march on the new man (who could
do nothing to catch up until pay-day), he took to wearing a
tie on these afternoon rides.

They were doing it to be noticed, but when one afternoon
I saw them cycling past, Andrew gave a smile, almost a
laugh, which was at once an expression of pleasure and a way

of saying that he knew the whole thing was quite ridiculous. Then immediately, for the benefit of his kinsman now, he tightened his mouth, looked ahead, and went serious again, and the two of them, very like one another, moved steadily away on the neat black-asphalted road with its whitewashed kerb, below the brilliant orange-and-yellow flowers of the tulip trees planted in colonial days, both of them pumping on the pedals in measured revolutions, the new man sitting on a saddle a little too high and straining to keep his feet on his pedals all the way down: celebrating their happiness and security and luck, Blair's houseboy and mine, in the land-scaped grounds of the compound which was like an echo of the oilfield compounds in Trinidad which both Blair and I had known only from the other side of the fence in 1949, when we were both at hopeful moments of our life, and when we felt that the world was beginning to change, though we could never then have seen the changes that were going to bring us here, to an African country that to us at the time was only a name.

IT WAS at De Groot's bungalow that I at last met Blair. De Groot was a lecturer in African history at the university. He was about my own age. He had done a certain amount of original work on the Swahili culture of the coast, and his position at the university was far too modest. He had been moved aside once or twice for Africans, but he thought that in an African country this was as it should be, and he didn't really mind. He had been born in East Africa and wanted to live nowhere else. That, in fact, was his principal ambition: to be always in Africa, to migrate nowhere else.

His father was a New Zealander who had gone to East Africa before the Great War. He was an engineer and builder and in East Africa he did small-scale construction work for the railways. His business failed during the Depression, and he lost the remainder of his money in his old age, when he quarrelled with his settler neighbours and started lawsuits against them. He had never been "a 'settler' settler," to use his son's words.

The same was true of the son (though he could mimic the settler voices); and he wasn't much of anything else either. De Groot, the son, understood all attitudes in this part of Africa, and was detached from them all. He divided the expatriate lovers of Africa on the compound into "cob-cullers," deer-hunters, people on an extended safari, and "*matoke*-eaters," plantain-eaters, people who wanted to pretend for a while that they were Africans. He saw himself as belonging to neither group (though he knew that to some people he looked like a *matoke*-eater). He never defined himself, but I think his attitude was that he was simply a man in his own setting, and fascinated by everything in that setting. In Africa he had no special cause; people looking for a man with a cause found him incomplete.

He was a bachelor. He liked friends, conversation, stories, jokes. His bungalow was the standard compound bungalow and absolutely the same as mine, in dimensions and plan and fittings, but it seemed much nicer. It was at the edge of the compound, on slightly sloping ground, with a view at the back, beyond a dip, of unregulated bush outside the compound stretching away to the next slope. Most people in the compound decorated their rooms with standard African artifacts—drums, spears, shields, zebra-skin pouffes, carved figures. (The vendors came around constantly; I bought some rubbish myself in the early days.) De Groot had an African eye, and apparently simple objects in his sitting room—like a wooden comb from a particular tribe, with variegated light-catching patterns carved with a relish that made you feel you would like to do some wood-carving yourself—were things you could give attention to and constantly see afresh. But the main reason why De Groot's bungalow was so attractive was because of the man himself. He was intelligent and quick, and without malice. He was completely open. You felt when you were with him that he took a delight in your character, your oddities, your presence.

(He was one of the people I thought I should go and see again before beginning this book. He had long ago left the university; he never said, but I believe life there had finally been made too hard even for him. Later he had done some semi-academic half-jobs; notes on Christmas cards had given me the vaguest ideas of those jobs. He had published a few things, but then he seemed to have drifted away from academic life altogether. I had no idea what he was doing when I wrote to him.

He misunderstood my letter: he thought I was going to be with him in a few days. He couldn't come to meet me, he said; he was going to send his driver; he described the driver. He said he had run out of Earl Grey tea; he wanted me to bring him some. He had a little farm now. Things were still chaotic, but there were a lot of books and he thought I would be comfortable. I knew the area where the farm was. It was scrubland, dusty, not welcoming. I felt that "farm"— with its suggestions of fields and fruitfulness—might have been too big a word for what he had. I imagined his house as a rougher version, but in wilderness, of his compound bungalow.

He wrote a second letter. This was clearly the work of an inflamed brain: the writer thought I was going to walk through the door at any moment. The letter was on an air-letter form; half-way through, the handwriting, that to me was so full of his character, broke up. Though the letter had been addressed, it hadn't been finished: some kind of failure had occurred during the writing, and he had saved his energy for the address.

De Groot had, in fact, written both letters from a hospital. I had written to him when he was dying. The planning and writing of a book can be attended by such coincidences.

For years after I left East Africa I used to think of going

back one day to have another look, do the long drives. That idea had always assumed that De Groot would be there, to guide, interpret, pass me on to people, and give me the news. He would have been the man to whom I would have brought back my stories. Without him there was no point in going back. I wouldn't have known how to move; it would have been another country.

I suppose it would have been possible twenty-five years before to foresee the shrinking of his life to the settler parody at the end. I know that worry about the future did come to him later. But while he was on the compound—still young and finding friends, and doing generous things like arranging the meeting between Blair and me—he was serene. The country had already begun to go very bad—and he knew it—but he was in the full joy of his African life.)

With his background De Groot would have understood the tensions between Blair and me. He didn't have to be told anything. And when he said to me one day that he had met Blair and got on with him, and that I should meet him too, I knew at once that De Groot had been doing a little work and that such a meeting would be all right. Blair would have felt the same. So even before we met a kind of goodwill had been established.

We met late one afternoon on De Groot's narrow back verandah, concrete-floored and perfectly open, just a few inches above the ground, with weathered wicker chairs and a low, bleached, ring-marked table, with a certain amount of junk pushed together in a corner against the kitchen wall. Beyond the little sloping strip of lawn—De Groot liked to water that—the land fell away, seemingly to bush; and from the hidden settlements below—settlements living off the compound—there came a sound of African voices.

In 1949, when I was seventeen, I had thought of Blair as a young man. Now he seemed to me middle-aged: he was close to fifty, and I was not yet thirty-four. The wonderful physique had thickened up, he seemed to be less neat in his movements, more assertive, to be taking up more room. Before I could think too much about that he put things right: he made the first gesture.

He said, "I tell people I saw you do your first piece of writing." Then he addressed De Groot as well. "It was in the department where we both worked. He wrote an article about a black beauty competition. He showed it to one of the typists and she didn't like it. She thought he mocked the black M.C. too much." He gave a deep laugh. "As soon as I began to hear about it I recognized the fellow."

I had often thought later—in England, when my writing career appeared not to be starting—of that joyous time of pretend-writing in the department. It took me six years to see what was wrong with that article about the beauty competition. The seventeen-year-old writer was too falsely knowing: his judgements, the angle of his observations, his jokes suggested he knew another, better world. That phantom world, which came with the first, innocent wish to be a writer, was hard to get rid of.

And it occurred to me now, considering Blair's freer movements in De Groot's verandah and a laugh bigger than I remembered, that at about the same time Blair might have come to the realization that the character he had been presenting to the world—the self-made man, still striving, looked up to by all, correct, with the manners of his special community—was in some essential way false to himself. He might have been granted another vision of his isolated community living in the debris of old estates; he might have taken their story back and back, to unmentionable times. And he might have decided then—like me as a writer—to remake himself.

We met at about half-past four. Blair left us at about six, when it was beginning to grow dark and cooking smoke from the chattering settlements below began to rise through the bush. We talked of meeting again. He mentioned dinner in his bungalow. (I thought of the burden on his houseboy, Andrew's kinsman.)

There was no further meeting. He didn't live. I was left only with those ninety minutes, and, as can happen after an unexpected or brutal event, ironies began to attach to every gesture and statement of Blair's that came back to me. It is hard to believe on such occasions that a person doesn't have, deep down, at some hidden level, an intimation that he has closed the circle and is near the end of things, and hard to believe that this knowledge doesn't break through a person's words and actions in a coded way.

And, in fact, at that last meeting Blair did speak, if not in code, in an oblique way of things that were important to him. Breaking into something De Groot was saying, he said, quite early on, spacing out the words, and with pointing gestures that made him seem enormous in the little verandah, "I *know* that the world I will be leaving is better than the one I came into." That was a simple racial statement, easy to understand. It explained his passion, his politics; and it was true: the revolution he had taken part in had succeeded.

But then a little later he softened the aggression of those big gestures. We were talking of insurance companies and medical tests, and he told a story of going to get a test in a clinic in New York. After his details had been taken down, he was given a dressing gown and told to go to a cubicle and undress. The dressing gowns were in four colours. The colours had no significance and the gowns were given out at random, but when the gowned men gathered in a waiting room, dressing-gown colour groups tended to form. He might have begun this as a serious story, but when De Groot and I laughed at the absurd picture he was creating, he laughed too.

Much later on, when De Groot was talking of tribal politics in East Africa, Blair gave the conversation an unexpected turn. We were all tribalists and racialists, he said; we could all easily fall into that kind of behaviour, if we thought we could get away with it. He told another story. He was in New York, at a railway station, and standing in line to buy a ticket. (He had a United Nations posting and New York was the setting of many of his stories.) The couple at the head of the line were causing a delay. They were an Asian couple: Blair couldn't say whether they were Filipinos or Malays or Indonesians or Chinese. They couldn't speak English. It took a long time for the clerk to establish where they wanted to go; and it was only after the clerk had given the tickets that the man began to look for money to pay. Blair found himself saying, "What's the matter with that damned Jap?" And the white man in front had turned and looked at Blair with great disregard.

It was a simple story; Blair and I had grown up surrounded by rougher racial manners and hearing much worse things about all races. But this was more than a story Blair was telling against himself. This was a story to tell us where he had got to; it was an offering to the two of us sitting with him in the fading light. Taken together with what he had said earlier in the afternoon, it was like a statement, made without excuse or apology, that after the passion of his politics he could now be another kind of man, ready for new relationships. De Groot, with his sensitivity in these matters, would have picked up something like that during his own meeting with Blair; and I found myself moved by what I thought Blair was saying. He expected his racial passion to be understood; he didn't think he had to explain it. That was impressive; it made me think afresh of his lost community in the blighted cocoa woods. I also liked the generosity, and the clumsiness, of his last story. The statement he had made could have been made only obliquely or in code, and with that kind of clumsiness; that was moving in itself. All three of us might have found plain words difficult.

For the rest of the time De Groot talked about the Swahili culture of the coast. This would have pleased Blair, the idea of the antiquity of Africa, the idea of African history, though he would not have been able truly to share De Groot's enthusiasms. He had got his certificates and external degrees, but he was not in any wider sense a well-read or educated man. He would have had no idea of the cultures De Groot was talking about, no feeling for the dates or periods.

But here too he wished to show himself in a new light. He played down whatever pleasure he might have felt at this talk of African history, and he said at a certain moment, "Sometimes here, when people start talking about gold and ivory, you can believe you're living in Biblical times. You almost expect them to start talking of peacock feathers."

This appeared to be a reference to the job he had come out to do for the government, and it appeared to confirm compound stories that Blair had run into trouble with some politicians. They had expected him only to put a squeeze on the Asian community. He was doing a lot more: he had begun to look at the smuggling out of ivory and gold. This was as much of a drain on the country's resources as the dealings of the harassed businessmen in the capital. It was well known that this kind of smuggling was being done by important men in the party, who (because of the regulations controlling the movement of people, and the innumerable new laws) now ruled in the interior with all the authority of old-fashioned chiefs, and (in spite of the talk of the socialist restructuring of society) often were connected to the old chiefly families.

De Groot said, after Blair had left, "He should be careful. They are not all like the president. There are some very wild men out there, and they can be pretty crude. The new power has gone to their heads. They feel they can do anything."

I got another version of the same message from Richard some days later. He stopped me in the compound and said,

"I have been looking up your friend's record. He's not exactly Mr. Clean, is he?" I knew then that Blair had begun to tread on important toes, and that Richard was already revolving in his head his defence of the regime, polishing his phrases, against anything that Blair might make public.

IT WAS as brutal and messy as De Groot had suggested it might be. And so shocking—even to Richard—that for some days no announcement was made of Blair's death; no one would have known how to present it. Instead, there were rumours, some of them inspired by people who would have wanted Blair out of the way. The first was that he was killed in a brothel just outside the capital. Another was that there had been some kind of Asian conspiracy. Yet another, coming very quickly afterwards, was that his bungalow on the compound had been burgled, his papers and everything else of value stolen, and his houseboy had vanished. There was some truth in the last part of the story. His houseboy, Andrew's kinsman, wasn't seen again.

What was established, after some days, was that Blair's body had been found in a showpiece banana plantation many miles from the capital. This plantation had been created with foreign advice and money, and was intended to be a model for the collectivized farms of the future. It had a special atmosphere. Old banana leaves, quickly drying and breaking down, and many inches thick, were used as a mulch. To walk on this mulch was like walking on a very thick, soft carpet. It deadened footsteps and seemed to absorb all other sound, and you very quickly began to feel uncertain about your footing. The people who had brought Blair or his body here seem to have intended to bury him below the mulch, but then they had been disturbed or had changed their minds. It was a day or two before the body was found and taken to the capital, and many days after that—and after a short official announcement of the death—before the body was flown back to Trinidad.

In the version of his death I carried in my imagination I saw Blair alive in that banana plantation, a big man floundering about in silence in his big, shiny-soled leather shoes in the soft mulch, between his sure-footed attackers. There would have been a moment in that great silence when he would have known that he was being destroyed, that his attackers intended to go to the limit; and he would have known why. And I feel that if, as in some Edgar Allan Poe story, at the moment of death, while the brain still sparked, a question could have been lodged in that brain—"Does this betrayal mock your life?"—the answer immediately after death would have been "No! No! No!"

Andrew grieved for his kinsman but didn't want to talk about him. He continued to drink on weekends. On Mondays he would be red-eyed, with a very bad headache, as before. But now, in addition, grief dulled his skin; his face was like a carving, without mobility, the lips seemingly clamped together, the lower lip jutting. For some weeks he appeared to be close to tears.

Moses Lubero didn't do his slow swivel of neck and eyes to look at me as I drove past. He took care now to look away, to be busy with what he was doing. Six weeks or so later the bicycle that had belonged to Andrew's kinsman (and had before that belonged to Andrew) began to be ridden about in the compound by a new houseboy.

And Richard. Two years ago I was in Paris for the publication of one of my books. In a restaurant one day, near the end of a lunch with an overworked French journalist who was bluffing his way through an interview, someone behind me said in my ear in English, "A voice from the remote past." It was Richard, without cigarette and ivory cigarette-holder. Twenty-five years had given him a lot of hair in his nostrils and ears. He was wearing a grey suit and he said he

was working in Paris for a foundation, arranging scholarships
for students from eastern Europe. He had left Africa and had
married again. "The male menopause," he said, in his brisk,
seemingly jovial way. "What they call the change of wife."
That was like Richard: the tested phrase. I said, "It must be
grim for you, seeing what's happened in so many parts of
Africa." He said, "I don't know what you're talking about.
I left Africa only because of what I told you. I wanted a
change, and what I am doing now is much more valuable.
Eastern Europe is much worse than anything in Africa. A
place like Hungary had a perfectly good communist government. They gave that up, and now they are on the brink of
ethnic conflict. Nobody says they are barbarians and sav-
ages." That again was like Richard, still concerned only with
the rightness of his principles, and somehow still safe.

I USED TO have a fanciful picture of the ceremonial return
of Blair's body to Trinidad: the aeroplane was at the airport,
and the big casket was being shouldered down the steps by
grave men in dark suits, four men or perhaps six. I knew the
picture was fanciful, but its stateliness seemed correct for the
occasion, until I began to question it. To take a casket of that
size down the steps would have been impossible for four
men or six men. Where would the casket have been in the
aeroplane? It would have had to be battened down to the floor
in some way. A number of seats would have had to be taken
out; that would have meant that a plane had been chartered.
That hadn't happened, so that picture of the casket and the
steps and the men in dark suits had to be set aside. The truth
would have been simpler. The body would have been in a
box, and it would have been placed in a refrigerated part of
the aircraft's hold. The body would have been embalmed
in Africa; that meant the internal organs would have been
removed. At the airport in Trinidad the flaps of the hold

would have opened, and when the time came the box would have been transferred to a low trailer, and perhaps in some way hidden or covered. There would have been formalities. Would the embalmed body in its box then have been transferred to a hearse? The hearse didn't seem right. I made enquiries. I was told that the box would have been taken away in an ambulance to Port of Spain, and then the shell of the man would have been laid out in Parry's chapel of rest.

December 1991–October 1993

A NOTE ON THE TYPE

The text of this book was set in Bembo, a facsimile of a typeface cut by one of the most celebrated goldsmiths of his time, Francesco Griffo, for Aldus Manutius, the Venetian printer, in 1495. The face was named for Pietro Bembo, the author of the small treatise entitled *De Ætna* in which it first appeared. Through the research of Stanley Morison, it is now acknowledged that all old-face type designs up to the time of William Caslon can be traced to the Bembo cut.

The present-day version of Bembo was introduced by The Monotype Corporation, London, in 1929. Sturdy, well-balanced, and finely proportioned, Bembo is a face of rare beauty and great legibility in all of its sizes.

Composed by Crane Typesetting Service,
West Barnstable, Massachusetts

Printed and bound by The Haddon Craftsmen,
Scranton, Pennsylvania

Designed by Cassandra J. Pappas